Frank Brennan is a Jesuit priest, professor of law at the Australian Catholic University, and adjunct professor at the College of Law and the National Centre for Indigenous Studies at the Australian National University. He has written a number of books on Indigenous issues and civil liberties. His most recent books are *Tampering with Asylum* (UQP, 2003), which compares Australia's asylum policies with those of other first-world countries, and *Acting on Conscience* (UQP, 2007), which looks at the place of religion in Australian politics and law. In 2009, he chaired the National Human Rights Consultation. He is an Officer of the Order of Australia (AO) for services to Aboriginal Australians, particularly as an advocate in the areas of law, social justice and reconciliation.

Other books by Frank Brennan

Too Much Order with Too Little Law
Land Rights Queensland Style
Sharing the Country
One Land, One Nation
Legislating Liberty
The Wik Debate
Tampering with Asylum
Acting on Conscience

NO SMALL CHANGE

THE ROAD TO RECOGNITION FOR INDIGENOUS AUSTRALIA

FRANK BRENNAN

UQP

First published 2015 by University of Queensland Press
PO Box 6042, St Lucia, Queensland 4067 Australia

www.uqp.com.au
uqp@uqp.uq.edu.au

© Frank Brennan 2015
Foreword © Patricia Turner 2015

This book is copyright. Except for private study, research,
criticism or reviews, as permitted under the Copyright Act,
no part of this book may be reproduced, stored in a retrieval system,
or transmitted in any form or by any means without prior
written permission. Enquiries should be made to the publisher.

Cover design by Luke Causby (BlueCork)
Author photo by Julia Charles
Typeset in 11.5/16 pt Adobe Garamond Pro by Post Pre-press Group, Brisbane
Printed in Australia by McPherson's Printing Group

The author is pleased to note the approval of Mrs WEH Stanner for the quotations from her husband's papers in the National Archives of Australia and at the Australian Institute of Aboriginal and Torres Strait Islander Studies (AIATSIS). He also acknowledges the approval of AIATSIS.

National Library of Australia
Cataloguing-in-Publication data is available at http://catalogue.nla.gov.au

ISBN 978 0 7022 53324 (pbk)
ISBN 978 0 7022 54499 (ePDF)
ISBN 978 0 7022 54505 (ePub)
ISBN 978 0 7022 54512 (Kindle)

University of Queensland Press uses papers that are natural, renewable and recyclable products made from wood grown in sustainable forests. The logging and manufacturing processes conform to the environmental regulations of the country of origin.

Dedicated to the late Liam Marrantya (1986–2009), a Ngangi-Wumeri man from Nauiyu Nambiyu, and others like him caught between the Dreaming and the Market.

CONTENTS

FOREWORD	by Patricia Turner, AM	ix
PREFACE	A Personal Journey	xii
INTRODUCTION	The Case for Modest Constitutional Change	1
CHAPTER 1	Approaching the Forthcoming Referendum	8
CHAPTER 2	The Collapse of *Terra Nullius* and Forced Assimilation	39
CHAPTER 3	The Promise of the 1967 Referendum	77
CHAPTER 4	After the 1971 Gove Land Rights Case	121
CHAPTER 5	Australia Day 1972	155
CHAPTER 6	The Need for Constitutional Change	183
CHAPTER 7	Aboriginal Concerns about Discrimination and Adverse Treatment	218
CHAPTER 8	The Road to Recognition for Indigenous Australians	248
EPILOGUE	No Small Change	280
APPENDIX 1	Previous Suggestions for Constitutional Change and Parliamentary Acknowledgment of Aboriginal and Torres Strait Islander Peoples	288
APPENDIX 2	Recommended Changes to the Constitution	301
ENDNOTES		302
INDEX		323

FOREWORD
by Patricia Turner, AM

Father Frank Brennan SJ AO is a highly respected academic, author and commentator on legal and human rights issues as they play out in Australia. He is also my good friend. I first met Father Brennan in Townsville in 1988 when I was based there to organise and run the international Fifth Festival of Pacific Arts. It was an event to promote the practice and maintenance of the indigenous cultures of the Pacific region. It is our mutual interest in the matters impacting on Aboriginal and Torres Strait Islander people in Australia that has cemented our friendship. One such key issue in this area that we will have to decide as a nation, depending on when the current Coalition federal government puts forward the legislation for the referendum, is the recognition of Aboriginal and Torres Strait Islander people in the Australian Constitution.

The question of recognition of Aboriginal and Torres Strait Islander people in the Australian Constitution is not a new one. However, it is a complex one. In this book, Father Brennan paints a picture of significant historical developments in the body of Australian law that now recognises and gives effect to some of the rights of Aboriginal and Torres Strait Islander people, especially in relation to their rights to land. As an Arrernte woman from Alice Springs, with a lifetime of working in

Aboriginal and Torres Strait Islander affairs, I know firsthand how long and difficult that struggle has been. In fact, in many cases Aboriginal people are still grappling with the complexity of securing their native title rights over their traditional lands.

To me, none of the rights of Aboriginal and Torres Strait Islander people have ever come easy. In most cases it has taken decades to get them recognised and then enacted. In regard to the Australian Constitution, only one referendum has ever been held to date about Aboriginal people. That was on 27 May 1967. It is regarded as the most successful referendum question ever put to the voting public as it received the majority of votes in the majority of states, a rare outcome indeed. It deleted all explicit references to Aboriginal people in the Australian Constitution. Specifically, section 51(26) was amended and section 127 was repealed. The deletion of the offending references to Aboriginal people meant that the Commonwealth Government was then able to legislate for Aboriginal and Torres Strait Islander people (section 51(26)) and they could be counted in the reckoning of the population (section 127).

With the Commonwealth Government now able to legislate for Aboriginal and Torres Strait Islander people, many assumed that it would only ever enact legislation that was beneficial to our people. But, alas, that was not to be. As Father Brennan outlines in chapter 7, the Commonwealth power to legislate can also be used against the interests of Aboriginal and Torres Strait Islander people. This book takes the reader on a very important journey, filled with interesting facts and often overlooked commentary by significant leaders. Father Brennan's background research enables the reader to be treated to such insightful gems.

The current prime minister of Australia, the Honourable Tony Abbott, has said he wants Aboriginal and Torres Strait Islander people recognised in the Australian Constitution. He said this would 'complete our Constitution rather than change it'. His government is yet to release further information about this matter. Hopefully, it will be very precise and clear. In the meantime, Reconciliation Australia has established a small team called 'Recognise', to promote the issue. They, too, eagerly await more clarity from the government of the day. Their role is important in spreading information across the nation about recognising Aboriginal and Torres Strait Islander peoples in our national Constitution. Their work follows that of an Expert Panel set up by former prime minister Julia Gillard to report on how such recognition should best take place. It is a comprehensive report, raising salient issues and a series of recommendations.

Father Brennan, among other important issues, discusses here the work of the Expert Panel and proffers alternative solutions. Undoubtedly, the single biggest challenge facing the question to be put in the referendum is whether the proposed change will gain majority support among Aboriginal and Torres Strait Islander peoples themselves. If it is not accepted by a clear majority of Aboriginal and Torres Strait Islander peoples, then what should we do? Obviously, as Australia's 'First Nation' people, coming from the oldest continuous culture in the world, this is a fact we want properly acknowledged. While many agree such recognition of this historical fact should be included in the national Constitution, others will put forward alternative views. But, the current prime minister has not put forward any other alternatives and is likely to stick by his wish for a referendum on the matter.

The position taken by Prime Minster Tony Abbott is a bold one. Why? Because as we have seen with the most successful referendum held in 1967, times change, issues change and the values held by the public at large also change over time. This is clearly laid out in this book.

Constitutional change in Australia is a serious matter. To gain a clearer appreciation of the issues involved and to assist the reader to clarify their own thinking about how to vote, I commend Father Brennan's perspective as a respectful and realistic account. I hope you agree.

Ms Patricia Turner, AM

PREFACE

A PERSONAL JOURNEY

We Australians are about to consider how to amend our Constitution in the hope that Aboriginal and Torres Strait Islander peoples might be more assured their due place in the life of the nation. We tried the same thing in 1967. Presumably we can learn from our successes and failures with that constitutional change and with all that followed. I am not an Indigenous Australian. I know there will be no constitutional change unless Indigenous Australians seek it and the rest of us are convinced about the necessity, correctness and certainty of the change.

I was a schoolboy in Toowoomba when the 1967 referendum was held. I have no recollection of it. As far as I know, there were no Aborigines at my school. I don't think I had even met an Aborigine. I do recall the ditty for the introduction of decimal currency on 14 February 1966. Which means I do remember some national events from my early secondary school days at a fairly isolated boarding school in a provincial Queensland town, the 'City of Flowers'. When I was a first-year university student studying law and politics in Brisbane it was 1971, the year of the last all-white Springbok rugby tour. They played their first game in Queensland on the weekend of two by-elections in which 'law and order' was an issue. The premier, Sir Joh Bjelke-Petersen, declared a state of emergency and won the by-elections resoundingly.

The university vice-chancellor, Sir Zelman Cowen, who later went on to become governor-general, complained about the police bashing of one of his students at a protest rally. He called for everyone to respect the rule of law. The police commissioner, Ray Whitrod, said there would be a police inquiry into the incident; Bjelke-Petersen said there would not be. No inquiry was held. Whitrod had to go, and he did.

On campus, the first generation of Aboriginal political leaders like Denis Walker, Len Watson and Cheryl Buchanan made regular speeches condemning racist Queensland laws, which denied Aborigines rights to their reserve lands while holding them subject to the whim of white administrators. The first Aboriginal legal service was established in Brisbane. I attended one day a week as a volunteer. Meanwhile the Whitlam Government had been elected and had established a royal commission into Aboriginal land rights. My father, later one of the High Court judges to decide the *Mabo* case, was the senior barrister for the Aborigines in the commission.

I moved to Sydney and joined the Jesuit order, training to be a Catholic priest. I spent a couple of months in 1976 with Father Ted Kennedy and Shirley Smith at Redfern. I was Mum Shirl's driver, going regularly to the courts and to the jails. I travelled to Canberra with Len Watson to watch the passage of the *Aboriginal Land Rights (Northern Territory) Act 1976* through the Senate. In the close familiarity of the Senate Chamber in the old Parliament House, I beheld the dignified satisfaction of Professor William Edward Hanley Stanner, who was listening attentively to the proceedings. I did not realise at the time that this was the culmination of his life's work as an anthropologist and advocate for Aboriginal rights.

My introduction to the complexity of Aboriginal issues came in 1981. I was the junior barrister in an Aboriginal murder trial back in Queensland. Alwyn Peter was the fifteenth Aboriginal male in three years to have killed another Aboriginal person on an Aboriginal reserve. In these cases, the victim was usually the accused's female partner. The senior defence barrister told the court that the homicide rate was the highest recorded among any ghetto group in the western world. In each case, the accused and the victim were shaped by life on a reserve; and each in their own way was destroyed by it. To be a member of such a group, you did not have to be bad or mad; you only had to be Aboriginal. We defence lawyers had a good win in the *Peter* case. Having pleaded a defence of diminished responsibility, Alwyn walked free within weeks of the completion of the court proceedings. A female anthropologist left me with the chilling observation that our forensic win had removed the one inadequate protection for defenceless women in remote Aboriginal communities – the minimal deterrence of the whitefella legal system.

In the following year, the High Court had cause to overturn a decision of the Queensland Supreme Court, which had increased to six months' imprisonment the sentence for Percy Neal, the elected leader of the Yarrabah Aboriginal Community Council, who was guilty of assault. With others, Neal went one evening to the home of Mr Collins, the white public servant who managed the community store. Neal was deeply upset about the management of the store and the Queensland Government's administration of the community generally. He twice spat at Collins, whose four-year-old daughter was present. He told Collins that he was a racist and that he and his family should leave the reserve. In the first instance a magistrate had sentenced Neal to two months' imprisonment. The magistrate said:

> Violence is something in recent times which has crept into Aboriginal communities. I blame your type for this growing hatred of black against white. You are not giving true representation as a leader to the people who voted you their leader. As a magistrate I visit four to five communities, and I can say unequivocally that the majority of genuine Aboriginals do not condone this behaviour and are not desirous in any shape or form of having changes made. They live a happy life, and it is only the likes of

yourself who push this attitude of the hatred of white authority, that upset the harmonious running of these communities.[1]

The appeal court of three Queensland judges then increased the sentence to six months' imprisonment. On appeal to the High Court, Neal succeeded in having the six-month term overturned. The High Court spelled out the relevant sentencing principles and, by majority, sent the matter back to the lower courts for consideration of appropriate penalty. Justice Lionel Murphy observed:

> That Mr Neal was an 'agitator' or stirrer in the magistrate's view obviously contributed to the severe penalty. If he is an agitator, he is in good company. Many of the great religious and political figures of history have been agitators, and human progress owes much to the efforts of these and the many who are unknown. As Wilde aptly pointed out in *The Soul of Man under Socialism*, 'Agitators are a set of interfering, meddling people, who come down to some perfectly contented class of the community and sow the seeds of discontent amongst them. That is the reason why agitators are so absolutely necessary. Without them, in our incomplete state, there would be no advance towards civilisation.' Mr Neal is entitled to be an agitator.[2]

Justice Brennan set down the relevant sentencing principle:

> The same sentencing principles are to be applied, of course, in every case, irrespective of the identity of a particular offender or his membership of an ethnic or other group. But in imposing sentences courts are bound to take into account, in accordance with those principles, all material facts including those facts which exist only by reason of the offender's membership of an ethnic or other group. So much is essential to the even administration of criminal justice.[3]

Six years later, Aboriginal academic Marcia Langton wrote the report *Too Much Sorry Business* for the Royal Commission into Aboriginal Deaths in Custody, documenting the plight of Aboriginal women suffering excruciating abuse on remote Aboriginal communities. In recent times, Peter Sutton, one of the leading anthropologists for land rights in decades past, has written *The Politics of Suffering*, recalling that by 2000 the Aurukun community in Cape York, 'the main home of the Wik people', had gone from 'a once liveable and vibrant community' to 'a disaster zone'.[4] I did not get that impression when the Wik people danced in Canberra after their High Court win in 1996. In the foreword to Sutton's book, Langton referred to 'the inland gulags and outback ghettos of remote Australia'. These are the communities that since 1967 have been granted land rights, sometimes over vast areas of traditional country. These are the communities that at great cost to the taxpayer were afforded a greater degree of self-determination on their traditional lands, attempting to make more real the choice between permanent settlement and migration, between self-determination and voluntary assimilation.

For more than 30 years, I have been preoccupied with the interrelatedness of Aboriginal dispossession, disadvantage and marginalisation and I have tried to state a publicly coherent policy of reconciliation, justice and recognition for Indigenous Australians. I come with fewer answers than I had 30 years ago. Noel Pearson says the 'symptom theory' underpinned our approach to the *Peter* case. Pearson says:

> All that was achieved by presenting a deeper historical understanding of the background to indigenous crimes and dysfunction was that the criminal justice system became sensitive to this background – and sentences became increasingly lenient. After a couple of decades we then reached a point where judges and observers – not the least Aboriginal people – started to wonder whether the loss of Aboriginal life was less serious than that of non-Aborigines. The criminal justice system may have

tried to accommodate an understanding of the factors which Brennan and those who followed him had illuminated in the *Alwyn Peter* case, but it did nothing to abate offending and the resultant 'over representation' of indigenous people in the criminal justice system. In fact I would say that it made this problem worse.[5]

These are troubling conclusions for any Australian committed to justice according to law for all persons, including Indigenous Australians, who are more likely than any other group to be appearing in court for a custodial sentence. Everyone must be treated equally under the law. A judge sentencing a criminal needs to consider both the gravity of the offence and the particular circumstances of the offender. This fair and proper application of the law may have unintended and negative consequences for Indigenous communities, where criminal assaults on victims are prevalent, while displaying an admirable commitment to the human rights of the individual offender.

In 2013, the High Court of Australia decided the case *Bugmy* v *The Queen* and affirmed the sentencing principle that had been set down by the High Court in the *Neal* case in 1982.[6] William Bugmy is an Aborigine who grew up in Wilcannia, a New South Wales country town marked by a high level of alcoholism and violence in the Aboriginal community. Bugmy had intentionally caused grievous bodily harm to a correctional services officer. The High Court considered Bugmy's circumstances as well as the gravity of the offence and concluded that the lower court had imposed too great a penalty. The majority of judges said, 'Of course, not all Aboriginal offenders come from backgrounds characterised by the abuse of alcohol and alcohol-fuelled violence.' But it is

> ... right to recognise both that those problems are endemic in some Aboriginal communities, and the reasons which tend to perpetuate them. The circumstance that an offender has been raised in a community surrounded by alcohol abuse and violence may mitigate the sentence because his or

> her moral culpability is likely to be less than the culpability of an offender whose formative years have not been marred in that way.⁷

There would have been no warrant for the High Court to make these observations about life on Aboriginal communities prior to the 1967 referendum.

Life for the contemporary Indigenous person is a life of choice and diverse possibilities. Law and social policy should provide the possibility of a realistic choice on a spectrum of possibilities from the pursuit of a traditional lifestyle on traditional lands to fully integrated participation in the social, economic and political life of the nation state, while maintaining cultural traditions and perspectives. In Australia, the resurgent opponents of land rights and self-determination think the former is not an option; thus this is an unreal choice, or at least a very cost-ineffective choice. They argue for laws and policies that provide no option but accelerated access to the benefits of mainstream society and the modern lifestyle, which is completely disconnected from the traditional hunter-gatherer lifestyle of Aborigines long past. The advocates for land rights confront the situation that many Aborigines are now 'land rich' but 'resource poor'. Those with land rights or native title are not able to use the land in any practical way for development. Aboriginal land titles cannot be readily sold, leased or mortgaged. We are yet to find the right balance between utility and security of Aboriginal land holdings – utility for the present generation and for individuals, security for future generations and for communities.

Indigenous Australians do now hold a secure title to a large part of the Australian land mass but, for most of those living in remote communities, the conditions are still terrible. Forty years ago, conservative politicians such as Sir Joh Bjelke-Petersen were expressing concern that the granting or recognition of land rights would result in Aborigines being more removed from and less responsive to the health and education services of the mainstream community. Sir Joh refused even to discuss the possibility of land rights with the Commonwealth Government. Prime Minister Gough Whitlam tried to push Queensland in the direction proposed by the Woodward Royal Commission, which proposed Commonwealth land rights legislation for the Northern Territory. After the dismissal of the Whitlam Government, Malcolm Fraser went ahead and the Commonwealth Parliament passed land rights legislation along the lines recommended by Sir Edward Woodward. Sir Joh thought the Commonwealth's legislation in the Northern Territory in 1976 was carelessly introduced and he was concerned that the granting of land rights and self-management to Aboriginal communities in remote parts of Northern Australia could contribute to social isolation. In Queensland he was particularly critical of the Uniting Church, which had encouraged Aborigines in their aspirations to return to traditional country, setting up outstations many miles from conventional facilities such as hospitals and schools, where reversion to the 'tribal' pattern of life was encouraged:

> School attendances dropped 40% and we cannot accept or tolerate a situation in this State where the young people of a community are thrust into an isolated situation, where by denial of fundamental education and health care services, and by an ideological indoctrination of Aboriginal separation and separate development, they would, by contrast with all other Queenslanders, be seriously impaired in choosing to pursue broader horizons of life in the future should they wish to do so. That Aborigines may be socially and educationally equipped to make such a choice in life is the fundamental aim of our Aboriginal advancement policy.[8]

These concerns are now being voiced by many Indigenous leaders, not to decry land rights but to plead for government intervention aimed at improving the health, education and employment prospects for Aborigines and Torres Strait Islanders living on their remote communities or seeking a life for their children in the urban areas of Australia. The children and grandchildren of the great land rights campaigners want to live in the best of all possible worlds, being Aboriginal but open to all the world has to offer, not being swamped by it, being able to stay afloat, able to make sense of it, able to embrace the mystery of it, even able to shape it, and to hand on to their children the uniqueness of their cultures and the universal possibilities of life in the modern world. Noel Pearson speaks of his people in Cape York as having a strong home base while having the confidence and opportunity to move in orbits as far afield as New York.

In Australia, life in the mainstream with some access, use and ownership of their traditional country may turn out to be the preferred option for most Aborigines. This will be an improvement on life in the mainstream without a secure land base, which is their entitlement in light of their historic dispossession. It will be different from living the life of a separate, sovereign Indigenous people, but since colonisation that has not been a realistic option. It may also be very different from life on a self-determining community, choosing the best of both lifestyles. This has appeal and possibility only for a minority of contemporary Indigenous Australians. It must remain an option. Bridging the gap between life in two worlds, under two laws, is the contemporary Indigenous reality. It ought be recognised and respected by the state; it ought be reflected in our constitutional arrangements.

Indigenous groups with some recognition of their land rights face this dilemma: how to live within the nation state and participate in its economy while maintaining distinctive culture and heritage. That ought to be their decision, and no one else's, even if that someone else is a government with a fresh political mandate. Those of us who are non-Indigenous members of the nation need to guarantee the minimum requirements for these Indigenous groups to make realistic life choices. In doing so, we have the opportunity, at some considerable cost, to ground our national identity and project the depth and complexity of the history of our land and all its peoples. Marcia Langton concluded her 2012 Boyer Lectures, which describe the benefits of the mining boom for Indigenous Australians, by recalling a conversation with an Aboriginal friend at Perth airport:

> He is a successful businessman, and he was heading home to attend Aboriginal law ceremonies for the next three months because, he said, 'the old people may not be around much longer'. These ceremonies will be held not far from the mines about which I have spoken. Aboriginal men and women have dedicated some proportion of this new social capital to cultural maintenance and renewal, and made Aboriginal endeavours commercially viable.[9]

These are no longer fanciful life choices. It is possible for some Indigenous Australians to be involved at high levels in economic enterprises that exploit land resources while at the same time remain committed to maintaining traditional ways, including ceremonies and obligations to the land.

In 1995, I made my first trip to the United States. I headed directly to Alaska. On arrival at the St Mary's Yup'ik Eskimo community on the Andreafski River, a small tributary of the mighty Yukon River, a local community member offered to show me around the community. Despite my jet lag, I readily agreed. I was keen to meet members of an indigenous community who were assured a significant degree of self-determination and land rights as far as the eye could see. This woman took me first to the local cemetery. I was perplexed. She told me the story of the lives and deaths of the three young men who had been most recently buried in the cemetery. She told me the story of the community without breaching the confidences or imposing on the privacy of any of the living. There were tales of violence, alcoholism and dreadful accidents. The similarities with so many tales that I had heard on Aboriginal communities over the years were stark – and far more immediate than the legal and political differences that distinguished the land rights and self-determination of Alaskan and Australian communities.

That night I was devastated as I reflected on what I had heard. One of the local Jesuits showed me a series of newspaper articles highlighting the dreadful social problems confronted by indigenous communities living close to the Yukon. But how could this be? These people had not only secure land title over their community lands but also other economic benefits flowing from the *Alaska Native Claims Settlement Act* of 1971. They had self-determination. They not only had their own law-making councils, they had their own courts and their own police, their own schools and a secure land base together with the economic security of a fishing resource, which was seemingly boundless in that part of the world – all we could have dreamed of in Australia. And they lived in such a remote place that very few outsiders had an interest in living there or disturbing them. They had been under both Russian and American governments and prided themselves on maintaining their traditions and identity no matter which flag flew at the post office.

Whichever country you survey, no matter what that government's policy, no matter what the present strategy of indigenous leaders, and no matter what the public understanding or sympathy about the position of indigenous minorities, land rights for indigenous people are an essential component in providing indigenous citizens with the choice and the potential to live an authentic indigenous life within the realistic confines of nationality and economy. Land rights are also the cornerstone for the settlement of historic post-colonial grievances in providing a land base for some indigenous persons and communities and economic and political bargaining power for others, assuring them a place at the table. With appropriate land rights measures, we can recognise the entitlement of indigenous communities to maintain and sustain their religious beliefs and practices, without threatening the public order of the society following colonisation. We can correct some historic injustices, which can be put right without occasioning injustice to other persons. These legal arrangements can help to validate the post-colonial legal system, providing a greater coincidence between law and justice. By drawing a line justly on past land grievances, the state's constitutional structure can then provide a necessary forum for the resolution of conflicting claims, assisting all citizens of the nation state to appreciate the place and entitlements of indigenous people and assisting all citizens of the nation state to reach a better understanding of their history and their place in the world.

Australia is distinctive because our history of land rights is so brief, our approach so pragmatic and belated, and our commitment so refreshingly new, fragile and wavering. Some Australians now entertain the hope or thought that Aboriginal problems could be solved if community land titles were changed to alienable individual titles that could be readily sold, leased or mortgaged, encouraging Indigenous communities to leave behind their traditional ways and enter the contemporary marketplace. Being able to sell, lease or mortgage their traditional lands, some Aborigines would definitely have an advantage in providing immediately for themselves and their dependants. But what then would be left for future generations who might look back and rightly claim that they were twice dispossessed, first by the British colonisers, and then by their twenty-first-century ancestors who were too quick to forfeit their heritage?

Whatever the content or success of any forthcoming referendum, we Australians need to harness the benefits of land rights so that Aboriginal and Torres Strait Islander citizens can have the option of real choices, participating in all the benefits that come with being part of a twenty-first-century pluralist democracy, which gives each their due, especially those with primary custodianship of the only heritage, cultures and traditions unique to this land. This is what the forthcoming referendum is about.

Indigenous and non-Indigenous Australians need to work together for the constitutional changes that are necessary, correct and certain. Those of us Australians who cannot claim any Aboriginal or Torres Strait ancestors need to be attentive to the aspirations of those who do. Together we need to assess those aspirations as moral entitlements. We then need to determine what realistic life choices they offer, and at what cost. We must assess which of them are politically achievable. And each of us will then decide how to make our contribution to our nation, which provides a place of belonging for all, especially those who are the embodiment and the owners of our Indigenous cultures, languages and heritage.

INTRODUCTION

THE CASE FOR MODEST CONSTITUTIONAL CHANGE

> The logical next step is to achieve full inclusion of Aboriginal and Torres Strait Islander peoples in the Constitution by recognising their continuing cultures, languages and heritage as an important part of our nation and by removing the outdated notion of race.
>
> *Patrick Dodson and Mark Leibler*

Australians are increasingly aware and dissatisfied that the Australian Constitution does not mention Aborigines and Torres Strait Islanders. In 1967, Australians voted overwhelmingly in favour of constitutional amendments to remove two negative and outdated references to Aborigines. John Howard when prime minister was committed to a constitutional amendment that would make positive reference to Indigenous Australians and their place in the nation's history and in national life. His successors Kevin Rudd and Julia Gillard repeated the commitment. Meanwhile, some Indigenous leaders were dissatisfied with court decisions and government policies, which they thought operated unjustifiably in a racially discriminatory way only towards Aborigines and Torres Strait Islanders. They wanted a constitutional guarantee that neither the Commonwealth nor the states could enact unacceptable laws or policies impacting only on Aborigines. They were upset at Commonwealth measures like income management, the 'federal intervention' on Aboriginal communities in the Northern Territory and state policies restricting access to alcohol on Aboriginal communities in areas like Cape York.

On New Year's Day 2014, Prime Minister Tony Abbott said, 'I will start the conversation about a constitutional referendum to recognise the first Australians. This would complete our Constitution rather than change it.'[1] Will completing the Constitution without making any substantive changes satisfy Indigenous Australians or make any real difference to their lives? Will proposing a change to the Constitution to the satisfaction of key Indigenous leaders satisfy the majority of Australians who are mistrustful of constitutional change? Many voters would be happy to sign on to a timely completion of the Constitution, making honourable mention of Aborigines and Torres Strait Islanders, bringing it into line with contemporary views but without making substantive changes. These are challenging issues requiring deep thought in the community and clear bipartisan leadership from our elected leaders.

The Australian Constitution is a fairly prosaic, legalistic document. It does not contain any great one-liners that could be readily learned by schoolchildren or repeated on talkback radio programs. Though democratically supported by the Australian people at Federation on 1 January 1901, the Constitution is simply an attachment to an act of the British Parliament. It sets out the basic structure of the Australian federation, bringing six former British colonies together as a Commonwealth. It sets down the relationships between the states and territories and the Commonwealth. It provides for a Commonwealth Parliament (House of Representatives and Senate), a Commonwealth Executive (the governor-general as the Queen's representative and the Queen's ministers of state), and a Commonwealth judiciary (the High Court and such other federal courts as the parliament establishes).

The Constitution specifies that the Commonwealth Parliament has the exclusive power to make laws with respect to customs and excise, which are the taxes placed on goods, especially when they cross a border from one jurisdiction to another. It specifies that most of the other law-making powers of the Commonwealth Parliament cover fields that can also be legislated by the states. These concurrent areas of legislative power are set down in section 51. Prior to 1967, section 51(26) provided that the parliament had power to make laws for the peace, order and good government of the Commonwealth with respect to 'the people of any race, other than the aboriginal race in any State, for whom it is deemed necessary to make special laws'. In 1967, the Australian people voted to amend that provision, taking out the words of exclusion 'other than the aboriginal race in any State', thereby granting the Commonwealth as well as the states power to legislate with respect to Aborigines within their jurisdictions. The High Court has made clear that the Commonwealth Parliament's legislative power in relation to Aborigines, though usually exercised for the benefit of Aborigines, extends to the making of laws adverse to Aboriginal interests or to laws that affected Aborigines might not want. Should there be a conflict between a valid Commonwealth law and a valid state law, the Constitution provides in section 109 that the Commonwealth law prevails and the state law to the extent of any inconsistency is invalid or inoperative.

The Constitution provides for amendment by a super-majority of voters – a majority of all voters and a majority of voters in at least four of the six states voting in favour of an amendment proposed by both houses of parliament. Amendment does not come easily. Only eight out of 44 referendum proposals have been passed since Federation. Since 1967, the Constitution contains no reference whatever to Aborigines and Torres Strait Islanders or to their presence prior to the assertion of British sovereignty. The Constitution uses the concept 'race' only in section 51(26) and in section 25, which is a completely outdated provision. Section 25 relates to the calculation of the number of seats from each state in the House of Representatives. Were a state to disqualify people of a particular race from voting in their parliamentary elections, those persons would not be counted in reckoning the number of seats to be allocated in the House of Representatives. No state does or is likely to disqualify people of any particular race from voting. Even if they did, such a racist action should not be permitted to affect the equitable distribution of seats in the House of Representatives. It is time for section 25 to go. When considering any reworking of section 51(26), we need to determine if there is any point in maintaining the concept of 'race' in the Constitution.

Australians are now being asked to consider how best to recognise Aboriginal and Torres Strait Islander peoples in the Constitution, which presently does not mention them, their history or their aspirations. Prime Minister Abbott's talk of completion without substantive change might quieten community apprehension and mistrust; it might also serve to modify the aspirations of some Indigenous leaders who, though they would like to see more substantive constitutional change, know that in politics the perfect is the enemy of the good. In 2012, Parliament passed a law requiring the minister for Indigenous affairs to appoint a review panel to consider the various proposals for constitutional amendment. That panel, headed by John Anderson, who had been leader of the National Party and deputy prime minister to John Howard, has recommended that the Abbott Government proceed slowly, cautiously and incrementally. Anderson says, 'It would be very much my view that we risk a terrible, terrible disaster if we go too early, if people are not ready and something put to the Australian people was knocked out.'[2]

Aboriginal panel member Tanya Hosch, who is deputy campaign director for Recognise, the community-based movement to recognise Aboriginal and Torres Strait Islander peoples in the Constitution, says, 'Every big moment like this in our country's history has been preceded by scare campaigns and mistruths. I trust the good judgment of the Australian people. In the meantime, we'll continue rolling out the thousands of conversations across the country as part of the Journey to Recognition.'[3] In September 2014, this review panel recommended that a referendum be held 'no later than the first half of 2017'.[4]

The parliament has also set up a committee of members from both houses to recommend the way forward. The committee is led by Aboriginal parliamentarians Ken Wyatt, a Liberal member of the House of Representatives from Western Australia, and Nova Peris, a Labor senator from the Northern Territory. Never before has there been Aboriginal representation on both sides of the parliament. This heralds a good start to the process. They are consulting Australians about the recommendations for change that were put forward by the Expert Panel on Constitutional Recognition, which had been set up by Prime Minister Julia Gillard and was co-chaired by the nation's father of reconciliation, Patrick Dodson, and lawyer Mark Leibler during 2011.

In their foreword to the Expert Panel's report, Dodson and Leibler say, 'The logical next step is to achieve full inclusion of Aboriginal and Torres Strait Islander peoples in the Constitution by recognising their continuing cultures, languages and heritage as an important part of our nation and by removing the outdated notion of race.'[5] This next step should commend itself to most voters and all members of parliament. The first proposed means for taking the step – the removal of the outdated section 25, which permitted a racially discriminatory determination of electorates – is already common ground in our parliament. Other proposed means for the removal of race will be strongly debated. Do we remove the notion of race by not mentioning the word 'race' at all, and by not mentioning any particular race in the Constitution? Or do we remove the notion of race ironically by constitutionally entrenching a guarantee against discrimination on the basis of race?

The Australian people will be invited to vote on measures that will have gained a broad cross-section of support in the parliament once the parliament has heard the findings of the joint parliamentary committee, which produced an interim report in July 2014 and will produce its final report in June 2015. In its interim report, the all-party committee agreed that any successful referendum proposal would need to meet three primary objectives. It must 'recognise Aboriginal and

Torres Strait Islander peoples as the first peoples of Australia; preserve the Commonwealth's power to make laws with respect to Aboriginal and Torres Strait Islander peoples; and in making laws under such a power, prevent the Commonwealth from discriminating against Aboriginal and Torres Strait Islander peoples'.[6] I agree with the first two objectives. I argue that the third objective is presently unachievable and unworkable.

For a modest constitutional change, I argue three aspects need to be considered: inserting a factual acknowledgment of Aboriginal history, culture, languages and land rights; deleting the racially discriminatory section 25; and amending section 51(26) to allow the Commonwealth Parliament to make laws with respect to the distinctive Aboriginal matters listed in the acknowledgment. I argue against a constitutional ban on racial discrimination. I think such a ban has no prospect of winning community endorsement at this time. Such a ban would also be unworkable and too uncertain in its application. Should Indigenous leaders see such a ban as a necessary precondition for their endorsement of any referendum proposal, I would argue that no referendum should proceed unless and until the nation is ready to vote for a fully fledged constitutional bill of rights (including a ban on all adverse discrimination) or at least for a comprehensive ban on all adverse discrimination, not just on the basis of race, but also on the basis of gender, age, religion, sexual orientation or disability.

If we are to make a substantive constitutional change, why should there be a constitutional ban on racial discrimination but not on sex discrimination? Why should there be a constitutional ban on racial discrimination only against Aborigines but not against newly arrived migrants? To place a ban on racial discrimination in the Constitution without a ban on other forms of adverse discrimination would be to put our constitutional arrangements out of kilter. To place a ban on racial discrimination against Aborigines and Torres Strait Islanders but not against other Australians would itself be an act of racial discrimination.

Neither of these proposals would complete the Constitution in its present form. They would change it substantially.

A constitutional ban on racial discrimination would require the High Court to second-guess every piece of legislation relating to Aborigines coming before the Commonwealth Parliament. The joint parliamentary committee has been advised by Neil Young, a leading barrister, that such a ban 'is likely to have wide-reading application and be heavily litigated'.[7] Nineteen years ago, I did propose a constitutional ban on discrimination on the ground of race, colour, ethnic or national origin.[8] I have since reversed that position and will argue strongly for the reversal in this book. Only a modest referendum proposal will have the prospect of being carried, of being workable and of being sufficiently certain in its future application. The lesson from the 1967 referendum is that a modest proposal overwhelmingly carried by the people provides the political imperative for governments to act.

CHAPTER 1

APPROACHING THE FORTHCOMING REFERENDUM

In the footsteps of Hasluck, Stanner, Dexter and Coombs

The Founding Fathers – and they were all male – who drew up the Australian Constitution saw little, if any, role for the Commonwealth Parliament to perform in relation to Aboriginal Australians. They did envisage the Commonwealth Parliament needing to make laws with respect to racial groups who had recently gained admission to Australia. No doubt there was a racial dimension to this perspective. Section 51(26) of the Constitution as enacted in 1901 provided that the Commonwealth Parliament had power to make laws with respect to 'the people of any race, other than the aboriginal race in any State, for whom it is deemed necessary to make special laws'. Edmund Barton, our first prime minister and one of our first High Court judges, justified such a provision on the ground that 'the moment the Commonwealth obtains any legislative power at all it should have the power to regulate the affairs of the people of coloured or inferior races who are in the Commonwealth'. Sir Samuel Griffith, who went on to become our first chief justice, said, 'What I have had more particularly in my own mind was the immigration of coolies from British India, or any eastern people subject to civilised powers.'[1] Our founders wanted the Commonwealth Parliament to be able to make restrictive and adverse laws aimed at people of 'inferior races' who, though lawful migrants or settlers, were in need of close, ongoing supervision by government.

A century ago, state policies in relation to Aborigines were aimed at protection of those Aborigines living on reserve lands in areas far removed from European settlement. In the Northern Territory, where the Commonwealth determined policy once it assumed control from South Australia in 1911, a distinction came to be drawn between 'full blood' Aborigines who were to continue living on reserves and 'part blood' Aborigines who, when children, were to be given the opportunity to live like Europeans. This required the removal of children from the reserve, from the Aboriginal community and from their parents. Patrol officers would seek parental consent; at times, they would proceed with removal even without that consent if they thought removal was in the best interests of the child.

Between 1951 and 1963 Paul Hasluck, the minister for territories (including the Northern Territory) in the Menzies Government, worked hard to implement and articulate the policy of assimilation. Early in life he was a journalist who had had the opportunity to see up close the living conditions of Aborigines on remote settlements in his home state of Western Australia. He wrote regularly for *The West Australian*. In 1934, he spent three months travelling with the Moseley Royal Commission in the state's north, observing the living conditions of the local Aborigines. He then researched an MA thesis at the University of Western Australia, studying the official policy and public opinion in relation to Aborigines in Western Australia between 1829, when the Swan River was settled as a colony, and 1897, when the Imperial Government surrendered control of Aborigines to the Western Australian Government. The thesis was published in 1942. In 1937 a national conference had been convened to formulate a national policy.

Hasluck was very critical of the policy announcement because it drew a distinction between classes of Aborigines – the half-castes, who were to be educated and absorbed into the white community, and the untouched natives in inviolable reserves, who were to be preserved in their tribal state.[2] Hasluck thought all Aborigines should be treated equally, being incorporated into the European style of life as quickly as was possible. Having been a lecturer at the University of Western Australia, he was seconded to the Department of External Affairs, spending some time at the Australian Mission to the United Nations, where he was introduced to the beginnings of international human rights jurisprudence.

Upon entering the Commonwealth Parliament in 1949, Hasluck resumed his strong interest in Aboriginal affairs. Guided by AP Elkin, a professor of anthropology at Sydney University, he had the chance to develop his assimilation policy in the 1950s. In retirement, he wrote with some satisfaction:

> In the post-war years considerable change has taken place and, without mock modesty, I can say that, because of the opportunities that political office gave to me, I was able to do a great deal myself – perhaps more than any other individual – to restore the status of the Aborigines so that today, as their right as citizens and not by gift or by 'exemption' from protective legislation, most of them have access to social services, voting at elections, freedom of movement, guardianship of children, property rights and testamentary rights, and, in general, a position under the law and under government much closer to that of all other British subjects and Australian citizens resident in Australia than it was in the 1930s. The handicaps which they continue to suffer today are social rather than official.[3]

Law and policy were said to be colourblind under the assimilation policy. Under the Northern Territory Welfare Ordinance, most Aborigines were declared to be 'wards' of the state. Regardless of their parental heritage, Aboriginal children were to be assimilated into the mainstream community. Those who showed greatest promise were often sent south for schooling. Today, some look back to the assimilation era under Hasluck's guidance as a time of certainty. They pine for a return to this clear path. But things were not so simple, even back then. There were no land rights. It was assumed that Aborigines had no legal rights to their traditional lands even if those lands had been left undisturbed by European settlers and even if the state had taken no action to appropriate them for any public purposes. Aborigines lived in communities on crown land set aside and reserved for their use.

By 1954, Hasluck and the government conceded that these reserve lands should be maintained for Aboriginal use and that activities such as mining and forestry should be permitted only after due consideration of Aboriginal concerns and with provision for an Aboriginal share in the revenue generated by such activities. Though no individual or group of Aborigines could effectively claim any legal rights to these reserve lands, the government was conceding that these lands were primarily for Aboriginal use and occupation. The government's moral concession that Aborigines had an entitlement to use these lands and to have some say over their use by others would be the seed for future ideas about land rights and self-determination.

In 1961, Hasluck succeeded in having all state governments agree to a common definition of 'assimilation':

> The policy of assimilation means in the view of all Australian governments that all aborigines and part-aborigines are expected eventually to attain the same manner of living as other Australians and to live as members of a single Australian community enjoying the same rights and privileges, accepting the same responsibilities, observing the same customs and influenced by the same beliefs, hopes and loyalties as other Australians.[4]

The government envisaged that there would be a need for some special measures for the benefit of Aborigines. But these measures were to be regarded as temporary and not based on colour, rather 'intended to meet the need for special care and assistance to protect them from any ill effects of sudden change and to assist them to make the transition from one stage to another in such a way as will be favourable to their future social, economic and political advancement'. Ideally, Hasluck foresaw that Aborigines would continue to live on reserve lands outside the major towns in the Northern Territory but only for as long as it took for them to make the decision to move into town, seeking the usual benefits of life, including health, housing, education and employment. Hasluck told Parliament on 14 August 1963:

> This clear tendency to dispense with any special laws affecting Aborigines only is directly relevant to the case that is sometimes urged for the amendment of the Constitution to enable the Commonwealth to pass special laws for the people of the aboriginal race. The train of our thought is that the Aborigines should not be made the subject of special laws and that consequently a power in this Parliament to pass laws concerning Aborigines only would be largely unnecessary.[5]

Hasluck saw the need only for greater consultation and co-operation between the state governments and the Commonwealth in its administration of the Northern Territory.

On 10 December 1965, CE Barnes, Hasluck's successor as minister for territories, told Parliament:

> In the Northern Territory there are now no laws which discriminate against aborigines; they are equal at law with all other Northern Territory residents though some special benefits have been retained to them such as special rights to reserved lands, including royalties arising from those lands and the right everywhere to take natural game and to use natural waters.[6]

Barnes made some subtle but substantive changes to Hasluck's definition of assimilation. In 1961 Hasluck had specified, 'The policy *means* that all aborigines and part-aborigines are *expected* eventually to attain the *same* manner of living as other Australians.' Barnes approved a change in this definition to, 'The policy *seeks* that all persons of Aboriginal descent will *choose* to attain a *similar* manner and standard of living to that of other Australians.' The element of Aboriginal choice was starting to creep in.

The idealism of Hasluck's original policy was sorely tested when the Commonwealth Conciliation and Arbitration Commission was required to review the Cattle Station Industry (Northern Territory) Award at the request of the North Australian Workers Union in 1965. Up until this time, many pastoralists were prepared to allow Aborigines to remain on their traditional lands, even if those lands were within the boundaries of a pastoral lease. Aboriginal groups would set up camp and the men would be expected to work at peak mustering times. They would be paid a pittance, but there was no expectation that they would work full-time. The Northern Territory pastoralists made it clear that there was no way they would continue to employ and provide ongoing community living for Aborigines living on pastoral leases if the commission required them to pay award wages. The commission observed, 'If the employers' application were to succeed and if the aborigines were to remain living on stations it seems to us likely that their assimilation or integration into our white economic society would be delayed.'[7] Pastoralists warned that the granting of equal wages would result in widespread 'disemployment' for Aborigines on pastoral properties. The pastoralists said they would have no option but to remove many Aborigines from their pastoral leases, even though Northern Territory pastoral leases had always contained some provision for ongoing Aboriginal access.

In its decision, the commission observed, 'There must be one industrial law, similarly applied, to all Australians, aboriginal or not. If any problems of native welfare, whether of employees or their dependents, arise as a result of this decision the Commonwealth government has made clear its intention to deal with them.'[8] Being fully apprised of the grave warnings issued by the pastoralists foretelling wholesale Aboriginal dispossession and unemployment, the commission, in handing down its decision on 7 March 1966, decided to delay implementation until 1 December 1968. The commission was untroubled by the inevitable effects of this delayed decision, noting:

> If, therefore, as a result of our decision, substantial numbers of aborigines move to settlements or missions it is our view that the policy of assimilation and integration will be assisted rather than hindered. Those aborigines who move will be those who are now having the greatest difficulty in understanding the concept of work and in fitting into our economic community, whilst those who remain will be the most advanced and therefore the easier to assimilate.[9]

The population flow did occur as predicted by the commission. The result was not the facilitation of assimilation and integration, but rather the beginning of the welfare mentality that Aborigines moving off cattle stations to missions and reserves would need to be paid 'sit-down' money for their survival in places where there was next to no prospect of realistic employment or training.

Though the commission made field visits to Brunchilly, Brunette Downs and Alexandria Station, as well as holding 33 days of hearings in Alice Springs, Darwin, Sydney and Melbourne, they never heard from any Aboriginal witness. Appearing as a barrister for the Commonwealth, James Gobbo, who later became a distinguished judge and the governor of Victoria, said in his final submission:

> All the chapters in the first part of the history of assimilation in the Northern Territory have been written – save for that of employment. All the gateways have been opened save that one. We have therefore come to the final and critical chapter. There is a great deal of work in the field still to be done – a great deal – but here we have it in our power – simply by applying the law of the land – to throw open this last gateway. Let the aborigines come into a body of laws that are typical of this commission

and typical of the industrial community of this Commonwealth. In short, let them come within the laws made for all Australians.[10]

In his autobiography written some 45 years later, Gobbo says:

> It may well be true that the union did not consult aboriginal stockmen, but I do not recollect any submission by the pastoralists on this matter, much less that they had themselves consulted and had been told that the aborigines did not want equal pay. What is certainly true is that the land rights issue which came to the fore after the Wave Hill stand was not canvassed by any party.[11]

At Wave Hill, the Gurindji people led by Vincent Lingiari had walked off Lord Vestey's cattle station, demanding better conditions and recognition of their traditional land rights. The stand-off is remembered in the protest song 'From Little Things, Big Things Grow' composed by Paul Kelly and Aboriginal songwriter Kev Carmody. Hal Wootten, who later became a great advocate for Aboriginal rights and one of the judges in the Royal Commission into Aboriginal Deaths in Custody, had appeared as a barrister for the Northern Territory Cattle Producers Council. Years later, when reflecting on the case, he would often make the point that no one asked the Aborigines what they wanted. He once made the insightful and accurate observation:

> The great tragedy of the case is that by reason of the application of this principle (equal pay) that was felt to be important to white fellows' consciences, Aboriginal communities were just suddenly removed from their traditional land. Their whole way of life was destroyed. They were thrown into artificial settlements, often mixed up with people who might have been their traditional enemies, certainly not people they were used to living with. There was enormous disruption of Aboriginal society as a result.[12]

The immediate grant of equal wages resulted in massive unemployment for these stockmen, who often then had to leave their traditional lands for the first time because pastoralists would not tolerate the presence of large numbers of idle Aborigines on their properties. The policy of assimilation was fraying at its edges and wreaking havoc. There was no clarity about the future of Aboriginal cattle workers and their dependants living on pastoral leases. There was no clarity about the long-term future of Aboriginal reserve lands and the people living on them. If Aboriginal stockmen were to be treated the same as white stockmen receiving the same pay and conditions, the reality was that most of them would not be employed. They would be receiving no pay at all.

Meanwhile, Hasluck's laudable commitment to non-discrimination had resulted in a legalistic policy approach requiring that most Aboriginal citizens in the Northern Territory be treated as wards of the state. They were then discriminated against not because they were Aboriginal, but because they, and only they, were wards of the state. If most Aborigines were wards of the state and most whites were not, then assimilation was a legal artifice. The complexities and exemptions from the policy had become too problematic. There was a need for a new narrative. Aborigines and their supporters were starting to talk about land rights. The United Nations was formulating international human rights instruments that spoke of the right of self-determination. With the fallout from the cattle workers' equal pay case and with political agitation in the cities, many activists were demanding that Aborigines be consulted and have a say in any laws or policies specifically directed at them.

In 1965, just prior to the decision in the equal pay case, the Menzies Government had given some consideration to constitutional reform. The Federal Council for Aboriginal Advancement (FCAA) led the charge for amending section 51(26). Labor parliamentarian Gordon Bryant, then vice president of the FCAA, published a leaflet in April 1965 urging that the words of limitation in section 51(26) be omitted because 'all Australian laws ought to apply equally to all Australians' and 'no one should be excluded from Commonwealth benefits on account of race'. The FCAA thought that the Commonwealth would then be able to discriminate in favour of Aborigines by passing special beneficial legislation. Billy Snedden, the attorney-general in the Menzies Government, submitted to Cabinet a proposal for an amendment consistent with the FCAA's position. He told Cabinet, 'I think the public believes that the underlying words in section 51(26) amount to discrimination. I do not personally accept that in truth they are; indeed, I think that their inclusion in the section constitutes a protection rather than a discrimination. But I think we must have regard to the electors' view of the matter.'[13]

Aware that the Labor Opposition was wanting to propose an amendment to section 51(26), Prime Minister Menzies told Parliament that it was curious to regard it as a discriminatory provision: 'In truth, the contrary is the fact.' He said that the unamended section 51(26) could not work adverse discrimination upon Aborigines. Being a constitutional lawyer, he offered this analysis:

> The words are a protection against discrimination by the Commonwealth Parliament in respect of Aborigines. The power granted is one which enables the Parliament to make special laws, that is discriminatory laws in relation to other races – special laws that would relate to them and not to other people. The people of the Aboriginal race are specifically excluded from this power. There can be in relation to them no valid laws which would treat them as people outside the normal scope of the law, as people who do not enjoy benefits and sustain burdens in common with other citizens of Australia.[14]

Professor Geoffrey Sawer, who was Australia's leading academic constitutional lawyer at the time, gave what the present chief justice of the High Court, Robert French, described as a 'prophetic warning' when he said, 'Having regard to the dubious origins of the section, and the dangerous potentialities of adverse discriminatory treatment which it contains, the complete repeal of the section would seem preferable to any amendment intended to extend its possible benefit to Aborigines.'[15] In the end, the Menzies Government did not proceed with any referendum proposal. With 2015 hindsight, many would now concede that Menzies was right. The inclusion of Aborigines within section 51(26) would permit the Commonwealth Parliament to make whatever laws it saw fit for Aborigines, whether benign or adverse. Naturally, the FCAA thought that if the power were granted to Parliament it would be exercised only in a beneficial manner for Aborigines.

When long-serving Prime Minister Menzies retired in January 1966, the Liberal Party elected Harold Holt as their new leader. As prime minister, Harold Holt committed Australia to signing the *International Convention on the Elimination of All Forms of Racial Discrimination* (*ICERD*), which was opened for signature on 7 March 1966. Australia signed the convention on 13 October 1966. At the international drafting meetings on the convention, Australian delegates were aware that the nation's treatment of Aborigines was problematic. Holt could see wisdom in committing to the public campaign for the amendment of those provisions of the Constitution that Aborigines and their supporters thought unacceptable.

In the Menzies Cabinet, Harold Holt had not previously shown much interest in Aboriginal affairs. Hasluck was left puzzled about Holt's belated interest and role as an innovator in Aboriginal affairs, saying, 'In sixteen years with him in Cabinet I had never known him to show any interest in Aborigines and when he was Treasurer from December 1958 to January 1966 he had certainly been much less responsive than Fadden had been to my bids for funds for Aborigines.'[16] Hasluck often thought himself on his own in Cabinet when seeking approval for Aboriginal programs. Holt's newfound fervour provided the opportunity for other Cabinet ministers to show some commitment to the cause.

The new attorney-general, Nigel Bowen, put a submission to Cabinet proposing the removal of those words in the Constitution that were 'alleged to be discriminatory against aboriginal people'. Bowen, like Menzies, was a very accomplished lawyer, and thus his qualification that the offending words in the Constitution were 'alleged to be discriminatory'. Cabinet members were adamant that this constitutional change would not strike a new balance of power between the Commonwealth and the states when it came to dealing with Aborigines living within state borders. Though favouring the amendment, Cabinet still thought that the public had widely misinterpreted the existing provision and that it did not work adverse discrimination upon Aborigines. Cabinet 'took the view that if the referendum was carried the Commonwealth role should not be to legislate itself but rather to participate with the states in the forming of policy'.[17]

On 27 May 1967, Australians voted overwhelmingly to amend the 1901 Constitution, repealing two provisions that were seen as racist. One unnecessary provision was to do with reckoning the number of people in a state. Aborigines were not counted. Section 127 had provided, 'In reckoning the numbers of people of the Commonwealth, or of a State or other part of the Commonwealth, aboriginal natives shall not be counted.' This section was simply repealed.

The other amendment was to take out the words of exception from section 51(26) so that the Commonwealth Parliament would have the power to make laws with respect to 'the people of any race, for whom it is deemed necessary to make special laws'. The amendment would allow the Commonwealth Parliament for the first time to make laws with respect to Aborigines. Australians were convinced that the Australian Parliament belatedly had at least some role to play in discharging the national responsibility to Aborigines and Torres Strait Islanders. The amendments were so uncontroversial that no one in the parliament put forward a 'No' case, with the result that electors were provided only with a 'Yes' case. The 'Yes' case was prepared and authorised by Prime Minister Holt, joined by John McEwen, the leader of the Country Party and deputy prime minister, and Gough Whitlam, the leader of the Labor Party and leader of the opposition. The case for repealing section 127 stated:

> Our personal sense of justice, our commonsense, and our international reputation in a world in which racial issues are being highlighted every day, require that we get rid of this outmoded provision.
>
> Its modern absurdity is made clear when we point out that for some years now Aboriginals have been entitled to enrol for, and vote at, Federal Elections. Yet Section 127 prevents them from being reckoned as 'people' for the purpose of calculating our population, even for electoral purposes!
>
> The simple truth is that Section 127 is completely out of harmony with our national attitudes and modern thinking. It has no place in our Constitution in this age.

The case for amending section 51(26) stated that the amendment would achieve two outcomes:

> First, it will remove words from our Constitution that many people think are discriminatory against the Aboriginal people.
>
> Second, it will make it possible for the Commonwealth Parliament to make special laws for the people of the Aboriginal race, wherever they may live, if the Parliament considers it necessary.

Importantly, the 'Yes' case addressed the concern of some voters that a successful referendum could result in the Commonwealth going its own way on Aboriginal policy, leaving the states behind. The 'Yes' case stated, 'The Commonwealth's object will be to co-operate with the States to ensure that together we act in the best interest of the Aboriginal people of Australia.'[18]

Of those who cast a valid vote in the referendum, 90.8 per cent voted in favour of the amendments. The size of the majority in support of constitutional change rather caught the Holt Government by surprise. Holt now felt obliged to take some domestic action consistent with Australia's newfound international stand against racial discrimination. The overwhelmingly positive result in the referendum convinced Holt that the Commonwealth should act more decisively in seeking better outcomes for Aboriginal Australians. But state rights were still to be sacrosanct.

After the referendum, the Holt Cabinet took its first tentative steps in setting the new Commonwealth direction for Aboriginal affairs. The Cabinet decision of 15 August 1967 noted 'that the Commonwealth should not be seeking to take a large-scale initiative either on policy or administration and should, as far as possible leave administration to the states (and to its own department of territories which, in this regard, has a state function), though, of course, if a conflict of policy were to arise, the Commonwealth would be in a position to prevail'.[19] The Cabinet noted 'that the states, at any rate in the early stages, are likely to be sensitive about Commonwealth intervention'.

Accepting that Aboriginal policies and programs would continue to be formulated and delivered largely by the states, Holt decided to set up the three-member Council for Aboriginal Affairs (CAA), which could provide advice directly to him as prime minister. Cabinet 'felt that, at least in the period while policy is being developed, this office might best be associated with the Prime Minister's Department and that this would give it status as the central Commonwealth agency coordinating policy issues affecting aborigines'.[20] There had been some talk about the establishment of a parliamentary committee on Aborigines following the referendum. The Holt Cabinet decided to oppose such a committee while being prepared to accept the establishment of a committee open only to government members.

On 31 October 1967, the prime minister outlined to Cabinet his proposal for the CAA, 'perhaps to be established by statute, to advise the government in the formulation of policies in relation to aboriginal citizens'.²¹ Holt wanted a financial wizard, and he found one in Dr HC ('Nugget') Coombs, who was to serve part-time as chairman on the understanding that he would continue as Governor of the Reserve Bank until mid-1968. Holt also wanted the best anthropologist in the country, and he found one in Professor WEH Stanner from the Australian National University. Just as Professor AP Elkin had been a key anthropological adviser to the Commonwealth Government when Hasluck was minister for territories, Stanner now filled that role. Finally, Holt wanted a competent public servant. After some delay and testing of other possibilities, Holt settled on Barrie Dexter. In his delightful self-deprecating mode, Dexter says Holt was looking for someone who was 'honest, just, sympathetic with underdeveloped or deprived peoples, knows his way backwards through the public service and [would] not squeal when he was kicked'.²² Being ambassador to Laos, Dexter happened to be visiting Canberra on an official state visit by Prince Souvanna Phouma. When asked by Holt to join the council, Dexter replied, 'But I don't know anything about Aboriginals.' Holt said, 'That's why I asked you to take on the job. I'm frightened by the people who think they do know something!' We will never know if he had Hasluck in mind. Dexter then said, 'Mr Prime Minister, you are asking me to open Pandora's box!' Holt replied, 'That is precisely what I am asking you to do, Barrie.'

From the outset the CAA thought it imperative that they be able to provide a special channel of communication with the government, 'by aboriginals themselves or by organisations representing them'.²³ The government had not been responsive to suggestions that the Aboriginal university graduate Charles Perkins be appointed to the CAA. In October 1967, the influential journalist Sam Lipski had written to Tony Eggleton, the press secretary to the prime minister, suggesting the appointment of Perkins, who had been described in the US mass-circulation magazine *Ebony* as 'Australia's Martin Luther King'. Lipski thought that Perkins, who had just returned from a recent overseas study tour, was 'impressed by the natural "openness" of Australian society and the willingness of some Australians to at least consider improving conditions for his people'. Lipski was hoping that the government might find a way for Perkins to channel his energy to the advancement of his people. Lipski's concern was that if Perkins 'should decide that his assessment of Australian society is wrong, namely, that in his eyes we remain paternalistic and cynical towards improving conditions for the aboriginals, he could become a destructive force of little use to himself and be more harm than benefit to his people'.[24]

Dexter had cause to wonder whether Holt had brought his Cabinet with him in support for the new initiative. Hasluck, by then minister for external affairs, had the most experience of any minister in relation to Aboriginal issues, having been the minister for territories for 12 years from 1951 to 1963, during which time he had oversight of policy in Papua New Guinea as well as the Northern Territory. Having been appointed, Dexter needed to return to Laos to pack up and move his family back to Australia. En route he had the opportunity to meet with Hasluck in Bangkok. 'Hasluck did not disguise his strong – almost bitter – antipathy to the arrangements now implemented, as well as to the composition of the Council.' Dexter was left with the impression that Hasluck was hostile 'to the prospect of anyone, especially amateurs, tampering with the assimilation policy'.[25] Hasluck went on to become governor-general and thus maintained a discreet vice-regal public silence but continued to have ready contact with ministers about the policy developments emanating from the CAA. Hasluck later wrote his own reflections about Holt's decision to set up the CAA: 'I have no first-hand knowledge of any discussions leading to these decisions. When I heard of the decisions it seemed to me that Holt may have purposely excluded me from any discussion about what should be done. Perhaps he worked on the principle that if you are getting a new broom, you do not mess about with the old broom.'[26] Having been the Cabinet minister with greatest involvement in Aboriginal affairs, Hasluck was very circumspect about what might be read into the voters' intentions when supporting the referendum in such numbers:

> My view is that the large majority who voted for a change were expressing a strong opinion that more should be done for Aborigines and that any appearance of discrimination against them should be removed. I doubt whether the voters were making a considered judgment on the question of Federal and State powers or that they required the Federal Government to take the principal role in the administration of aboriginal affairs.[27]

Both Coombs and Dexter acutely felt their lack of experience in Aboriginal affairs. They thought their approach would be 'pioneering and adventurous, with an element of hit and miss in it, if we were to make any impact'.[28] They were delighted to receive a letter of congratulations from Professor Elkin, who thought that Coombs' prestige and Australia-wide experience were 'just what is needed to guide the Commonwealth's activities in this field, and to weigh the representations, claims and plans from states and from miscellaneous bodies'.[29] Elkin was heartened that with the recent grant of franchise many Aborigines had started 'realising and desiring that they should accept responsibility for their own community life'. On a recent trip to the Northern Territory he 'noticed a growing resentment to the doctrine that "Father knows Best" – that is, that what they do must be decided in Darwin'.

Speaking to a Canberra church group two years after his appointment to the council, Stanner expressed his longstanding reservations about government advisory committees but when asked to be a member of the CAA, he thought he had little choice: 'I felt that, if I refused, I would not again be able to look an aboriginal in the face.'[30] The council got down to work very promptly. At its first meeting, the council listed the issue of land rights. At its second meeting on 15 November 1967, the members met with Professor Charles Rowley and considered the question, 'Who is an Aboriginal?' At the end of the discussion Dr Coombs said, 'Perhaps the best definition of Aboriginal is a person who so describes himself.'[31] They discussed the policy of assimilation. Dexter recalls:

> As to assimilation, we were at the outset of the view that Aboriginals, and indeed other non-Anglo-Saxon Australians, were not in fact being assimilated – and that this indeed was contributing to their deprivation. We concluded that the Aboriginals would not be effectively incorporated into a single but diverse Australian society unless or until they actually wished to be so. On the basis of our knowledge of experience in other countries and of the situation of immigrants into Australia we were each convinced that minorities identify with the dominant culture more effectively when the decision is their own, when they are attracted to it by the benefits it confers, and when identification does not involve a repudiation of ethnic or national identity and tradition. We found ourselves in agreement that any people without link with the past, without social and family cohesion, without material resources and without self-respect and hope for the future was unlikely to be able to cope with the demands of a complex industrial society, largely alien and indifferent to its difficulties.[32]

From the start, Coombs set out his opposition to what he called omnibus welfare agencies. He was strongly opposed to any sort of Department of Aboriginal Affairs that would risk perpetuating the difference between Aborigines and other Australians. He proposed that 'the CAA should get the functional Commonwealth departments working in the specialist fields at the request of the Council after it had advised the government of the order of priorities'.[33] The CAA's first action was to have the prime minister write to state premiers proposing that the Commonwealth would provide financial assistance for all Aboriginal children wanting to attend secondary school.

The council's first flush of enthusiasm was short-lived with the tragic news of Mr Holt's disappearance in the surf at Portsea on 17 December 1967. Coombs wrote to Stanner four days after the disappearance of Holt wondering whether to accept the invitation to address the annual meeting of the Federal Council for the Advancement of Aborigines and Torres Strait Islanders (FCAATSI): 'My impression is that, despite some weaknesses and perhaps undue sectional influences on its activities, it is as close to a representative body of Aborigines as exists at present. Consequently, although it is somewhat inconvenient for me, I am inclined to think that I should accept the invitation.' Exercising his mind about Aboriginal representation, Coombs wrote again to Stanner two days after Christmas saying:

> I like Perkins, although he has his problems. I think it would be wise to find a role for him in which he feels that his special training and experience are really used. I think we have to give a great deal of thought to the development of some technique for enabling aborigines to choose their own representatives. These could, of course, be different persons from one whom we chose to consult in a specialist capacity.

Professor Stanner delivered the ABC Boyer Lectures entitled *After the Dreaming* a year after the referendum. The Boyer Lectures had by this time become a feature of national life, being broadcast on the ABC and providing a stimulus for public discussion. Stanner's lectures undoubtedly changed the way Australian opinion-makers thought about Aboriginal issues. In his third lecture, 'Appreciation of Difference', Stanner reflected on the referendum result:

> In 1967 nearly nine people in every ten who voted at referendum declared that the Commonwealth should have full power to legislate for all Aboriginal citizens wherever situate. No one knows or can say exactly what message that signal sent. The great reforms of the recent past – the full

suffrage, the end of discriminatory laws, and such other things – all real, all valuable, all in their way courageous, did not damage real interests or pockets to an alarming extent, and hardly a nervous voice was heard. The psephologists missed their biggest bus in not analysing what the voters had in mind.[34]

Not even Stanner, who was to be one of the great architects of the pending changes after 1967, had the least idea what those changes might be. At the time of the referendum, Aborigines did not have any recognised rights to their traditional lands. Assimilation was the government policy. Governments were committed to programs aimed at Aborigines leaving behind traditional ways and traditional lands, moving and becoming like other Australians, and as quickly as possible. These policies were pursued by state governments without any intervention by the Commonwealth, which pursued similar policies in the Northern Territory. After the referendum, state governments were assured that the Coalition Government led by Harold Holt would make little change to policy. The Commonwealth would be a voice at the table, offering some co-ordination and additional finance for ongoing state initiatives.

The CAA served governments of both political persuasions between 1967 and 1976. They were always at war with public servants and politicians, agitating their new ideas. Their chief antagonists were the Queensland Government, led by Sir Joh Bjelke-Petersen, and the Commonwealth departments of Territories and later Interior, which had responsibility for Aboriginal welfare in the Northern Territory. The council provided the ideas but, more often than not, was not responsible for implementation. While agitating for land rights and self-determination, they did not need to worry too much about the limits on these concepts. That was more the concern of the state governments and service-delivery departments like Health, Employment and Education at the Commonwealth level. The strong vote at the 1967 referendum provided the political impetus for the changes sought by the CAA, even though there was nothing in the wording of the constitutional amendments that pointed necessarily to these changes.

Between 1967 and 1976 these three white men, sometimes labelled by Aborigines as 'the three wise men', had the task of formulating national policy for Indigenous Australians, taking the country from the mindset of *terra nullius* to land rights, and from the template of assimilation to self-determination. When the term 'assimilation' was abandoned, various terms were tried in its place: integration, self-management and self-determination. Whatever term their political masters were using, the CAA members would constantly exercise their minds on how best to include Aboriginal Australians in the decision-making processes of government and in service delivery, but without an Aborigine ever becoming a member of their council. The narrative of land rights and self-determination provided a comprehensible focus for the law and policy for the next 20 years, in much the same way as Hasluck's narrative of assimilation had served the country between 1951 and 1967.

In his last book, *Shades of Darkness*, published in 1988, Paul Hasluck looked to the future and set out what he regarded as the basic questions:

> … whether Australians of aboriginal origin are to live together with other Australians, or apart from them; are they to have the same opportunities or different opportunities; are they to bear the same responsibilities and be subject to the same laws or are they to be regarded as a 'lesser breed' from whom less should be required? Is Australia to have one society or two societies?[35]

Noel Pearson appeared to be on the same page as Hasluck when he said in his 2013 Whitlam Oration:

> There is no contradiction in saying we recognise the importance of the nation's unique Indigenous heritage and history, while at the same time

confirming that we are all equal on the basis of our shared and equal Australian citizenship. The two propositions are complementary. The one entails the other. What's more, both propositions are politically necessary.

It is the confirmation that all Australians are equal before the law that legitimises and makes acceptable the symbolic recognition of Indigenous history and heritage. It confirms we are not creating a separate category of special treatment or collapsing into cultural relativism. It confirms that the same rules should apply to all Australians.[36]

If the Australian Constitution is to be completed rather than radically changed, the referendum proposals will need to further the possibility of one society in which all members, including Indigenous Australians, are accorded the same responsibilities and opportunities. There is no going back to the *terra nullius* template. Land rights are here to stay. The challenge is to design laws and policies which both allow the present generation of Aboriginal landowners to enjoy and make economic use of their lands and guarantee future generations a share in the Indigenous patrimony which is essential if Aboriginal cultures and heritage are to be maintained. Presently too many remote Aboriginal communities are landlocked. Meanwhile, government policies have continued to move along the spectrum from assimilation to self-determination and back. Any process for constitutional change and any new provisions placed in the Constitution need to provide the space for the robust but respectful dialogue to continue, about the limits of self-determination and the extent to which governments are justified in taking measures to attract Aboriginal Australians into the post-colonial society that respects Indigenous cultures and heritage while providing the opportunities and imposing the responsibilities for full participation in the life of the nation.

With an Abbott Government leading the pace and direction of constitutional change, there is no point in overlooking the strong resistance and antipathy of those like Paul Hasluck who thought the country went too far with notions of self-determination leading to separate development and social and cultural isolation. In *Shades of Darkness* Hasluck went on to ask about Aboriginal Australians:

> Are they to be a minority living an artificial, pampered and separate life, not supported by their own participation in what all other Australians are doing but by the bounty of those who earn the national income? Or are they to be living museum pieces? Or a sort of fringe community whose quaint customs are stared at by the tourists? Will the drone of the didgeridoo, the clicking of the boomerangs and stomping in the dust in the red centre of Australia still be the sufficient employment for the grandchildren of the people of Ularu [sic]? Will the separate development that is being pursued with a beneficent purpose today have the result after two or three generations that persons of Aboriginal descent find that they are shut out from participation in most of what is happening in the continent and are behind glass in a vast museum, or are in a sort of open-range zoo? Or is it intended that their separate development will be carried to a point where they become virtually a nation within a nation. That seems to me to be a dangerous absurdity – dangerous to Australia as a national entity in the world, dangerous for the future relationship between peoples of different ethnic origins in this continent and dangerous to the expanding hopes of aboriginal persons themselves. It is an idea that makes separate development not simply a transitional method but the permanent solution. That is abominably racist thinking.[37]

I had read these words in the past and discounted them as the musings of an old man disaffected that his ideas, which had been formed after deep reflection on the years of his personal dealings with Aborigines and had formed a lifetime of commitment, had been surpassed, and perhaps even discredited, by his colleagues without his having been adequately consulted. But then I was invited in October 2013 to speak at the launch of the Miriam Rose Foundation in Darwin. Miriam Rose Ungunmerr-Baumann was the first Aboriginal principal of a school in the Northern

Territory. She had also chaired her local community council at Nauiyu Nambiyu, Daly River. I have known Miriam, her family and her community for 30 years. One of the strong inspirations for Miriam wanting to establish her foundation was the death of her nephew Liam, aged just 22.

In November 1986, Pope John Paul II had come to Alice Springs, met Aboriginal people from across Australia, walked the Dreaming track, donned the Aboriginal colours of black, red and gold, and then held up baby Liam Marrantya, who had been handed to him by Liam's mother, Louise. The world knew Liam's baby face but the world knew little of his story thereafter. As a baby he evinced the warmest expressions of love and admiration from the strangers across the globe who saw him on their television sets. As a young man, he found no place of belonging in the world. He had no sense that he was being held as he experienced the whirlwind of life in remote Aboriginal Australia. The photo became an international icon. Coming into adulthood, Liam found himself all alone with nowhere to go, nowhere to belong and nowhere to be held. He lived out his life at Daly River, where Stanner had done much of his early anthropological work. He was isolated from all that he saw on television and from so much that he experienced whenever he went into Darwin. He drank too much, and then, like too many others, he took his own life. Miriam knew that Liam's journey had been travelled in far too many Aboriginal families. Something had to change. Land rights were not enough. Self-determination was meaningless for those whose lives were gripped by such a cycle of despair.[38]

The Australian way has always espoused equality for all, differential treatment and a social welfare net for those who need a helping hand, and recognition of difference for those who are the custodians of our unique Indigenous cultural heritage. Owning our history, entrenching equality, overcoming disadvantage and proudly embracing Aboriginality as central to our national identity are key elements of the Australian way. These elements must underpin the nation's commitment to recognising Aboriginal and Torres Strait Islander peoples in the Constitution.

Whether this is a task of completion or change is debatable. Talk of completion will still some community fears and tailor some Aboriginal aspirations. It is timely to attend to our Constitution now so that we can better move forward, agreeing on the appropriate limits on land rights, assimilation and self-determination so that all Australians might have the opportunity to participate in the benefits of a society that accords each their due and provides opportunities and demands responsibility for optimal health, education and employment.

What we need is a Constitution that provides the legal foundation and national responsibility for the recognition of land rights – land ownership, land access and protection of sacred sites – and realistic life choices for Aboriginal Australians. Assimilation collapsed because it was premised on *terra nullius* and governments deciding what was best for Aborigines, forcing them to become part of the mainstream by not providing them with any option. Self-determination collapsed under enormous human and financial waste caused by too many people presuming that land rights entailed choices, which in the end were unrealistic, unwanted or artificially contrived, as there was no capacity for the state or for Aboriginal communities to sustain the choices made. Just because an Aboriginal community has land rights, that does not guarantee a life of promise nor should it entail a limitation on their individual realistic choices for a life of potential for full human flourishing.

What we need is a referendum which kick-starts the political process for all parties coming to the table to determine the balance between security and utility in land rights and to set parameters on realistic choices for Aboriginal communities within which individuals and families can make informed decisions about their futures, including education and training, employment and business, and religious and philosophical disposition, whether they live in cities, country towns, remote communities or outstations. This referendum provides the opportunity for the nation to affirm belonging and realistic life choices for those who are the primary custodians of Aboriginal heritage, wanting to share equitably the benefits of our pluralistic, democratic society.

During the 1988 bicentenary, John Howard, as leader of the opposition, visited Alice Springs. On his return he told Parliament about his meeting with the respected Aboriginal leader Wenten Rubuntja, a noted artist and chairman of the Central Land Council. Rubuntja told Howard, 'We are all one mob but some of us have more problems than others.' Howard told Parliament, 'In a sense that sums up what I think a lot of Australians would like to be the approach towards improving the lot of Australian Aborigines.'[39] We can only do this by respecting land rights, culture and history, and providing realistic life choices for the future. That is what a successful referendum could achieve. No matter what the ultimate formula of words put to the people at referendum to amend the Constitution, the proposals will not succeed unless there be a general community consensus that the amendments accurately and simply state the basis for the distinctive moral entitlements and realistic life choices of Aborigines and Torres Strait Islanders, including those who are no longer poor, disadvantaged and dispossessed.

Today the country is once again searching for a new narrative, as it was in 1967. But we know that narrative must result from an informed dialogue between Indigenous and other Australians. We have experimented with various modes of Aboriginal representation at the national level. All have been found wanting. There was the National Aboriginal Conference and the Aboriginal and Torres Strait Islander Commission. Now there is the cumbersome, under-resourced National Congress of Australia's First Peoples, which is yet to develop any significant national traction and profile. The Abbott Government has handpicked an Indigenous Advisory Council of 12 members, including business leaders and respected Aboriginal leaders. This council will advise primarily on economic issues. There is no focal point for Indigenous participation in government decision-making. There is no credible, well-resourced national forum for the expression of Indigenous viewpoints. So the task of consultation about constitutional reform is not easy. Reconciliation Australia, the independent, national not-for-profit organisation committed to national reconciliation, has set up Recognise, a people's movement that has attracted over 200,000 supporters in the quest to have Aborigines and Torres Strait Islanders recognised in the Constitution.

The Howard, Rudd, Gillard and Abbott governments have tried to explain the benefits of an ongoing 'federal intervention' in the Northern Territory, which has included laws and policies that target only Aborigines, restricting their economic freedom and land rights without their consent. We continue to wrestle with the limits to be imposed on the concepts of land rights and self-determination. The term 'self-determination' continues to have appeal for those schooled in international human rights instruments and for those who, while conceding Aboriginal sovereignty is an impossibility or a problematic legal construct, favour maximum Aboriginal independence within the nation state. It is not a term that has broad public appeal or understanding. It is not the sort of term to be readily invoked in a referendum campaign. Aborigines seek practical land rights and realistic life choices. Practical land rights would address Noel Pearson's concern that his people are presently 'land rich and dirt poor'. They hold a land title but often can do nothing with the land. Realistic life choices have to include drawing on the strengths of traditional culture and having access to all that modern life has to offer. Practical land rights and realistic life choices may well be the two new paradigms.

Those who think that a resounding vote for constitutional recognition of Indigenous Australians in the near future will simply be a matter of minor legal housekeeping, while we all get back to business as usual, need to take a closer look at the post-1967 history. I am not suggesting that a successful referendum will lead to similar tectonic paradigm shifts as occurred in 1967 with the move away from *terra nullius* to land rights and the move from the ideal of assimilation to the ideal of self-determination. But due recognition of Indigenous Australians will occasion a reassessment of the chief policy parameters. It will mark a re-commitment by the Australian public to attend to unfinished business concerning the moral entitlements and the realistic life choices for Indigenous Australians, many of whom still weigh in at the bottom end of social indicators whether in relation to life expectancy, health, education, employment or imprisonment.

In the context of the contemporary discussion in Australia, it is important to remember that prior to the 1967 referendum no political leader was suggesting that a successful referendum result would occasion any massive change in policy or responsibility. No parliamentarian or Aboriginal advocate was suggesting to the public that the referendum would be the pathway to land rights or to the abandonment of assimilation. Today, it is not as if we have found the ideal policy solutions, given our faltering steps at closing the gap and providing realistic training and work opportunities for Indigenous Australians, especially on remote communities where people continue to live on their traditional lands, often without any economic prospects or practical training opportunities.

Half the Northern Territory landmass is now held by traditional owners with an inalienable freehold title. All states now have some form of land rights legislation. Following upon the High Court's 1992 *Mabo* and 1996 *Wik* decisions, the parliament's *Native Title Act 1993* sponsored by Paul Keating, and the amended Act sponsored by John Howard in 1998, Australia now has a very complex network of laws for dealing with native title, in addition to the Aboriginal statutory titles under state schemes. The *Native Title Act* is now 551 pages in length. There is a lot of work to be done to provide a right balance between security and utility of land. While 18 per cent of the continent has been subject to native title determination, and another 18 per cent of the landmass is covered by indigenous land use agreements pending ultimate native title determination, prospective native title holders are often constrained from being able either to use the land themselves or to authorise others in the economic use of the land.

Even if we agree only to complete the Constitution, rather than change it, we will be taking a bold step as a nation, seeking a new national partnership between Indigenous and other Australians committed to a just and proper settlement for Indigenous Australians wanting to belong again in this land and in the society built upon their dispossession. Despite large expenditures and goodwill on both sides of the political aisle, Australia's Indigenous policy is in a mess. There is no clear narrative comprehensible to the Australian public. There is a complex web of legislation and administrative arrangements for Aborigines and Torres Strait Islanders wanting to access government funds allocated for their benefit.

In the present time of transition it is difficult for non-Indigenous Australians committed to the rights and aspirations of their fellow citizens who are Indigenous to know how to contribute to the formulation of a new narrative, and how to help give voice to diverse Indigenous aspirations. For example, we hear strong, passionate and coherent voices such as Noel Pearson in support of income management for welfare recipients on Aboriginal communities, and equally passionate and coherent voices such as Nova Peris in opposition. As we search for the new narrative and for the new processes to ensure that Indigenous voices are heard prior to the institution of laws and policies specifically directed at them, it is timely to look back on the era of the CAA, learning lessons from these three white men who took seriously both the Dreaming and the Market. Some think that Coombs, Stanner and Dexter were incurable romantics who easily got their way in the corridors of power around Canberra. Nothing could be further from the truth. They worked with hostile and supportive governments, with competent and incompetent ministers, with co-operative and obstructionist departments, and with radical and conservative Aboriginal leaders. They were misunderstood and lampooned in the media as they were praised and idolised.

Delving into the history of post-1967 referendum developments, I hope to provide pointers for a satisfactory completion of the

Constitution in the next referendum, confident that any change will kick-start further reflection and national commitment to put right the injustices of the past and to set in place laws and policies that ensure justice for all Australians, including the first Australians. This requires a national conversation about morality and not just law. It requires experienced realism about what works and not just academic commitment to freedom of choice. The idealism and tenacity of Hasluck, Coombs, Stanner and Dexter provide some inspiring pointers for those of us, whether we are Indigenous or not, seeking a better way.

It would be unhelpful for a non-Indigenous Australian such as myself to engage in gratuitous commentary about contemporary debates on policy within the Indigenous community, especially when there is no cohesive Indigenous voice in the marketplace of ideas. Unlike the situation in 1967, there is now a bevy of Aboriginal thinkers and activists whose views are well published and whose alliances are well known. There is no point to be served by identifying as a Patrick Dodson supporter or a Noel Pearson supporter, as a Marcia Langton backer or a Michael Dodson backer. The country is the richer for a plurality of Aboriginal perspectives. Looking back to the work, achievements, frustrations and hurdles of Coombs, Stanner and Dexter, I hope we might come more quickly to a new national paradigm of moral entitlements and realistic choices for Indigenous Australians. I have been privileged to know all three men.

I spoke at Coombs' funeral in St Mary's Cathedral, Sydney, and his funeral instructions were simple: 'Bach at the beginning, "Waltzing Matilda" at the end, and no God-bothering in between.' I attended Stanner's funeral, having received the last letter he ever wrote. Just a month prior to his death, Stanner had given anthropological evidence to the court in Alwyn Peter's case. As the junior barrister appearing for Peter, I had thanked Stanner for his evidence. He replied:

> I am fascinated by the question: how do general ideas about human conduct change so quickly? I can recall about fifty years ago appearing as

a witness for the defence in an Aboriginal murder case in Darwin before Wells J. He was notably unimpressed by my arguments but nevertheless reluctantly took them into account in mitigation, while looking round the court as if expecting trouble. Or do I mean 'remarkably quickly'?[40]

He died four days later, still awaiting the decision in the Daly River land claim in the Northern Territory on which he had worked. Aboriginal claimants, their lawyers and anthropologists received news of his death as they anticipated the verdict at Daly River. 'Old men such as Pincher Mulluk Mulluk told young anthropologists how they had been carried on Stanner's shoulders while he hunted and talked with elders long since gone.'[41] I have also enjoyed many a fine conversation with Barrie Dexter at his home in Canberra while preparing this book.

I write for competent conscientious 'whitefellas' convinced that we still have an unfinished national agenda, and for those Indigenous Australians still minded to give us the benefit of the doubt despite the gap between rhetoric and reality in accommodating their legitimate aspirations in the life of the nation. I do not pine for a return to the template of Stanner, Dexter and Coombs any more than I pine for a return to the template of Hasluck and Elkin. I think we can learn lessons from them all as the next generation of Australians negotiates terms of settlement and recognition.

CHAPTER 2

THE COLLAPSE OF *TERRA NULLIUS* AND FORCED ASSIMILATION

The lead-up to the 1967 referendum needs to be seen in terms of the collapsing paradigms of *terra nullius* and forced assimilation that had informed Commonwealth Government policy and relations with Aboriginal communities in the Northern Territory, and had been the basis for Aboriginal policy in the states since 1788. *Terra nullius* is the idea that the land belonged to no one prior to the arrival of the British because, before then, no one living on the Australian continent had developed the notion of land ownership.

On Australia Day 1961, Minister for Territories Paul Hasluck convened a meeting of state ministers and government officers in Canberra – those who had 'an administrative responsibility in the advancement of native welfare'. Hasluck had been the minister for territories for ten years. Back in 1951 he had convened a Native Welfare Conference, which agreed to a national policy of assimilation rather than the longstanding policy of protection of Aborigines living on remote communities. He now saw a need for a further conference to discuss the meaning of the policy and to see if there could be better co-operation between the Commonwealth and state governments in advancing the policy. He also wanted better co-ordination across Australia to ensure that the same definitions were used in determining which 'natives' or 'wards' of the state came under special protective or restrictive legislation and in deciding the grounds for exemption. In his opening remarks, Hasluck observed:

> Such a meeting is a time for business rather than piety. But, at the same time, all of us know that we would not be here, engaging in these talks if we did not share a belief that this is a work that touches our humanity, our faith and our national self-respect. This is a work that demands a clear head but it also warms the emotions. It calls for idealism as well as common sense.

Hasluck noted that the anniversary of the founding of the first European settlement in Australia was 'a fateful day for the aboriginal people of this continent'. He urged the participants to find ways in which governments and society could work more closely to create the social reforms necessary to give Aboriginal Australians a helping hand and 'the chance of a full and happy life'. Hasluck displayed both equanimity and optimism, describing Australia as the land of the fair go, and concluded, 'I am confident that a country like Australia, which has already mastered so many of the problems of living together in a free society, and has achieved so large a measure of social justice, respect for human rights and equality of opportunity, has it well within her capacity to deal with the situation of 70,000 aborigines in a community of 10 million.'[1]

After the conference Hasluck received, out of the blue, a letter from the young Charles Perkins, an Aboriginal soccer player in Adelaide hoping to complete his secondary education. Hasluck had already met Perkins briefly. On hearing about the conference, Perkins had written expressing an interest in attending. He wrote, 'If there is any possibility of myself attending this most important of all meetings, with an opportunity of voicing the coloured people's opinion, then I would be most honoured as I am sure I can be of some help.'[2] Hasluck did not receive the letter until after the conference but he replied immediately, pointing out that the conference was for government personnel only. Hasluck undertook to provide Perkins with copies of the proceedings. He also commenced inquiries with the bureaucracy to see if anything could be done to assist Perkins with his ongoing education. Perkins wrote:

> If the conference has dealt fully with most of the points accounted for on the Agenda, then we, the Aboriginal blooded people of Australia, can hope for a more enlightening policy from the respective governments in our States. My most determined intention in life Mr Hasluck is to, if possible, have some influential opinion in determining this policy and it is to this end that I am and will always be striving.[3]

Over the next six months the two shared a regular correspondence, culminating in Perkins accepting the offer of a clerkship in the Northern Territory.

In April 1961, the House of Representatives set up a Select Committee on Voting Rights for Aboriginal and Torres Strait Islander people. Kim Beazley Snr, the member for Fremantle, was the main representative from the Labor Party. Peter Howson, elected in 1955, was the main representative for the Liberal Party and the member for Fawkner. This committee made visits to 39 Aboriginal communities and heard from over 300 witnesses, of whom at least 140 were Aboriginal.

The committee was troubled to find that 17,000 Aborigines in the Northern Territory were classified as 'wards', unable to enjoy the usual benefits of citizenship. The committee was firmly of the view that all adult Aborigines and Torres Strait Islanders should be permitted to vote in federal elections. In 1962, they were given that option. The work of this committee was very formative for Peter Howson, who later became the first minister for Aboriginal affairs in the Gorton Government in 1968. Looking back on his career, Howson said, 'I'd seen and listened to Paul Hasluck right from the time I first got into Parliament because he really knew so much more about this than anybody else at the time in Parliament.'[4] The committee found that fewer than 2000 Aborigines were living in traditional tribal cultures. The report noted that, 'As a situation of complete integration is inevitable, your committee considers that the aim of the Commonwealth should be to assist integration to continue as smoothly and speedily as possible.' The committee recommended that there be strong Commonwealth investment in education, industries, land tenure and housing. There was cross-party support in the committee.

Two years after the creation of the select committee, the Yolngu people from Yirrkala on the Gove Peninsula in north-east Arnhem Land presented a petition to the Australian Parliament, expressing concerns about proposed bauxite mining on their traditional lands. This community was part of a Methodist mission on an Aboriginal reserve. The Yolngu grievance about proposed mining was to become a litmus test for so much of the work to be done by the Council for Aboriginal Affairs from 1967 to 1976.

Prior to Federation in 1901, the governments of the colonies had treated Aborigines as if they had no rights to their traditional lands. At Federation, the area now known as the Northern Territory was under the jurisdiction of South Australia. On 1 January 1911, the Northern Territory was handed over by South Australia to the Commonwealth Government and, for the first time, Canberra had to consider making provision for Aboriginal Australians. Much of the Northern Territory during the latter part of the nineteenth century had been made available for pastoral leases, which were granted over vast areas of land for a fixed term, usually 30 or 40 years. The pastoralist would use the land for cattle raising, and Aborigines would be allowed continued access to the land for hunting and gathering.

In 1886, John Arthur Macartney was granted a pastoral lease over the Yirrkala lands. The land was hardly used, and the last lease in the area concluded on 10 January 1913. No more pastoral leases were granted. The land was not suited to cattle raising. In 1931, the Commonwealth

Government proclaimed a reserve in Arnhem Land for 'the use and benefit of the aboriginal native inhabitants of the Northern Territory', including the land originally part of the Macartney pastoral lease. Then in November 1935, Reverend Wilbur Chaseling arrived in the area and founded a Methodist mission. The Methodist Missionary Society of Australia Trust Association was granted a lease over the land for a term of 21 years from 1 July 1938. With this lease, the missionaries were able to take up residence and conduct a mission, starting to provide the makings of a small township on the Yolngu land. At this time, all Australian governments encouraged the churches to provide personnel who could care for Aborigines in remote parts of the country. For 20 years, the Methodist missionaries were the only white people to maintain significant contact with the local Aboriginal population at Yirrkala. Then, in 1955, surveyors and miners started arriving to conduct exploration activities on Yolngu country. The land was found to be rich in bauxite, a newly sought mineral that could be refined to produce aluminium.

In 1958, the government commenced issuing mining leases in the area. Though Paul Hasluck had claimed in 1954 that economic activity on Aboriginal reserves would be permitted only after due consideration of Aboriginal concerns, he and his fellow ministers saw no need to deal directly with the Yirrkala people or the local Methodist missionaries. They did, however, consult with the Sydney-based Methodist Overseas Mission Board, which gave general agreement in principle for mining to proceed, and Reverend CF Gribble, general secretary of the board, became involved in discussions with government and prospective miners.

When the Australian Government first decided to open up the Gove Peninsula to prospecting for bauxite mining, there was no mention of the concerns or rights of the local Aborigines even though Hasluck as early as 1954 had given the assurance that Aboriginal concerns would be considered when Aboriginal reserve land was being dedicated to other purposes. The first leases were granted to the Commonwealth Aluminium Corporation Pty Ltd (a partnership of British Aluminium

Company Ltd and Consolidated Zinc Pty Ltd) in November 1958. Hasluck announced the granting of further permits to the Gove Bauxite Corporation on 19 July 1961 and indicated that the government would be agreeable to a smelter being constructed locally so that aluminium could then be exported to Japan.

The Yirrkala Indigenous community and the local Methodist missionaries found they had been left out of any discussions within the church's hierarchy as well as with government. The deals between the church and the state were being cut down south. The Aborigines trusted the Reverend Edgar Wells, who became superintendent of the mission in 1962. They had many discussions together. Wells knew more than his prayers. He was in the habit of sending telegrams to the press and to other key contacts in the south to inform them about Yirrkala developments. Though Wells was kept in the dark by his mission superiors, at one stage Arthur Calwell, the leader of the opposition, provided him with critical information about proposed excisions of land at Yirrkala. The Yirrkala Aborigines decided to contact Gordon Bryant, the Labor member of federal parliament and the member of the Federal Council for Aboriginal Advancement. Bryant asked his party elder Kim Beazley Snr to accompany him to Yirrkala. While there, Beazley went to the mission church to look at the magnificent bark paintings: 'Suddenly, I had an idea. We met again with the tribal council, and I urged them to petition parliament with a bark painting. I was sure this would catch the attention of the press. Then it could not be ignored in the way that most petitions are.'[5] Wells and the Aborigines liked the idea.

Reverend Gribble attended a meeting with Hasluck and representatives of the Gove Bauxite Corporation in Sydney in February 1963. Gribble reported that the mission board then unanimously approved 'the assurances given by the Minister and the Company as it has the right to do in an emergency of this kind'.[6] The only 'emergency' was the rumblings of discontent coming from people on the ground in Yirrkala. The mission board was anxious to give mining the go-ahead despite the objections coming from their own mission superintendent and the Aborigines at Yirrkala. The government granted special mining leases within the Aboriginal reserve in the Gove area to the Gove Bauxite Corporation and the French company Pechiney on the understanding that Pechiney would divest its interest in an Australian subsidiary. The only mention of Aborigines was the announcement that double royalties would be paid, 'the proceeds of which are to be paid into a trust fund for the general benefit of aborigines in the Territory'.[7] Agitation had commenced in the ranks of the Methodist Church. The Victorian Methodist newspaper reported, 'No consultation had taken place at any level between Rev. C. F. Gribble or Methodist Overseas Mission and the people of Yirrkala.'[8]

On 23 May 1963, Kim Beazley Snr proposed an opposition motion in the House of Representatives that 'an Aboriginal title to the land of aboriginal reserves should be created in the Northern Territory'.[9] In hindsight, Peter Howson thought this was the first indication of the breach in bipartisanship on Aboriginal policy. It was the first time that any senior politician in the Commonwealth Parliament had suggested that Aborigines might be granted a legal title to their traditional lands.[10]

The Yirrkala people presented their petitions to Parliament, mounted on bark paintings as Beazley had suggested. Copies were then tabled in the House of Representatives on 14 August 1963 by WC Wentworth on the government side and Jock Nelson, the member for the Northern Territory, on the opposition side, and then on 28 August 1963 by Arthur Calwell, the leader of the opposition, and Kim Beazley Snr. The petitions are now proudly and permanently displayed in Parliament House, together with a copy of the Magna Carta. They read:

To the Honourable the Speaker and Members of the House of Representatives in Parliament assembled:
The Humble Petition of the Undersigned Aboriginal people of Yirrkala, being members of the Balamumu, Narrkala, Gapiny, and

Miliwurrwurr people and Djapu, Mangalili, Madarrpa, Magarrwanalin-irri, Djamparrpuynu, Gamaitj, Marrakulu, Galpu, Dhaluangu, Wangurri, Warramirri, Naymil, Rirritjingu, tribes, respectfully showeth —

1. That nearly 500 people of the above tribes are residents of the land excised from the Aboriginal Reserve in Arnhem Land.
2. That the procedures of the excision of this land and the fate of the people on it were never explained to them beforehand, and were kept secret from them.
3. That when Welfare Officers and Government officials came to inform them of decisions taken without them and against them, they did not undertake to convey to the Government in Canberra the views and feelings of the Yirrkala Aboriginal people.
4. That the land in question has been hunting and food gathering land for the Yirrkala tribes from time immemorial; we were all born here.
5. That places sacred to the Yirrkala people, as well as vital to their livelihood are in the excised land, especially Melville Bay.
6. That the people of this area fear that their needs and interests will be completely ignored as they have been ignored in the past, and they fear that the fate which has overtaken the Larrakeah tribe will overtake them.
7. And they humbly pray that the Honourable the House of Representatives will appoint a Committee, accompanied by competent interpreters, to hear the views of the Yirrkala people before permitting the excision of this land.
8. They humbly pray that no arrangements be entered into with any company which will destroy the livelihood and independence of the Yirrkala people.

And your petitioners as in duty bound will ever pray God to help you and us.

It is commonplace for citizens to present petitions to Parliament about all manner of things. But never before had petitions been presented to the Australian Parliament with such solemnity. When the petitions were discussed in the House, Paul Hasluck took the opportunity to explain the developing policy of assimilation that was replacing the policy of protection. He said:

> Over the past 30 years there's been a growing sense of responsibility among the Australian people and by all Australian governments and the growing belief that their obligation towards the aboriginal people is greater than simply to provide, as it were, an isolation ward in which they may die in peace. Increasingly, year by year, greater efforts have been made for the advancement of the aboriginal people. Today the agreed policy of all Australian governments is a policy of assimilation, which means that conscious efforts are to be made to advance the aborigines to a stage where they may live to the same advantage on the same standards and in the same places as every other Australian and where they may have the same opportunities as all other Australians.[11]

As the minister for territories, Hasluck was belatedly trying to correct the bureaucratic mentality that Aboriginal reserves could be readily revoked if the land were required by other persons for another purpose. He continued to insist that Aborigines derive some benefit from any mining occurring on Aboriginal reserve lands. He thought it sufficient that the government obtain a double royalty from any mining operation with the proceeds being dedicated to Aboriginal projects in the Northern Territory.

Hasluck was anxious to demonstrate that he was solicitous of Aboriginal interests in land, even though he had not suggested the granting of land titles. During the parliamentary debate on 12 September 1963, following the presentation of the Yirrkala petitions, Hasluck published for the first time a minute he had circulated to his departmental officials 11 years previously on 28 April 1952:

> There is no policy of reducing aboriginal reserves. We expect that, as and when our measures of the social advancement of natives may succeed, there will be a lesser need for the natives to use native reserves in the way in which they are used at present by the natives, but this expectation that circumstances will change as time goes on cannot be stated as a policy. As and when the needs of the natives change, decisions will be made in each separate case whether an aboriginal reserve should, in the light of the new needs, be abolished, reduced or increased.
>
> In all matters relating to reserves the phrase 'use and benefit' should not be interpreted only to mean wandering over the reserves for the purpose of hunting, food gathering or practising tribal rights, even if those were the only uses to which the reserve was put at the time of its creation.[12]

Hasluck's hope and expectation was that eventually there would be no need to maintain any Aboriginal reserves because all the people living on them would have made the transition to assimilation, living elsewhere and having no need to return. But until that time came, Hasluck was committed to maintaining the Aboriginal land base on the gazetted reserves so that Aborigines could continue to live there untroubled until they were ready to move and be assimilated into the mainstream community. Hasluck was able to tell Parliament, 'From that point on the files will show that we have consistently resisted the excisions from native reserves.' He also shared with the House a departmental minute he had circulated in August 1962 stating:

> No excisions from reserves or abolition of reserves are to be made for purposes of settlement or subdivision unless the circumstances are such that the aboriginal wards can themselves take part in the settlement or benefit from the subdivision. These reserves are being held today, not as a refuge to which aborigines can retreat and live in a tribal state, but as reserves of land to meet the future needs of these people when they have advanced further

towards civilisation. Particular application of this policy can be seen in the mining laws under which special royalties are paid for the benefit of wards if any mining is done on reserves or on land excised from reserves.[13]

Between 1952 and 1962, Hasluck had become more accepting of the idea that not all Aborigines were likely to leave the reserves and migrate to the towns and cities. Some would want to remain on their traditional lands and ongoing provision should be made for them. He also became more accepting of the idea that these reserves could be made available for commercial development, with the Aborigines directly benefiting from the development on the land. He was inching towards land rights. Though wanting to avoid the possibility of segregation of Aborigines, Hasluck insisted:

> Country with economic potential on reserves is to be held untarnished until such time as the Aboriginal wards can themselves share in the benefits which arise from its development. With an increasing Aboriginal population the maintenance of this policy is more important than ever and while there is justification for retaining as reserve the land that is at present remote (for openness will cease to be a disadvantage), there is no justification for leaving them only the land that is bad. We have to keep the good land on the existing reserves.

As early as September 1963, Hasluck, having for the first time shared the content of these earlier memos with Parliament, was able to declare, 'I say explicitly that if it would give greater firmness to a policy which is now enunciated in ministerial minutes, our line of thinking is that it should be given statutory form.'[14] By the time of receipt of the Yirrkala petitions, both sides of Australian politics were starting to think about land rights.

The Yirrkala Indigenous community had given the Australian Parliament its first opportunity to focus on land rights. Having spent years on the opposition benches, the Labor Party felt a greater liberty than the government to raise some of the moral quandaries surrounding Aboriginal ownership of land. After all, there was little prospect of Labor having to enact the policy of transferring ownership and control of vast land reserves to Aborigines. In opposition, they could agitate the moral questions without setting the limits on land rights. Kim Beazley Snr moved the motion for the establishment of a parliamentary select committee to inquire into the grievances of the Yirrkala residents. He said, 'The moment the petition was presented to this parliament, this parliament was put on trial. In fact, I think, the Australian nation is on trial. Morally, the nation is on trial in any event, even if this matter had no international implications. Internationally, in fact the nation is on trial.'[15] While not questioning the government policy of assimilation, Beazley suggested, 'If they are members of the community of the Australian Commonwealth they cannot be dispossessed of land that they occupy without consultation.'[16]

At this time, the parliamentary notice paper, which lists the business that members of parliament want debated, included an item proposed by the Labor Party espousing some kind of title to land for Aboriginal Australians in places they occupy as living areas. Beazley argued that some form of land title would be a precondition to avoiding constant crises developing whenever there was a demand for mining or pastoral activity to occur on Aboriginal lands. Gordon Bryant was more confrontational, questioning how the policy of assimilation could be applied in a remote place like Arnhem Land. He asked:

> Assimilation into what, into what are we going to assimilate these people? There are 4,000 aboriginal people in Arnhem Land and there is not one policeman. In what other part of Australia could you have 4,000 people and not one police officer? It might be better in some ways if we were assimilated into the traditions of the people of Yirrkala.[17]

In September 1963, following Beazley's parliamentary motion, the House of Representatives voted to set up the Select Committee on the Grievances of Yirrkala Aborigines. The committee held hearings in Yirrkala, Darwin and Canberra. Significantly, they heard three days of evidence in Yirrkala and thus were able to hear directly from the Aborigines, including Yolngu elder Milirrpum and the Methodist superintendent, Reverend Wells. The committee heard plenty of evidence about sacred sites and the Aboriginal relationship with the land. The chairman of the committee, Mr RL Dean, asked Milirrpum, 'Do you think it is a good idea for the mining people to come here and work on some part of the area? Do you think that this will bring advantages to your people?' Milirrpum replied:

> We did not know what people came here. First of all aboriginal people not get whisper nowhere. Other people really plunder this country – only take from this country. We did not know, first of all, why they came. But later on, we soon get a little bit of word. But all aboriginal people did not get the word from mining people to mission. After that, when mission people get a little bit of word from mining people and mission tell us they went to all the marks. After mission tell us, we were worrying a little bit about our country. All aboriginal people did not know anything about why they mine bauxite. That is why the people little bit worry. They see men plunder this country. We were worrying about our children and our country. We want to hold all the country. All generations of our people here. The people here little bit worry because of all this whisper, and that is why we people come together this afternoon for this business.
>
> If this country taken, we want something else from mining people. This aboriginal people's place. We want to hold this country. We do not want to lose this country. That is how the people are worrying about this country. We want to get more room for our hunting and our fishing, because later on we got more people. Our children are to come. All my

children at school in this country. They want to hold this country. We fought the law for our children for all this country. Please, we do not want to lose this country. We stand on this country. The Aboriginal people were the first Australians here. Then you people come along. Please, that is my word I am telling you. That is my last word. Thank you.[18]

Three days before he gave evidence, Superintendent Wells received a castigating letter from Reverend Gribble, who was greatly disturbed by Wells' activities in relation to the mining proposal. Gribble wanted Wells to understand that the mission board's support for the mining proposal came 'after long and careful negotiation' and that 'no strong objection was taken either by the District or the people to this'. It was not appropriate for Wells to be adopting a contrary position and he should not be commenting publicly 'on questions of policy and missionary work generally without the knowledge of the Chairman of the District and without his consent'.[19] Wells was undeterred. He gave evidence at some length and explained the Yirrkala people's connection with the land:

> After living among these people, I accordingly advised my superiors to indicate to the Prime Minister [Sir Robert Menzies] that this mining deal should only be brought about by negotiations using the utmost delicacy, or otherwise even a security problem could arise. Even after such an agreement, and none was suggested to the best of my knowledge at any level with the aboriginal people, men would remain for many years disturbed at a primary, psychological depth that would need careful and constant watchfulness. A man's territory can be defined as the area within his range of movement that he will defend to hold.
>
> As a result of certain camp-fire meetings at one stage of this suggested land take-over, a most able and senior leader of these said, 'Tell them they can have the rocks from the middle [the bauxite deposit], but they cannot have the coastal lands and the sea. We are sea people.' The vigorous response they displayed when a fisherman found a surveyor's peg on Bremer Island

convinced me that the 'territorial hold' and depth of mental awareness must be dealt with. There has been a constant guard on Bremer Island ever since, under the people's own initiative.[20]

Wells was given free rein in the presentation of his evidence, and he took it, probably realising that his days as a mission superintendent at Yirrkala were about to end. He favoured the development of the mining project, but he believed it should be owned by an Aboriginal trust set up by agreement with the government rather than with the private sector. He told the committee, 'I believe the response from other, and some far distant, sections of the aboriginal community in Australia indicates that the Government will make a great mistake in pursuing a policy without the full consent and awareness of the original holders of primary title in Arnhem Land.'[21]

CE Barnes, shortly to become Hasluck's successor as the minister for territories, was a member of the parliamentary committee. He asked Wells if he agreed with the policy of assimilation as explained by Hasluck. Wells replied:

> My comment is that the Department of Territories treats different groups of indigenous people under different terms of association. For instance, what has happened over Gove mining bauxite development simply could not, in terms of Mr. Hasluck's own reference to the matter, have taken place in New Guinea – could not. That would indicate that one group of indigenous people could have certain privileged property rights and ownership values. I believe that part of the content of assimilation, viewed from a certain social point of view, is that the Australian aboriginal is now enjoying what other people do not enjoy; that is access to certain lands without, as it were, specific title being paid for by some way or other. Assimilation to some people means that they can be moved from the land in order to be made equal. I do not believe that to be the proper way of bringing about the Government's policy of assimilation, but it appears now that we are confronted with a case in

point that assimilation could be interpreted to be the policy of movement whereby somebody else acquires what is now the aboriginal person's land value. I do not share that approach.[22]

The House of Representatives select committee reported to Parliament on 29 October 1963, finding that there had been no discussion between public servants and the Yirrkala people before the decision was made to excise land from the Aboriginal reserve to allow mining. The only discussion had been with the Methodist Mission authorities.[23] The Sydney-based church leaders had unilaterally decided what they thought was best for the Yirrkala Aborigines. The local residents and the local mission staff were strongly of the view that they had not given their consent to the mining development and they had not been adequately consulted. The all-party committee of politicians agreed. The committee learned that the government's chief welfare officer who covered Yirrkala was away on leave at the time. The committee felt 'that the Welfare Branch's lack of proficient linguists also led to a failure in clear communication in May 1963, after excision and the granting of the lease, when officers met representatives of the people to explain the proposal'.[24] The committee found that there were 'many sacred places within the whole of the excised area'.[25]

The committee reported that Aboriginal landholding arrangements seemed somewhat fluid, with ownership or control changing hands fairly readily. They heard reports that land in the Cape Arnhem area had 'recently changed hands'.[26] The available literature, including the published writings of the Reverend Chaseling, indicated that there was a 'changing pattern of hunting rights over the total area'. It is important to note that the committee quoted without criticism some of Chaseling's observations about warring groups displacing each other. Chaseling's observations were to become critical in the later court proceedings instituted by the Yirrkala Aborigines against the Commonwealth and the miners. In those later court proceedings, the lawyers and expert witnesses appearing for the Aboriginal landholders were very critical of Chaseling's interpretation that Aboriginal relationships with land were quite so fluid as he suggested in his writings. Even though there had been minimal disruption to Aboriginal life in this part of the world by outsiders coming onto the lands, there had clearly been internal land disputes and some land transfers by the local Aborigines. It was not possible to view the Aboriginal landholding arrangements as fixed from time immemorial.

Committee members of both party allegiances were of the view that compensation should be paid for the taking of any lands that the Yirrkala people thought they owned. Never before had Australian members of parliament spoken with one voice about the moral entitlement of Aborigines to some recompense for the loss of their traditional lands. The committee stated, 'Where, upon investigation, it is clear that there was claim to an area of land which was felt by the Yirrkala people to constitute ownership, your Committee believes that a direct monetary compensation should be paid for any loss of traditional occupancy, even though these rights are not legally expressed under the laws of the Northern Territory.'[27]

The committee recommended that compensation for loss of traditional occupancy be made by way of land grant, capital grant and monetary compensation. The committee favourably quoted the Reverend AF Ellemor, state secretary of the Methodist Overseas Mission of Victoria, who was realistic enough to accept that mining would proceed while thinking it would be wrong to move the mission to another site without Aboriginal consent simply so as to make mining easier or more economical. He was troubled that Aborigines would have to bear the consequences of others deciding how and where mining would proceed. He invited the members of parliament to see the mining issue in the broader context of the fraying policy of assimilation: 'I believe that this bauxite development – because it is in this area – presents us with a challenge to the whole policy of assimilation ... I further believe that the place to grapple with this problem of assimilation is here.'[28]

Neither Reverend Ellemor, representing the Victorian Methodists who thought their national mission board had sold the Aborigines short, Reverend Wells, the superintendent of the Yirrkala Methodist mission, nor the committee realised at the time that the Yirrkala mining development would spell the end of the formal policy of assimilation and the beginning of land rights. The select committee successfully recommended the establishment of a standing committee, which would be charged with making regular visits to Yirrkala and reporting on the proposed mining by the Gove Mining and Industrial Corporation and its social impact. Parliament rose within the week and Australia went to the polls on 30 November 1963, returning the Menzies Government with a healthy majority.

Hasluck tried to make out that the parliamentary committee report had changed nothing and that the government was already attentive to all legitimate Aboriginal concerns. The Methodist mission board saw no need to change its approach; it simply needed to bring their local mission superintendent to heel. During the election campaign, Hasluck wrote to Reverend Gribble, assuring the mission board that 'Most, if not all, of the recommendations of the Committee had already been covered by the recommendation written into the lease or accompanying agreement. Personally, I always appreciated the way in which your own Board had assisted us in trying to do what is best.'

Gribble wrote again to Wells restating the board's objections to Wells' improper opposition to its decisions. The national board had decided that Wells should leave Yirrkala and return to Milingimbi, where he had previously worked for ten years.[29] Wells decided to give notice of retirement by mid-year. He was immediately ordered back south. He was in no doubt that he was being punished for his evidence to the parliamentary committee contradicting the position of his national board, which had agreed to the government's proposal to grant the mining leases. Wells was being sacked for standing up for his people, the members of his local church congregation at Yirrkala. Some members of parliament offered to institute contempt proceedings against Gribble. Wells wrote to the chairman of the committee, saying that he could not be party 'to the possible legal condemnation of a brother in Christ'.[30] Though out of sorts with Gribble and the national board, Wells was not going to wash the church's dirty linen in public.

After the election, Hasluck was promoted from his long-held portfolio of territories to defence. He was succeeded by CE Barnes, who at least had the benefit of having heard firsthand the Aboriginal grievances at Yirrkala when he served on the parliamentary select committee. The newly elected government decided to postpone the mining proposal by the Gove Mining and Industrial Corporation because it was not sufficiently advanced and it did not include the provision of a local alumina plant, which would have provided a value-added product and additional local employment. The government invited further bids.

Two major consortia of Australian and foreign companies put in bids. Announcing the successful bids for bauxite mining leases to Parliament on 15 September 1965, CE Barnes insisted that the successful bidders would need to demonstrate 'a preparedness to respect the rights of the Aborigines in the area',[31] whatever that meant, given that the government was still firmly of the view that the Aborigines had no legal rights to land. The government had done nothing to follow up the parliamentary select committee's recommendation that direct monetary compensation should be paid for loss of traditional occupancy. The consortium led by BHP missed out, and the consortium led by Nabalco Pty Ltd, in which CSR had a major interest, together with Swiss Aluminium Ltd was successful. The seven Australian companies in the successful consortium were committed to underwriting 50 per cent of the project. The successful bid included commitments to build an alumina plant with a capacity of 500,000 tonnes per annum, as well as wharf and township facilities. Barnes told Parliament: 'The company has undertaken to respect the rights of the Aborigines in the Gove area and will provide them with suitable employment opportunities.'

There was a growing public understanding and sentiment in support of Aborigines having recognised rights to land and having some say in what should happen on their land. In the parliament, this was no longer just the isolated opinion of the occasional Labor member in opposition. The Yirrkala saga had awakened the consciousness of Australians that the *terra nullius* mindset, backed by a commitment to forced assimilation for Aborigines, was unsustainable. There was now a permanent standing committee of the House of Representatives, which had the ongoing task of monitoring the situation at Yirrkala against the benchmark of the recommendations made by the 1963 parliamentary select committee, including the need to protect sacred sites and traditional hunting grounds, the need for the local Aboriginal community to be consulted about the location of the proposed mining town, and the entitlement to compensation for loss of traditional occupancy by way of land grant, capital grant and monetary compensation. Yirrkala was the national test case of new policies, given that all members of the 1963 parliamentary committee had optimistically stated that the proposed Gove development 'gives the Commonwealth for the first time in history' the opportunity 'to demonstrate that urban development by Europeans does not automatically reduce Aborigines to the status of fringe-dwellers, and that land development does not reduce them to the status of dispossessed people'.[32]

These were the new policy parameters to which all members of parliament now needed to give at least notional assent. There was no public disquiet with this new policy direction. It provided the backdrop for the 1967 referendum campaign, which encouraged the Australian public to vote for a constitutional change that did the right thing by Aborigines, providing them with a fair go and the full benefits of citizenship. The protection of sacred sites, the protection of traditional country, appropriate consultation and compensation were now part of the mix when determining fair laws and policies. Once the 1967 referendum was carried so overwhelmingly by the Australian public with the unqualified encouragement of both sides of parliament, it was inevitable that the 1963 recommendations for Yirrkala would become a test case for real change.

Prime Minister Harold Holt announced the formation of the Council for Aboriginal Affairs (CAA) on 2 November 1967. He gave the council a free hand in determining its priorities. At its third meeting on 7 December 1967, the council decided that land rights would be a key priority. They decided to make Yirrkala the national test case. But then came the tragic news of the death of the prime minister a week before Christmas in 1967. The new prime minister, John Gorton, who took office in January 1968, did not share Holt's commitment to making a fresh bold start in Aboriginal affairs. He did appoint the nation's first minister in charge of Aboriginal affairs, Mr WC Wentworth. The old Department of Territories, which had administered overseas territories as well as internal Commonwealth territories such as Christmas Island and the Northern Territory, was split in two. There was now a separate department for dealing with overseas territories such as Papua New Guinea. The internal territories, including the Northern Territory, would now be administered by the Department of the Interior. The CAA, having spent its first couple of months directly under Prime Minister Holt and within the Department of Prime Minister and Cabinet, would need to negotiate Northern Territory policies through officers from the Department of the Interior. This would also require the council and its minister to have regular dealings with the minister for the interior, who was always a member of the Country Party, the Coalition party least sympathetic to any new direction in Aboriginal affairs.

The CAA was very disappointed at the governor-general's speech at the opening of parliament in 1968. Having forwarded a detailed action plan, which they confidently expected to appear in that speech, Lord Casey merely made reference to the co-ordinating role of the CAA and noted that the council would 'consider ways in which aboriginal citizens can choose their own representatives to consult with and advise the council'. The council, wrongly as it turned out, took heart from the governor-general's observation that 'the responsibility for the Northern Territory will, except in certain respects as regards the welfare of aboriginals, education and national development matters, be transferred to the Department of the Interior'.[33] They thought they would have a clear path to implementing their policy agenda in the Northern Territory. This was not to be the case.

Barrie Dexter describes this as the beginning of five lean and terrible years during which, for the most part, they had no allies, but many enemies, in Cabinet.[34] While Harold Holt had promised CAA members that he would promulgate and perhaps even legislate a special charter for the CAA, Gorton was to show no interest in entrenching the role or status of the council, who would then find they were something of an anomaly within the Commonwealth bureaucracy.

The CAA's direct access to the prime minister was gone even before it started. Instead, their conduit was the enigmatic and disorganised WC Wentworth. There was no doubting Wentworth's personal commitment to Aboriginal advancement, but as minister he was not a team player and he was given to sporadic, disjointed policy announcements. One of his earliest ministerial fiats was a request for thousands of outdoor toilets to be erected in the Northern Territory. Coombs said it was no wonder that his initials were WC.

In April 1968, Coombs proceeded with his planned address to the Federal Council for the Advancement of Aborigines and Torres Strait Islanders (FCAATSI) Conference. Speaking of the CAA, he told the Aboriginal delegates and their supporters, 'It is not intended that the Council and its office will become large or involved in administering day to day matters of concern to Aboriginal citizens.' Wrestling with how best to ensure Aboriginal representation and access to government, he told them:

> There is one task, however, which the Council will perform itself. In his statement announcing the establishment of the Council the late Prime

Minister said that one of its important jobs would be to maintain touch directly with Aboriginal communities so that their views could be heard effectively in the making of policies affecting their welfare. A good deal has been said and done from time to time about the views of Aboriginal citizens being heard, but I think there is a growing feeling amongst Aboriginal Australians that their spokesmen should be chosen by themselves. This is certainly the council's view and the Minister, the Hon WC Wentworth, in various statements has expressed it forcefully. It was good to hear the Governor-General endorse it in his speech at the opening of Parliament last month.[35]

On 22 May 1968, the Gorton Cabinet had its first opportunity to consider a detailed Cabinet submission from Minister Wentworth. The CAA had produced a very detailed set of policy proposals for Wentworth, including suggestions about land rights and non-discriminatory legislation. Outlining their vision, they had set out principles including co-operation with the states, the need for the Commonwealth to lead by example in its own territories, and the establishment of conditions for Aboriginal citizens to live with dignity, commanding their own activities and enjoying full opportunity for their aptitudes. They steered clear of the term 'assimilation'. They then proposed a number of programs, including funding to the states to enhance Aboriginal housing, health and education, a capital fund for Aboriginal enterprises with an associated technical advisory service, and a commitment to increased Aboriginal employment in the Commonwealth public service. They recommended legislation establishing a court or tribunal to determine land claims by Aboriginal communities on the grounds of traditional occupancy. They readily acknowledged that there were difficult problems to be resolved in relation to land that would require further study.

The CAA was not a government department, and nor were they situated in the minister's office as advisers. But they were the formal advisory body to the minister. Wentworth was not interested in detailed policy proposals coming from the CAA. He had his own ideas. He wanted to sideline the CAA and simply do his own thing. He proposed that the CAA instead be made advisers to the small Office of Aboriginal Affairs, which consisted then of a few public servants resourcing the CAA. Tension ran high between the CAA and Wentworth when, without any discussion, Wentworth reworked the whole policy document, omitting any reference to land rights. Dexter later wrote:

> Our proposals, long-pondered, discussed with the States and with numerous Commonwealth departments and amended to take account of their valid suggestions, were emasculated and unrecognizable, and the general form of the redraft was uncoordinated and illogical, and the language incoherent.[36]

Coombs was in Sweden and so he was unable to respond, but Dexter and Stanner regarded it 'as the first tangible evidence of what we have suspected – as the complete rejection by the Minister of the concept of the council as both the major policy forming body and his own adviser'.[37] Dexter was very disturbed that the minister was attempting to develop different lines of policy 'by going behind our backs and dealing directly with his ministerial colleagues', and thought it would damage the CAA's standing with other departments.

Cabinet decided to delay consideration of the policy proposals, asking that an interdepartmental committee provide a paper for the Cabinet's consideration.[38] This greatly frustrated Dexter, who then had to sit on the interdepartmental committee and deal with exasperated public servants from other departments, who had already provided the CAA with their views on the various policy proposals.

Though the CAA had already expressed reservations about the assimilation policy, Wentworth, backed by Hasluck, by now the minister for external affairs, had his way in Cabinet once the proposals had passed through the interdepartmental committee. There was no one in Cabinet to represent the CAA position that the assimilation policy was now discredited and unworkable. The detailed Cabinet decision of 2 July 1968 'declared firmly that the ultimate objective would continue to be assimilation – a single Australian community':

> While recognising that it will take generations for the Aboriginals to become fully assimilated into the Australian community, the Cabinet's position is that it will hold patiently and purposefully to this aim. It will measure any policy proposals against it and would want to avoid proposals which, by identifying Aboriginals as such and setting them permanently apart from other Australians, are likely to have the effect of acknowledging and establishing a policy of continuing separate development leading to an eventual racial problem.[39]

Cabinet wanted Prime Minister Gorton to take the opportunity at the forthcoming meeting of Commonwealth and state ministers on Aboriginal affairs to 'reaffirm the objective of assimilation as distinct from permanent separate development'. Cabinet was open to provision of special transitional arrangements that would help to accelerate the progress towards assimilation. Cabinet insisted on the need for close consultation with state governments, and was willing to take a pragmatic approach in providing assistance for housing, health and education. Coombs had easily convinced his fellow CAA members that the Commonwealth should take economic initiatives, not just directing funds to the states, but also directly funding local Aboriginal groups wanting to start their own businesses or service delivery operations. Cabinet was willing to adopt the Coombs initiative of funding co-operatives but with some qualifications. 'Whenever appropriate opportunity occurred', these co-operatives were to include white people as well as Aborigines. The Cabinet also wanted to see those Christian churches that were working among Aborigines to be 'drawn on by the Government in its policies and planning and brought into activities, where appropriate, as a stabilising influence'. Given the activities of the Methodist missionaries at Yirrkala and the Presbyterians on some of the Queensland communities, who were also starting to stand up for land rights and self-determination, this was looking less likely.

Cabinet planted the seeds for ongoing tension and misunderstanding between the small Office of Aboriginal Affairs overseen by Dexter and the Department of the Interior. The ministry in charge of Aboriginal Affairs was acknowledged as having 'overall responsibility ... for policy in relation to Aboriginals on an Australia wide basis'. However, Cabinet noted that the Department of the Interior's 'responsibility for the implementation and administration of the program within the Northern Territory remains'. This was a recipe for bureaucratic turf wars in the future with both the CAA and Interior thinking they were primarily responsible for the policy aspects, rather than service delivery, in relation to Aboriginal affairs in the Northern Territory.

In the years ahead, the Department of the Interior would maintain a firm assimilationist stance consistent with the 1968 Cabinet decision and true to the vision articulated for so long by Paul Hasluck. Meanwhile, the CAA, when negotiating funding arrangements for Aboriginal programs in the states, would gradually shift national policy away from assimilation towards voluntary integration and long-term assistance for those Aborigines and their communities wanting to maintain their cultural identity on traditional lands. The battle lines were drawn.

Cabinet agreed to an initial lump sum payment of $9.9 million to an Aboriginal Advancement Trust Account. Half this amount was to be available to provide capital grants for viable business enterprises in line with Coombs' vision. In the Northern Territory, Minister Wentworth as minister-in-charge of Aboriginal affairs was to have responsibility for deciding the projects on which expenditure would be made, but in consultation with the minister for the interior.[40]

On 12 July 1968, Prime Minister Gorton addressed a conference of Commonwealth and state ministers responsible for Aboriginal affairs who met at Parliament House in Melbourne. This was the first major address by an Australian prime minister outlining Indigenous policy since the May 1967 referendum. Gorton said, 'Our ultimate objective is, of course, the assimilation of Aboriginal Australians as fully effective members of a single Australian society.' He quoted the policy as it had been enunciated at the 1965 conference between the states and the Commonwealth on Aboriginal affairs: 'The policy of assimilation seeks that all persons of aboriginal descent will choose to attain a similar manner and standard of living to that of other Australians, and live as members of a single Australian community.' Gorton said that all policy proposals would be measured against this objective and that the Commonwealth wished 'to avoid measures which are likely to set aboriginal citizens permanently apart from other Australians through having their development based upon separate or different standards'. Gorton was anxious to reassure the states that the Commonwealth would not be taking over and that any independent Commonwealth action would occur only after consultation with them. Emphasising the need for Aborigines to be self-supporting as fully and as quickly as possible, he announced the establishment of the Aboriginal Advancement Trust Account. Gorton said that 'effective assimilation is dependent upon aboriginal citizens being able to stand on their own feet'.[41]

Though pleased that Gorton had agreed to establish the trust account, the CAA was very worried by the assimilationist tone of Gorton's remarks and the clear indication that he would not be proceeding any more quickly along the path of encouraging local Aboriginal initiatives than the states might want to move.

Uncertainty about policy direction was heightened by the CAA's tensions with Interior and by their frustrations with Minister Wentworth. While recovering from surgery on 18 August 1968, Stanner read the papers for the next CAA meeting and wrote to his fellow council members from his hospital bed, observing:

> The various papers all read, and wept over. You know what? Our Bill [Minister Wentworth] makes me think of one of those infuriating slot machines on old railway stations. You put in your penny for advice or counsel; wait for the click that never comes; turn away in despair; and, just as you're walking away, there is a queer rattle, and out pops – not a bar of chocolate or even an acid drop – but a card saying 'A tall dark man is coming into your life'. Send regards to all deserving cases.

Addressing officers of the External Affairs Department about a year later, Stanner expressed the view that 'we are moving into a new phase of aboriginal affairs … The great challenge is to adapt policy and to develop new practice to meet the factual situations of the next decade or so. The policy and practice of the Hasluck era are overdue for re-examination.'[42] He readily conceded that the idea of assimilation when first thought up two decades previously seemed a true breakthrough: 'People latched onto it gratefully. It cleared the vision, or seemed to do so, mainly, I think, by contrast with the past. Since that time the whole context of aboriginal affairs has changed.' Some of those changes included Australia's embracing of diversity in migration, new thinking about how to achieve development for poor and marginalised groups with an emphasis on their human dignity, a staggering increase in the Aboriginal population, a marked drift of Aborigines to the cities, a change in Aboriginal self-perception and self-expression, the distinct possibility of a pan-Aboriginal movement, and a change in the public mood. Though not proposing any one-word description of the new policy being pursued by the CAA, Stanner thought the CAA had much work to do in moving beyond the stereotype of assimilation and that it would be 'to everyone's advantage to have frank discussion within the family'. He said, 'My impression is that the policy of assimilation has been hardening into a sort of dogma, which no one is supposed to assail on pain of being thought a reactionary, or an agitator, or worse, an idealist, or worse still, an academic. This is surely the danger point for any idea.' Later critics of the council could well have said the same about the ideas of land rights and self-determination.

Meanwhile, the Aborigines at Yirrkala had received no satisfaction from government about their concerns relating to the proposed bauxite mine. They had sat down for numerous meetings with federal politicians but they still thought they had not been heard or sufficiently respected since they had first sent their bark petitions to Canberra. The constitutional referendum had changed nothing for them. The CAA was unable to further their cause within the political process marred by the bureaucratic turf war with Interior. However, Professor Stanner had delivered the 1968 ABC Boyer Lectures, in which he drew attention to the plight of the people at Yirrkala. In his second-last lecture, entitled 'Confrontation', he spoke of the anomie that characterised so much of Aboriginal relations with other Australians. He identified four causes of this anomie: homelessness, powerlessness, poverty, and the disparity between plans and styles of life. Speaking of homelessness, he conjured images that decades later were to help inform High Court judges make sense of the Aboriginal relationship with land. Stanner said:

> No English words are good enough to give a sense of the links between an Aboriginal group and its homeland. Our word 'home', warm and suggestive though it be, does not match the Aboriginal word that may mean 'camp', 'hearth', 'country', 'everlasting home', 'totem place', 'life source', 'spirit centre' and much else all in one. Our word 'land' is too spare and meagre. We can now scarcely use it except with economic overtones unless we happen to be poets. The Aboriginal would speak of 'earth' and used the word in a richly symbolic way to mean his 'shoulder' or his 'side'. I have seen an Aboriginal embrace the earth he walked on. To put our words 'home' and 'land' together into 'homeland' is a little better but not much. A different tradition leaves us tongueless and earless towards this other world of meaning and significance. When we took what we call 'land' we took what to them meant hearth, home, the source and locus of life, and

everlastingness of spirit. At the same time it left each local band bereft of an essential constant that made their plan and code of living intelligible. Particular pieces of territory, each a homeland, formed part of a set of constants without which no affiliation of any person to any other person, no link in the whole network of relationships, no part of the complex structure of social groups any longer had all its co-ordinates. What I describe as 'homelessness', then, means that the Aborigines faced a kind of vertigo in living. They had no stable base of life; every personal affiliation was lamed; every group structure was put out of kilter; no social network had a point of fixture left.[43]

Stanner then put to the nation the Aboriginal case for land rights, rather than assimilation, with an eloquence that moved many listeners and brought him to the attention of those determined to assist the Yirrkala community. He thought he had 'perhaps given the impression that these things all happened long ago and far away'.

Only the other day I went to the corner of Arnhem Land where a great mineral industry is taking shape within an Aboriginal reserve. I thought it would be interesting to see at first-hand the response the Aborigines are making to it, and whether they grasp what it may hold in store for them. On the few evidences I could gather in a brief visit they could not be said to be opposed to it in an outright way. I would say, rather, that they were simply overborne by the weight of external initiative, authority and advice that all will be well. But, for all that, those I spoke to or listened to were perplexed and worried in spite of a hope that great things would come to them.

Perplexed, understandably enough, because none of them can really grasp the scale and complexity of the enterprise; or gauge the changes it will bring into their lives at its peak; or foresee the place they will have in the new world it will bring. A new world indeed! Apart from a very large industrial complex which, according to published statements, will cost several hundred millions of dollars, there will be a new port, a new township for several thousand Europeans, not all directly concerned with the industry, and a whole new infrastructure to carry out the developments. The Aborigines of course have no comprehension of what lies ahead. The adjustment they will have to make will be greater relatively than that which the Aborigines of Botany Bay and Port Jackson had to make to the smaller and more leisurely events of Phillip's time. At present they are shielded by a little distance from the immediate hurly-burly of first-stage development, but before long a wave will burst over their heads. The Industrial Revolution engulfing 18th century rural England could not have been more devastating.

They were worried by one fact already patent to them: that some large tracts of country which they believe, in their innocence, to belong to them, will be foreclosed for a long time, perhaps lost forever.

I listened to one elderly man speaking on the matter. He was something of an orator, with a power of words, a sense of pause and gesture, and very evident ability to phrase the conventional wisdom of his audience. I had the sense that he expressed well what many of his fellows were feeling and thinking. He turned his back to the open waters of Carpentaria, and looked north, west and south to the great stretches of Arnhem Land which no one – no one, that is, except the Aborigines – wanted only a few years ago when we knew nothing of the mineral riches that have been discovered. In a dramatic way he pointed to and declaimed the names of territories and places within the tribal domain. 'All of them', he said, 'are our country'. He then named the places already or soon to be lost under the special leases created over them. I could not follow all he said because I depended on an interpreter but there was no mistaking the substance of his remarks or the fact that he was unhappy and unreconciled. Were they to be compensated? Would yet more land go? Would the sacred places really be protected? These were among the questions he asked, but no one present could answer him with the scruple and certainty that alone could set his doubts at rest. The upshot was that he and others made the response that must have happened a thousand times since 1788. They said, in effect: our homeland is being whittled away; we have no power to control what is happening; we do not understand; we are in your hands; by ourselves we can do nothing. There was no long ago and far away about this: it happened in August 1968.[44]

By this time, the views of Reverend Wells, the outspoken mission superintendent at Yirrkala, had carried the day in the Methodist Church. He had received strong backing from Victorian Methodists, upset with the national mission board members' actions in Sydney. With assistance from the Methodist missionaries, the Yirrkala people decided to try the law. On 23 December 1968, Frank Purcell, a solicitor from Werribee in Victoria, wrote to Stanner informing him, 'We have received instructions on behalf of aboriginal clans of the Gove Peninsula in the Northern Territory to take legal action on their behalf regarding aboriginal land rights.'[45] He said that his clients were being assisted by the Aboriginal affairs commission of the Methodist Church in Melbourne. They wanted Stanner to assist in supplying material and giving evidence at the hearing.

Stanner was not only available, he dedicated extraordinary energies to the case for the next three years. Coombs was easily convinced to come on board. Dexter was also strongly supportive, but being a public servant he was restricted in what he could say. The CAA had earlier been cautioned by the Department of the Interior about providing public commentary in support of Aboriginal land rights. Officials at the department had not been impressed with Stanner's Boyer Lectures. On 5 January 1969, Coombs, as 'Guest of Honour' on ABC national radio, threw caution to the wind and spoke about the injustice confronting Aborigines at Yirrkala:

> Recently, you may have read reports of a new agreement between the Government and a joint overseas and Australian company for the development of a mighty bauxite and alumina project on Gove Peninsula in the

> Northern Territory ... Nowhere did I see any reference to the fact that this development is to take place in an Aboriginal reserve – on land which Mr Paul Hasluck, when Minister for Territories, pledged would be reserved or withheld from development, until it could be developed for the use and benefit of the Aboriginal people. And nowhere did I see any discussion or controversy about the effects of the agreement on the Aboriginal residents, or how far these developments are in fact for their use and benefit.

Coombs concluded with his heart on his sleeve:

> All my working life, it has been my good fortune to have worthwhile and exciting work to do. For this I have been and am grateful; but above all, I find myself grateful now that, while I still have eyes to see with, a tongue to speak with and a mind to understand with, I can help build a place for our Aboriginal Australians in a society diverse enough, culturally rich enough, and politically wise enough to welcome them with honour.[46]

First thing the next morning, Minister Wentworth was on the phone to Dexter insisting that members of the council were not free to engage in such public commentary. Dexter insisted that he was the only one of the three who was a public servant, and Dr Coombs and Professor Stanner were free to exercise their discretion as citizens unless and until a charter for the CAA was finalised. The land rights genie was out of the bottle, and there was nothing Wentworth could do about it. The assimilation cork had reached its use-by date.

On 9 January 1969, Stanner received a very complimentary note from the esteemed Julius Stone, Professor of Jurisprudence at the University of Sydney. Stone wrote: 'Let me voice my admiration to your excellent Boyer Lectures, which I found both deeply thoughtful and courageous and moving. It is encouraging to have minds like yours and Nugget's playing on the side of Australia's responsibilities. With best wishes to 1969.' Stanner replied, attaching a copy of his sixth undelivered Boyer

Lecture, dealing with his own interpretation of the jurisprudential aspects of the pending litigation with the Yirrkala Aborigines suing the Commonwealth and Nabalco, claiming legal ownership of their traditional lands which were subject to the Commonwealth mining leases granted to Nabalco. Stanner suggested to Stone:

> A court could be asked to rule that the Commonwealth's legal duty should now be made fully coincident with its moral duty. That is to say, the Commonwealth, being recognised as the owner in law of the Reserve lands, should now consent that the aborigines be recognised as the owners in equity. It could be demonstrated that the Yirrkala aborigines for a long time have considered the relation with the Commonwealth to be of this kind, and only because of that have abstained from the violence formerly shown towards non-aborigines who intruded into the region.[47]

Though not a lawyer, Stanner was willing to investigate ways in which a court could be convinced that the Aboriginal moral entitlement to their traditional lands could be translated into legal concepts familiar to those trained in the British legal tradition. Though conceding that the crown was the legal owner of these lands since European settlement, Stanner was suggesting that a court might be convinced to find that the crown held the land in trust for the Aborigines, and that as trustee the crown was obliged to have due regard for the entitlement of the beneficiaries, the local Aboriginal community.

The CAA set about convincing politicians and the public that there was a need for fundamental legal and policy changes – from *terra nullius* to land rights, and away from assimilation to a policy that allowed Aborigines more control over their identities and destinies. In time, people would use the term 'self-determination'. Unlike the pre-1967 changes from protection to assimilation, these reforms would come at some considerable cost to other interests because if implemented, Aborigines would be recognised as the owners of lands in which miners and pastoralists also had an interest. There would be a legal requirement for Aborigines to be adequately consulted about any future developments on their lands. There may even be a need for Aboriginal consent to these developments. It was no longer true to say that 'hardly a nervous voice was heard', which was the way Stanner had described the public reaction to his Boyer Lectures.[48]

On 25 September 1969, Stanner circulated to the council 'a premonitory note on the apparent certainty that after the election there will be a Department of Aboriginal Affairs', no matter who won government at the election due one month later. If Labor were to win, he accurately predicted that it would be a more omnibus department than the Coalition would have proposed. That is precisely what was to happen once Labor won the election after that one, in December 1972. Rather than accepting this as inevitable, Stanner counselled putting a strong counter-case:

> (a) the marked success of our efforts to use the Federal and State functional departments, (b) the immense difficulty of Australia-wide administration without a complex Federal machinery, (c) the certainty of serious friction if competing or overlapping Federal functions were started in State territories, (d) the contradiction between a policy of assimilation and a practice of administrative segregation, and (e) the general anachronism of omnibus Departments of Aboriginal Affairs.[49]

Though the CAA had ongoing difficulties with Interior in the Northern Territory, it had been making steady progress with the agencies in the states, and even with the service delivery departments in Queensland, despite ongoing tensions with Queensland's powerful Department of Aboriginal and Islander Affairs. The CAA members were great believers in co-operative federalism, with the Commonwealth being able to provide the money and policy goals for the state departments delivering the services that they were best equipped to provide. Stanner added a strong footnote:

'A Department, once established, would be most difficult to disestablish. It would discourage assimilating and integration, keep aboriginal separation in being, stimulate the movement for ethnic identity, and provide dissident interests with a unifying target.' How right he was. How ironic that, in later years, conservative critics would lay the blame for these very developments at the feet of Coombs and his colleagues. It was the politicians, not their advisers, who sought the omnibus federal department. The advisers accurately predicted the problems.

Not having a fully fledged parliament, the Northern Territory was governed primarily by an administrator appointed by the Commonwealth Government. The key public servants were Commonwealth officers from the Department of the Interior. When Fred Chaney Snr (the father of Fred Chaney who later served as the minister for Aboriginal affairs and then in 2011 as a member of the Expert Panel chaired by Patrick Dodson and Mark Leibler) was taking over as administrator of the Northern Territory in March 1970, Coombs took the opportunity to write to him setting out the role of the CAA and its major concerns about the Northern Territory administration. He explained, 'Generally speaking the Council seeks to avoid executive responsibility relating to Aboriginal affairs, feeling that it is in the main preferable for this responsibility to be borne by the executive department or agency concerned.' He provided Chaney with three key research papers from the CAA relating to: Aboriginal communities on pastoral properties; a visit to Wave Hill, where the Aborigines had gone on strike at Lord Vestey's cattle station; and the situation at Gove and Yirrkala. The priorities of the CAA were clear. He expressed concern that the Welfare Branch of the Northern Territory Administration, being the successor of the old Native Affairs Branch, was still too much an omnibus department responsible for delivering all services to Aborigines. So, although the CAA wanted to have government move away from the policy of assimilation, they were at the same time strongly in favour of what we would now call mainstreaming. Coombs told Chaney:

> There is, we believe, good reason for Welfare to shed responsibility for health, education, local government, economic development, and other matters in so far as they affect Aborigines, and for these responsibilities to be picked up by those branches of the Administration functionally responsible. Thus, basically, we consider it wise that Aboriginal communities, even on reserves, should be administered as much as possible as are other small towns and communities, i.e. by the branches and departments concerned with the provision of community services, rather than by the Welfare Branch.[50]

The CAA could see no sense in maintaining a bureaucracy that purported to be a jack of all trades and master of none. If it was sensible to have specialist departments such as Health and Education delivering services to non-Aboriginal communities, then the same should go for service delivery to Aboriginal communities. Also, the CAA was concerned that the Northern Territory Administration in the past had treated 'town-dwelling part-Aboriginals' as part of the general community and distinguished them from 'Aboriginals' and did thereby 'make more difficult the incorporation of Aboriginals themselves into the general community'.

Coombs was going out of his way to make it clear that the CAA did not have any separatist agenda. It wanted mainstreaming and it wanted to maximise the prospect that 'Aboriginals' and not just 'part-Aboriginals' would seek voluntary incorporation into the general community. The CAA was accurate in their prediction: 'We believe there is an increasing tendency for part-Aboriginals to identify as Aboriginal rather than as European Australians and it is our view that, when being of Aboriginal descent is found in practice in no way prejudicial to the welfare or advancement of a citizen, this tendency will be even the greater.' The CAA saw no point in distinguishing between Aborigines on the basis of whether they had a mixed racial or cultural heritage. Increasingly, those with any Aboriginal heritage tended to identify as Aboriginal and it was no concern of the state to draw arbitrary distinctions. The CAA was anxious to work with all government agencies to ensure that the era of forced assimilation was put to rest and to provide specialist assistance through service delivery departments for Aborigines making their own life choices, including continuing to live on their traditional lands, hopefully with legal recognition of their title. The concern of the assimilationists was that this would create a regime of separate development founded on the legal entrenchment of unequal rights. This concern continues in Australia today, at a time when we are considering constitutional recognition of Aborigines and Torres Strait Islanders.

The greatest and most experienced advocate of assimilation, Paul Hasluck, died in 1993. His son Nicholas published some of his last papers in *Light That Time Has Made*. Paul had been troubled by the 1988 visit to Australia of Professor Erica-Irene Daes from the UN Working Group on Indigenous Populations. She had reported, 'Australia stands in violation of her international human rights obligations.' Hasluck was worried that the country was slipping from harmony to discord and that 'in some quarters the idea that all Australians have equal rights has given place to a view that they have unequal rights'. Any assertion of unequal rights would heighten racial antipathy. He concluded, 'There surely can be no other view of the coming century than that both Aboriginal and non-Aboriginal persons in Australia will live together in the Australian continent. That future will be a troubled one if we do nothing but assert rights against each other and forget our common responsibility to work for a common future.'[51]

During Hasluck's lifetime, land rights had become a precondition for the exercise of the Aboriginal responsibility to make realistic life choices, especially for their children. Constitutional recognition must be about the recognition of the rights and responsibilities necessary for all Australians to live together on this continent, having the opportunity to achieve their full human flourishing, peacefully and justly.

CHAPTER 3

THE PROMISE OF THE 1967 REFERENDUM

The possibility of land rights and better life choices

In 1964, a patrol officer with the Northern Territory Administration's Welfare Branch, Jeremy Long, published two articles about patrols among the Pintubi people in the Central Desert in which he had participated between 1957 and 1963. These articles provided unique insights into the contemporary dilemmas confronting public servants encountering Aborigines in remote areas where there had been minimal previous European contact. He wrote evocatively and empathetically about the plight of a thinning population in harsh terrain that crossed from Western Australia to South Australia and up to the Northern Territory. After the 1957 patrol in the Lake Mackay area, the government officers considered sinking wells to provide a more assured water supply. But by 1961, 'the whole group settled at Mt Doreen and later moved to Yuendumu. Here they settled in quickly, and, although they sometimes spoke of going out to collect relatives still in the desert, it was clear that they would not take up a hunting life again.'[1] All three governments co-operated to do what they could to help these people while at the same time insisting that there be no revocation of the Aboriginal reserve lands and that 'the three governments concerned should develop facilities for the Aborigines living on them'.[2] Government was committed to maintaining the option for the people either to return to their traditional country, which would be maintained as an Aboriginal reserve, or to remain at Yuendumu, where they would be provided with housing and basic services. Long gave a heart-rending description of the patrol in which he participated in August 1963:

> All the people we had met were eager to be taken out of the desert to Papunya, and it was arranged that we would return after the summer, with a truck to take them in. These groups were not only lonely because of the departure of so many of their relatives, but had health problems and were evidently ill-nourished. Of the 39 people seen during the patrol, 15 had been seen first in 1962. Reasonably reliable information was gathered about some 45 others, and it was estimated that some 40 or 50 would be living in the country between Jupiter Well and the Warburton Range Mission.
>
> At the next meeting of the Officers' Conference on the Central Reserves, it was agreed that a joint patrol be made in April 1964, with the aims of contacting as many people in the desert as possible and offering transport out of the desert to all who wanted to leave. It was recognised that, desirable as it might be on many accounts to leave the people to follow their traditional way of life undisturbed in the desert, it would be inhumane to neglect them, now that it was known that their social life had been impoverished by the depopulation of the area; that there were some who were ill and undernourished; and that they had clearly expressed a wish to be taken in to a settlement.[3]

Long was the intellectual of the Northern Territory Welfare Branch, having the benefit of protracted firsthand experience with Aborigines, including some who had hardly ever met a white man before. While Long was conducting patrols in the Central Desert, Professor Ronald Berndt from the University of Western Australia was in the Top End conducting academic research, familiarising himself with the circumstances of the Aborigines at Yirrkala in Arnhem Land. In November 1964, Berndt published a lengthy article on the Gove Dispute.[4] The director of the

Welfare Branch of the Northern Territory Administration sought Jeremy Long's opinion on Berndt's paper; Long at this time was being described as an Investigation Officer (Social Welfare).

Long professed 'no special knowledge of the history of the difficulties at Yirrkala relating to the mining leases'. He had visited the area briefly in 1961 before there had been any dispute. He had met the leaders from there from time to time but he had 'no opportunity to have the leisurely and painstaking discussions with the Aboriginals there which would be necessary to form any opinion of their view on the use of land in the peninsula'. Long compared Berndt's twofold classification of Aboriginal relationships to land – the land-owning group and the land-occupying and utilising group – with that adopted by anthropologist Les Hiatt: those with a ritual relationship and those with an economic relationship. Long thought, 'The land-using groups are fluid and it would be impossible to define the limits of land used by any Aboriginal group precisely.' Even if one were to accept a twofold classification, Long said it was 'clear that neither amounts to ownership of land in our sense'. He went on to say, 'This is not, of course, to say that Aboriginals do not have an interest in land nor that they should not be recognised as having rights in land.' Long was not convinced that Berndt had established 'that the rights of Aboriginal groups with inherited custody of totemic sites amount to land ownership'. He concluded:

> That the principles of consultation and compensation where reserved land is to be leased have been well-established for some time and that it has been accepted that rights of access should be maintained as far as possible and that sacred areas should be preserved from interference. The only problem is to establish procedures in these matters and ensure that these are followed.[5]

Not all public servants in the Northern Territory were opposed to the protection of Aboriginal interests. Given the social flux they were encountering in remote areas of the Northern Territory and the novelty of land rights claims, they were in unmapped territory and, although perplexed, they were seeking what was in the best interests of the Aborigines. It was common ground in the government bureaucracy that sacred sites should be protected, Aborigines should enjoy continued access to Aboriginal reserve land, and they should be consulted and compensated if others were to be allowed to use the land. There were no laws in place to achieve these ideals.

The Yirrkala Aborigines, upset by proposed bauxite mining on their traditional country without their permission, issued proceedings in the Supreme Court of the Northern Territory in late 1968, claiming that their lands had been unlawfully invaded by both the Commonwealth and Nabalco Pty Ltd, the company to which the Commonwealth had purported to grant various mining leases in the Gove Peninsula. Thus began one of the long games of legal and political ping-pong in which the cause of land rights went backwards and forwards between the courts and the parliaments, over the net of public opinion. No one surmised that the 1967 referendum result would provide an impetus for ultimately recognising the land rights of the Yirrkala Aborigines and of all those similarly situated. Milirrpum and Mungurrawuy were the leaders of the two clans that were the land-owning groups – the Rirratjingu and the Gumatj. These landowners were joined by Daymbalipu, the leader of the Djapu clan, who, though not claiming to be owners, had access to the Rirratjingu and Gumatj lands for hunting and foraging.

There was a complete stand-off within the Commonwealth ranks. Initially, the Council for Aboriginal Affairs (CAA) wanted to do whatever it could to avoid a legal showdown, being hopeful that some settlement could be negotiated, while the Department of the Interior were intent on defeating the Aboriginal claim. By early 1969 it was clear that there would be no negotiated settlement. Stanner prepared a paper for the CAA arguing that the Commonwealth's main object in the litigation should not be to secure the development and execution of the mining project but rather 'to determine once for all what rights if any the aborigines have in common law and equity'. Stanner was in no doubt that this was the needed test case on Aboriginal land rights. If the question were left undetermined, Stanner argued that it would 'continue to plague Australia long after the inconvenience and monetary loss of interruption or collapse of the project have been absorbed'. Interior were adamant that the mining must proceed and that, if the Aborigines were to succeed in gaining an injunction from the court, the Commonwealth should promptly acquire compulsorily any interests in the land that the court might say the Aborigines held. Stanner said that Interior's advice was bad and 'it would be widely held to point to a defective morality'. Coombs and Dexter agreed with Stanner's proposal that the Commonwealth 'appear in the suit, not as an adversary but with the sole intent, in the national interest, including the interest of the aborigines, to assist the court towards a common law ruling on stated matters which affect areas other than Yirrkala'.[6]

The CAA provided Minister Wentworth with a copy of Stanner's paper. On 25 January 1969, Peter Nixon, the minister for the interior, issued a press statement indicating that the Commonwealth had agreed in principle to contribute to the legal costs incurred by the Aboriginal plaintiffs. Without such a Commonwealth commitment, there would have been no way that the Aborigines and the Methodist missionaries could have bankrolled the litigation. Nixon said, 'Because of the very important issues involved the Commonwealth has no alternative to defending the action so that an authoritative ruling will be given by the Court on the far-reaching questions involved. At the same time, the Government does not wish the Aboriginals to be at a disadvantage in conducting their case because of lack of funds.' He wanted to make it quite clear that in defending the case, 'the Government was not acting in a spirit of opposition to the Aboriginals, but was seeking a determination of the legal issues that had been raised',[7] and that the Commonwealth would conduct the case on this basis.

Two days later, Crown Solicitor HE Renfree advised Frank Purcell, solicitor for the Aboriginal plaintiffs, that the Commonwealth intended to grant the bauxite leases to Nabalco 'as soon as convenient' and that the Commonwealth intended to 'file a summons seeking judgment for the defendant', thereby avoiding the need for any protracted trial of the issues. So even though the Commonwealth was prepared to fund the Aborigines having their day in court, it was anxious to have the litigation concluded as quickly as possible, claiming that the Aborigines had no arguable case. Purcell engaged Stanner as an expert anthropologist for his clients. Stanner set out his initial thoughts on Aborigines and the land in a paper for Purcell on 29 January 1969:

> What, in the main, I have led towards saying is that the Yirrkala land, to which I consider these general principles applied, though with some regional variation, was risibly treated when included among the King's or Queen's 'wastes' or 'wild' and 'unoccupied' lands and on which the aborigines were allowed, as our legislation puts it, 'to be'. They were lands dealt with, interestingly and rationally, by *leges* not *scriptae* which even now will repay respectful study. I hope to have made plain that there was an anciently established code of rights in land; that the rights were vested, not in individual persons as such, but jointly in a particular kind of kinship group; that the right went beyond usufruct; a proprietary right was well recognized; and that the qualifications of proprietary rights had to do with the rational ordering of activities and the well-being of people in a particular form of society.[8]

Stanner was arguing that the British common law, as determined by the courts if and when there was a need (the unwritten *leges*), rather than the statutes (the written laws, which he classified as *scriptae*) could be invoked to establish that Aboriginal rights in land survived and were recognised. Aborigines actually owned the land; it was not just a matter of them having access to unoccupied wastelands for their use.

Stanner then wrote to Purcell, making some general remarks in support of the affidavit he had sworn for the case. He wrote:

> I am not in principle opposed to projects for the economic development of the aboriginal reserves. I have long been an advocate of that course. I expressed recently [in] the Boyer lectures the opinion that under modern conditions the aborigines have no satisfying prospects of life except in and through measures for their advancement and development. I consider, however, that development projects within the reserves should observe three conditions, and that the conditions should be mandatory for both private and public enterprises.
>
> The first condition is that any project of which Europeans are to be the main beneficiaries should have the prior consent of the aborigines of the reserve in which it is to go on. The second condition is that the aborigines should be treated as having, of right, a contractual relation with such an enterprise in their areas, directly, or through a trust on which they are represented by aborigines. The third condition is that private enterprise should accept a significant degree of responsibility towards the aborigines in the area.
>
> These are minimal conditions. Unless we observe them we have no philosophy of development that suits the place and the time. We are elbowing the aborigines out of the way, and emptying words such as 'aboriginal reserve' and 'reserve for the use and benefit of aborigines' of any significant meaning. I do not consider that the conditions have been adequately met in the Gove project.
>
> ... Past intrusions invariably broke up aboriginal society. They did so over a wider area than was immediately concerned. There were reasons inherent in aboriginal social organization why this was so. The effects are visible throughout the Northern Territory. Mission stations and government settlements illustrate the effects of small-scale intrusions, at a slow rate, under conditions in which aborigines were, and are being, given a degree of protection.

Pastoral properties illustrate the effects of small-scale intrusions, at a slow rate, under conditions in which aborigines were, and are being, given a lesser degree of protection. Towns such as Darwin, Katherine and Alice Springs illustrate the compounding of two things – the effects of large-scale past intrusions, at a slow rate, under which aborigines had almost no protection, and the effects of recent developments, at a higher rate, under conditions in which aborigines are being given a higher degree of protection.

No one is particularly pleased with the end-products. The present scale of welfare services and expenditures, and the insistent demand for progressive increases, are the best evidence of our disquiet with the state and prospects of aboriginal life deriving from past intrusions.

The plan for the Nabalco project is for an unprecedented concentration of all the forces which, on a smaller scale, at a slower tempo, and in a less intensive combination, produced the situations just described. I know of no parallel in Australian history in which European and aboriginal elements were forced together on a scale, at a rate, and in a situation, comparable with that which exists at Yirrkala.[9]

Stanner followed up with an ANU seminar paper on the case under Chatham House rules. Coombs and Professor Julius Stone were in attendance, as were other legal academic luminaries like Tony Blackshield and Sam Stoljar. Stanner's paper states:

In other circumstances it might be reasonable to say that even if the clans have rights, they have slept far too long upon them, and are out of time. But the record of history, and the experience of anthropologists, is that to the aborigines generally the possibility of their being ousted was unthinkable. While the 'unthinkable' was slowly becoming patent they did not really comprehend that their rights were in danger, and were at a loss what to do when the shock of full comprehension finally came. There is no reason to suppose that the attitude and response of the Yirrkala clans was different. In such a context the long-continued actualities of the situation and the extrinsic matters I have mentioned may be thought to go beyond the law as it stands and to raise considerations of prudence, as well as of good conscience, natural justice and equity.[10]

Despite Stanner's views and the advice of the CAA, the Commonwealth maintained its position that there was absolutely no merit in the Aboriginal claim to land rights and saw no need to engage in a full-blown trial of the case, delaying the granting of mining leases. The Commonwealth's application for summary judgment striking out the claim, so as to avoid a trial calling many witnesses, was heard by the Northern Territory Supreme Court from 18 to 21 March 1969. The Department of the Interior continued to recommend that, win or lose, the Commonwealth should compulsorily acquire the Yirrkala lands so that the mining project might proceed promptly with minimal disruption. Stanner wrote another paper for the CAA arguing that any win for the Commonwealth would be 'at best a "victory" of law in the most pejorative sense':

> The Commonwealth will wish to contemplate the effect of such a victory following on the forcible seizure recommended by Interior. It will have conserved the agreement with Nabalco, but will have raised to a new level the question of moral liability to the aborigines; at the least not helped its own public standing; and, at the least, made much more imperative the skilful handling of the field difficulties.[11]

Stanner would not be budged from his moral certainty about the validity of the Aboriginal claims. He had read enough law to know that the law could be developed or expressed by judges so as not to be too far distant from what decent people would regard as just. He was in for some surprises. He insisted that the Commonwealth needed to set up a reserves land trust and charge it with the duty of managing and developing the reserves, always attending to Aboriginal interests in the land.

The mining company could then negotiate with the trust and hold its interest in the land from the trust. Stanner proffered a defensible interpretation of the Aboriginal claim. They wanted to negotiate a fair outcome, including recognition of their land title and the payment of rent, royalties and compensation, perhaps with an equitable interest in the project. Stanner proposed a way forward:

> If the Commonwealth were to say before the first stage of the hearing, that, irrespective of the court's decision, it will give an honourable undertaking to treat with the aborigines on such matters, it could well also say before the first stage of hearing that, irrespective of the court's decision, it must insist in the national interest that the project shall go on. But not otherwise.

Professor Stanner attended the proceedings in Darwin in March, made extensive notes, and then wrote to WC Wentworth, the minister-in-charge of Aboriginal affairs. Stanner circulated his notes widely around Canberra, asserting that Bill Harris, the senior barrister appearing for the Commonwealth, had submitted:

> The Crown would make its primary attack on the whole substance of the case as plainly bad and misconceived. The action was an attack on the constitutional law, the law of real property, and Australian practice over a period of nearly 200 years. It was so obviously untenable that it cannot possibly succeed. No possibility of good cause of action. The statement of claims, even if proved, could not succeed. Frivolous and vexatious. Plainly hopeless. Would lead to a useless trial. Australian law did not recognise tribal rights to land.[12]

Edward Woodward, the barrister appearing for the Aboriginal plaintiffs and being instructed by their solicitor Purcell, had replied, 'Nothing is further from the truth than that the aborigines are making a misconceived and remarkable attack on the law of property.' As Stanner summarised it, 'On the contrary they were invoking the protection of the law. The aborigines sincerely believed they are the rightful owners.' Woodward went further: 'they know they are the owners: the land was given them by their spirit ancestors and they had held it ever since.' Having looked to the law developed in other civilised countries, he concluded:

> It was not too much to hope that the same might be done here to give some protection to the aborigines who established a claim to land. But they were being met at the door of the court by the Commonwealth and Nabalco with an allegation that the claim was frivolous, vexatious and an abuse of the privilege of the court.[13]

Stanner said he had attended the hearing with three expectations. He thought that the Commonwealth's main interest would have been to assist the court to determine the law of Aboriginal land rights. He presumed the Commonwealth would not want to antagonise the Aborigines. He hoped that if hard things had to be said against the Aboriginal interests, they would be said by the barristers appearing for the mining company and not the barristers appearing for the Commonwealth. Stanner was blunt about what eventuated: 'I was wrong on each count.' He thought the Commonwealth had done the company's work and that Aborigines would think that the Commonwealth was standing up for the company and opposing them. With great prescience, Stanner advised his minister, 'In my opinion, even if Woodward's submission finally fails for reasons of law, his reading of Australian history will be widely disseminated, and will have an appeal to public sentiment that your Government would be unwise to ignore.'[14]

Dr Coombs took up Stanner's clarion call. He asked the minister to have the government change its anti-Aboriginal stance in the litigation. The CAA was gravely concerned with the approach of the government lawyers and 'feels that if it is maintained it can only damage the Government's credit domestically and internationally, and seriously impair especially with Aboriginal citizens your own standing as Minister-in-Charge of Aboriginal Affairs'.[15] Given that the case was to resume hearing in one of the southern capitals, Coombs wanted Wentworth to be aware that the case from here on would attract significant publicity. He needed to be aware that:

> ... at least a significant minority of Australians believe that Aboriginals still living on lands traditionally occupied by them and their ancestors possess some rights in those lands, and that a vast majority of Australians believe our community has an obligation to Aboriginal citizens, part of whose traditional homelands are being handed over to private industrial enterprises to ensure that their economic and social welfare is protected.

Coombs then wrote, as one Canberra mandarin to another, to Ted Hook, the secretary of the Attorney-General's Department, indicating that the CAA members were greatly concerned about the Commonwealth's conduct of the case. Having wielded power around the corridors of Canberra for a long time, Coombs probably thought he could get Hook to exercise some moderating influence on government lawyers, who were failing to consider the longer term ramifications of the Commonwealth being perceived as hostile to untested Aboriginal claims. He reported that Stanner, having sat through the Darwin proceedings,

> ... was distressed at what he felt to be an antagonistic attitude on the part of the Commonwealth Counsel which he felt to be incompatible with the assurance given by the Minister for the Interior some time earlier that the Commonwealth was entering this case not in a spirit of opposition to the aboriginal people but simply in order to have the legal issues determined in an appropriate way.[16]

Hook got the first assistant crown solicitor to provide him with an assessment of Stanner's paper. The departmental assessment contained more than black letter legal opinion, providing some insight into what was likely to be the pervasive public service mindset at the time, and not just in Interior. Stanner's report filled the solicitor with 'considerable apprehension' that the false premises on which it was based 'could be highly detrimental not only to the Commonwealth's interest, but to the aboriginals themselves'.[17] He thought the Aboriginal claim from a legal point of view had a forlorn hope of success, and that it may have been launched so that the court could be used as 'a forum to support other political aims'. He thought both Stanner and Coombs were causing great harm to the Commonwealth and to Aborigines. Having been in Darwin for the initial hearing, he proffered a parting sociological observation:

> I was informed in Darwin during the course of the proceedings that whatever the outcome of the Court action may be, there are indications that it and other actions by the aboriginals are having a detrimental effect on the relations between the aboriginals and the white people of the social strata in which the aboriginal normally mingles. I was given to understand that in this strata, there has at least been a tolerance, if not a complete acceptance of the aboriginals, but recent activities of the Government in relation to specific sections of the aboriginals combined with the institution of the present court proceedings was creating a noticeable atmosphere of hostility towards the aboriginals that has never previously existed. I wonder if Dr Coombs is aware of this.

Hook did not hand on any of this gratuitous advice – at least in writing. He was not able to provide Coombs with much satisfaction about what was 'basically a problem of policy', pointing out that the government lawyers, not being policy-makers, 'are concerned with the establishment and advancement of the legal position as we see it, and that position is not to the benefit of the aboriginals'.[18] He did try and console Coombs that there was no need to fear because, even if the Commonwealth succeeded completely in the case as he expected, the

Commonwealth would still 'do what it thinks is the right thing in regard to the Yirrkala tribe'. Coombs was supposed to be satisfied that there was no need for legal recognition of land rights when government out of the goodness of its heart and guided by upright public servants would do the right thing.

Wentworth provided Nixon with a copy of Stanner's notes from the Darwin proceedings. Nixon was quite unapologetic for what clearly was a confrontationist stance adopted by the Commonwealth. Nixon conceded there were political implications in the Commonwealth's handling of the case and recoiled at the thought 'that the Commonwealth should not fully defend the action in the Courts so that the legal position can be clearly determined'.[19] He conceded that there were 'political implications in maintaining the position against recognition, at this stage in history, of customary land rights'. He said:

> Any criticism can, however, in my view be met by pointing to the extensive programmes of educational, social and economic assistance to aborigines as both affecting any claims they may have for past dispossession of land and as being of more value to them by encouraging and assisting them to enter the mainstream of Australian life.

Nixon's view was that the Commonwealth was doing more than enough for Aborigines so they should not take offence at the Commonwealth strongly contesting any claim to Aboriginal land rights in the courts. In view of the 'many substantial implications, political and other, involved in any suggestion that traditional land rights should be recognised', Nixon warned Wentworth against taking any action in trying to modify the Commonwealth's approach to the litigation as the matter came within his responsibility as minister for the interior. He assumed Wentworth would not take any further action without first consulting him. He provided a copy of his letter to the attorney-general. On 15 May 1969, Justice Blackburn rejected the Commonwealth's application to strike out the action and all parties then prepared for a hearing of the substantive matter.

One positive outcome from Coombs' approach to Ted Hook was that Hook did bring together the government lawyers, Bob Swift from Interior and the members of the CAA in a search for a more coherent joint position on the case. Swift provided Interior with a detailed briefing after the meeting. Hook had said there could be no such thing as a friendly legal action. The Commonwealth might need to test any evidence given by Aborigines. Swift was sure that the witnesses would be treated with full consideration and not with a spirit of antagonism. Coombs was 'to consider the possibility of putting forward to the Government a proposal which would take the issue out of the legal forum and remove it for political consideration'.[20] Hook made it clear that all government lawyers, including the attorney-general, Tom Hughes, and the previous solicitor-general, Anthony Mason, 'held the view that it was not possible as a matter of law for the action by the Aborigines to succeed'. Confident that Aboriginal court action had no prospect of success, the government lawyers were sticking to their tactics and hoping that Aboriginal supporters at the CAA would have the good sense to convince the Aborigines to abandon the case and seek some political resolution to their grievances.

Back at Interior, Jeremy Long was asked to prepare a paper answering the question, 'What do Aborigines mean when they say they own land?' as a basis for finding agreement among the parties. He described the most foundational relationship with land as 'a ritual or spiritual one' over sacred sites. There were other relationships that entitled others to visit and forage. He said that 'the ritual relationship extends in a less precise way to the areas surrounding the sites, the boundaries of which are not everywhere precisely defined'.[21] The assistant secretary advised the acting secretary of Interior that Long's paper did not offer a way forward: 'If the plaintiffs accepted the proposition of a ritual relationship with certain sites we could expect that the Gove people would argue that the whole of the land in dispute was encompassed by this special relationship. This would be difficult to disprove.'[22]

Interior's search for common ground got nowhere and Coombs' proposal came to nothing during June 1969. The Commonwealth gave consideration to Interior's original idea that it might acquire the contested land immediately under the *Lands Acquisition Act* and proceed forthwith to issue the bauxite leases. The Commonwealth's barristers, Bill Harris and Malcolm McLelland, agreed that 'it would not be proper for the Commonwealth to purport to compulsorily acquire the land', 'so long as the Commonwealth maintains that the subject land is owned by the Commonwealth'. Such a course would be 'contrary to what the Commonwealth claims and the executive believes to be the case'. The barristers also provided some political advice supporting the same conclusion as to why acquisition would be inadvisable: 'It would tend to confer upon legal claims to land rights by Aboriginals generally a degree of substance in the public and perhaps a judicial mind which in our view would not assist future resistance to such claims.'[23]

On 1 July 1969, Stanner gave a speech to the Belconnen Churches Group in Canberra. As ever, his remarks were in writing and painstakingly edited, regardless of the modesty and limited size of the audience. He spoke of the policy change from assimilation to integration with disarming honesty:

> The Commonwealth since the Referendum of 1967 has the power to override the states but is unlikely to use its powers other than concurrently and persuasively. The strategy of what we are doing is not agreed or even clear. When we speak about 'assimilation' or 'integration' we are speaking about ultimate targets and final purposes, not about immediate or early methods to attain them.
>
> Even those who tried hardest, that is, the religious missions, for a long time worked rather uncomprehendingly, and destroyed rather than formed. We waited until 1967 to bring the national resources and the

national imagination to bear on the difficulties. It was in that year that the Commonwealth set up the Council for Aboriginal Affairs of which I am a member.[24]

Stanner said that he could speak only circumspectly about the Yirrkala land case because it was *sub judice* but that, when he delivered the Boyer Lectures in 1968, he had no information or expectation that the Aborigines would take their case to court. Insofar as he had any conscious purpose at all in speaking about the Yirrkala claim in those lectures, he was 'appealing against the obvious run of events, to the sensibility of Australians generally, and putting the argument that it was not yet too late to try to compose the most fundamental grievance that the aboriginal people have against us'. The CAA was working behind the scenes to try and convince government, including the bureaucracy, about the legitimacy of land rights; they were also doing what they could to convince the public and to educate citizens about the practicality, as well as the morality, of Aboriginal claims.

Stanner then wrote to Purcell, 'I had some hope, as had Dr Coombs, that there might be a chance that the Government would conduct the next phase of the case along non-adversary lines, even if the Company did not, but I now believe that this will not be so.'[25] Until this point in the litigation, the company's barristers had been able to take a back seat and simply endorse the arguments that had been put by the Commonwealth. In the lead-up to the hearing of the full action, Purcell put various suggestions about compensation, seeking the Commonwealth's views. Even at this stage, the Aborigines would have been prepared to agree to some mining if they were to be paid some compensation for the disruption to their community life and for the interrupted access to their traditional country. Meanwhile, the Commonwealth was sounding out other anthropologists who might counter the evidence to be given by Berndt and Stanner. They approached Les Hiatt at the University of Sydney, and he wrote to Stanner seeking advice. Stanner reminded Hiatt that these were adversarial proceedings, and that the parties were probably seeking to divide anthropological opinion. He wrote, 'There are statements in things you have written in recent years which can be turned to the Crown and the Company interest. It cannot be because of your charm, brilliance and bright blue eyes that you have been approached. It is because of the prospect that your testimony can be used to argue the law and/or the facts against the aborigines.'[26] Stanner was right. Interior already had Jeremy Long's paper in which he had contrasted Berndt's views with Hiatt's. In the end, Hiatt did not give evidence.

When preparing for the *Milirrpum* litigation, Stanner had spent a week in November 1969 at Yirrkala, a community he had previously visited only once. Pondering what role he might play in the case given his extensive anthropological experience in other parts of the Northern Territory, he went 'in order to see as far as I could, by brief tests, to what extent I could say ... that knowledge gained in other parts of Australia would have some relevance to my opinions about the state of community life, the kind of customs they are following, the extent to which they follow those customs in Arnhem Land'.[27] While there he attended the Sunday morning service at the Methodist Church. He noted: 'About 100–125 there, including 18 Nabalco etc, employees, some Catholic and Greek. 3 Aboriginal youths and 15 girls in choir. A "dead" service – uninspired music, no liturgy, hackneyed and unilluminating sermon. Christianity suffers by comparison. Hymns from MHB [Methodist Hymn Book].'[28] He was often given to musings, many of which were never published and some of which verge on the poetic or lyrical. After returning south, he typed an unfinished reflection, which he filed away with his notes of the visit. He commenced with these remarks:

> If you pass through the door of the Methodist church at Yirrkala on Gove Peninsula in Arnhem Land your eyes are at once taken by two symbols. One is the cross. The other is a set of iconographs painted by aboriginal artists. They stand there, on the far end wall, beyond the altar, in some

way sanctifying each other in the turbulent life that now confronts the Yirrkala people.

On a Sunday morning a few weeks ago I went through the door. The heat was oppressive. The high cumulus clouds were building up to a half-promise of rain. The choir sang sweetly about 'what tares the evil one hath in His Garden sown' and 'behold me standing at the door, and hear me pleading evermore'. We heard that 'Jesus said, I am the door', and came to the benediction: that 'it is through Christ that all of us, Jew, Gentile (Aboriginal and European), are able to come in the one spirit into the presence of the Father'.

I have to confess that some of the time my thoughts wandered. Perhaps it was the heavy electrical charge in the atmosphere, or the ceaseless wailing of the aboriginal children in the congregation, or vividness of the flame-tree flowers against the blue of the lower sky. Or perhaps the conjoint symbols on the wall.

I kept wondering: if the wall should still be standing in a few thousand years time, could an archaeologist of the day imaginably deduce from them anything of the torment of choice that has become the stuff of life – and conscience – at Yirrkala?

The answer had to be 'no'. The data would be insufficient. Other things would be needed. I began to conjure them up as we sang, 'I bore the cruel thorns for thee. I waited long and patiently.'[29]

His thought then turned to bauxite and money 'less as holy symbols than as oafish graffiti making a palimpsest on the erased cross and iconographs'.

Stanner returned to Canberra convinced that the iconographs would enrich the local community and the nation for generations to come. He had work to do, ensuring that bauxite and money did not erase them any more quickly or completely than the Aborigines would wish. Those iconographs had inspired the artistic design of the petitions presented to the Australian Parliament in 1963, capturing the imagination of the nation. The stuff of life and conscience at Yirrkala had taken on national significance in the wake of the 1967 referendum, arming Stanner, Dexter and Coombs with the leverage to play off law, politics and morality. The courts, the bureaucracy and the parliament all had a role to play as the public wondered for the first time about what was due to Aborigines whose interests had been espoused at the referendum, and as some of those Aborigines were heard in court, in parliament and on the airwaves describing their modest, just claims. Persons of goodwill disagreed about how those claims might or might not assist Aborigines to live a better life in modern Australia but the modest referendum had unleashed changes unimagined by its proposers, its supporters and the voters.

On 2 December 1969, Coombs accompanied Bob Swift from Interior to a meeting with Reverend Gribble and his assistant at the Methodist Overseas Mission Board. They discussed the conduct of Aboriginal missions. Gribble told them that the board had decided three years previously that 'the eventual outcome must be the taking over from the mission by community organs of all secular activities', but that these things could not be rushed. Clearly there had been some institutional learning result from the board's showdown with the Reverend Wells back in 1963. The board was being more attentive to the views of the local Aborigines and was no longer purporting to speak for their interests when meeting with government. In relation to developments at Yirrkala, Gribble 'stressed that it took a long time to find out what Aboriginal attitudes really were. He felt that the young people at Yirrkala would be very interested in participation in the activity generated by the mining project but that the old men would exercise a very conservative influence for a long time yet.'[30]

On 31 December 1969, the Commonwealth advised that it would compensate the Aborigines for any interest in land which was found to exist and which needed to be acquired so that the Commonwealth could honour its undertakings to provide the bauxite leases to Nabalco.

Should the Yirrkala Aborigines receive such compensation, they would no longer be eligible for payments from the general programs established by the Commonwealth to provide welfare assistance for Aborigines in the Northern Territory. The Commonwealth rejected the suggestion that some compensation be paid immediately. It was known by this time that some of the key Aboriginal leaders were open to the mining proceeding without a court case, provided only they received what they thought to be adequate compensation. RB Hutchison, the first assistant crown solicitor, advised the plaintiff's solicitors:

> Nor does the Commonwealth wish to be a party to any action which might be taken to suggest that the discharge of the responsibility it accepts in respect of all Aboriginal communities in the Territory, including the Yirrkala people, is in any way dependent on the plaintiffs forgoing the opportunity of establishing in a Court any legal rights which they may have.[31]

The Commonwealth was anxious to avoid any perception that it would make assistance to Aborigines conditional on them not pursuing their rights in the courts.

The hearing of the full action commenced in Darwin on 25 May 1970. There was one major change to the line-up of barristers: the Commonwealth was now led by its new solicitor-general, Bob Ellicott. He had taken on the position in May the previous year and immediately been involved in various international legal disputes and consultations for the Commonwealth. Usually the solicitor-general appears only in the High Court, leaving most matters in lower courts for the attention of other barristers briefed by the Commonwealth for the purpose. Ellicott's predecessor, Anthony Mason, who was later the chief justice at the time of the *Mabo* case, had no interest in appearing in the proceedings before the Northern Territory Supreme Court. When Ellicott was apprised of the pending litigation by Hutchison in the crown solicitor's office, he thought he should become directly involved:

> I come from a Methodist background. So this case is about an Aboriginal community at Yirrkala. Some of them are Methodists and some of them have been trained as Methodist local preachers. There's a fellow there called Galarrwuy Yunupingu, aged 19, who was to act as interpreter. He had learnt good English at bible college. This to me is an unusual case, so I'm not going to reject it. And I decide to take it on.
>
> I don't think I had any confirmed views about Crown land or who owned the land. Except, I was a property lawyer and I knew the history of Australia and its land law. My initial reaction was: if the land has been claimed by the Crown then all interests have been subsumed to it. And there is no basis on which you can say any part of Australia hasn't therefore become free of any Aboriginal interests in the land. I obviously would have thought of the difficulties of proving what had taken place. The government of the day, in the context of the 1967 referendum, had a strong view that it wanted to be seen, and to be genuinely seen, to be concerned about the Aboriginal people and their future. There was no malevolence or adverse motive in its attitude.
>
> There was an attitude I was aware of that probably found its main exposition in members of the Country Party who were very concerned about the Aboriginal people – wondering what we should do, what we can do to raise their status, and to look after their health and wellbeing. They did not, however, see land rights as being of significance in that pursuit.[32]

On the first day of the hearing, Ellicott told the court, 'The Commonwealth in its defence of this action is not wanting to prevent the aborigines in any way putting their case factually.' He had no objection to Justice Blackburn gaining some benefit from Stanner's anthropological evidence but was insistent that this evidence was not admissible and that 'Your Honour should not rely on it at all when it comes to the question of the nature of the relationship of the aboriginal with the land, because that is a matter of fact as to what the aboriginal law and custom is'.[33]

Ellicott's argument was that Stanner's anthropological experience was from other parts of the Northern Territory and that Stanner had spent only a short time in Yirrkala, listening to the stories of the local Aborigines. Ellicott did not view Stanner as an expert on Yirrkala. Further, Ellicott argued that Stanner only knew things about Yirrkala that he had heard from the locals, so the court should hear directly from the locals and not from Stanner, who was not in a position to attest the truth of what he had heard. Ellicott knew that the court would have to rule on the admissibility of 'hearsay' evidence from Aboriginal witnesses testifying that they had been told details about traditional landholdings by their deceased ancestors. It was painstaking work to adduce the evidence through translators in Darwin while ultimately leaving it to the judge at the end of the case to rule on the admissibility of this evidence. The Darwin hearings ran until 10 June 1970. The case was not to resume in Canberra until September.

The day after the Darwin hearings concluded, Ellicott wrote to the attorney-general, indicating that in past meetings with ministers, 'the Minister for the Interior has emphasised the desire of the Commonwealth that this action should not, if at all possible, go off on some technical ground without the question of aboriginal rights in relation to the land being determined'.[34] He indicated ways in which he thought the litigation could be run, ensuring that it did not run off the rails and giving the judge the opportunity to rule on the substantive questions of law. He highlighted a number of problems relating to the plaintiffs' evidence which, if not overcome, 'could mean that a Court might decide the case without deciding the main issues'. The main issues were whether the Yirrkala Aborigines had rights to land prior to 1788 that would be recognised by an Australian court applying the British law, whether those rights could survive the assertion of British sovereignty over the Aboriginal lands, and whether the Aboriginal plaintiffs in the case had the same rights over the same areas of land as their ancestors had prior to 1788. Ellicott accurately forecast that the plaintiffs 'may have considerable difficulty in establishing that their clans were in fact on these lands in 1788 or that other aboriginal clans regarded the Gove lands as their country in 1788'. Ellicott was prepared to concede to the plaintiffs' barristers 'that whatever land relationship is proved by admissible evidence to have existed immediately before the Mission came, also existed in 1788'. The mission had been established in 1935. He made it clear, however, that he 'did not think the Commonwealth could, on the evidence, concede that the particular clans (ie. The Rirritjingu and Gumatj) were the aboriginals who in fact had that relationship with the Gove land in 1788 or since'.

Meanwhile, Bob Swift, the deputy secretary of the Department of the Interior, was continuing discussions with Nabalco about prospective Aboriginal employment on the proposed mine site. The company saw the good sense in providing local employment possibilities. The company distinguished between the young and mature Aborigines, who 'in many cases had not developed settled work habits and did not want to continue working for sustained periods'.[35] The company suggested that a pool of 60 older workers might share 20 full-time jobs not in the mining sector as such but in the provision of town services. The company was agreeable to training younger Aborigines for mining work but warned about the risks of employing Aborigines from elsewhere: 'Nabalco had employed a very good Aboriginal driver who came from another area. This man eventually resigned because he was not able to mix with the Yirrkala Aborigines nor visit the Mission.'

Trouble was bubbling away at Wattie Creek (Daguragu), the other Northern Territory location that was in the national spotlight with local Aborigines expressing concerns about outside interference in their lives. In August 1966, Vincent Lingiari had led his people off Lord Vestey's Wave Hill station, striking over wages and appalling conditions, including the exploitation of their women by European workers. In September 1968, the CAA discussed whether it might be possible to organise a sub-lease from Lord Vestey of some of the land on the Wave

Hill station for use by those camped at Wattie Creek. Coombs and Dexter visited Wattie Creek in November 1969 and continued to put suggestions about a sub-lease but could get no agreement from Interior. By now the strike was in its fourth year. Aborigines were protesting their living conditions and reduced access to their traditional country now that the equal-wages decision was impacting on their permission to remain as communities on pastoral leases. On 3 September 1970, four days before the *Milirrpum* litigation was to recommence in Canberra, Peter Nixon, the minister for the interior, decided it was time to speak in Parliament and correct some of the simplistic public narrative about land rights, especially at Wattie Creek:

> The picture most frequently presented is of a valiant band of people, united by tribal ties, fighting the all powerful Government and influential vested interests for the right to establish themselves in an area of land to which they have some tribal attachment deeply rooted in their ancient history. If they could only get title to this land, they would establish a flourishing enterprise, restore their dignity and confidence, and move forward to a glowing future. This picture is a misleading one.[36]

Nixon expressed strong concern about the ongoing plight of Northern Territory Aborigines on remote communities but warned against the attraction of easy solutions. He was adamant that land rights was no answer:

> The Government believes that it is wholly wrong to encourage Aboriginals to think that because their ancestors have a long association with a particular piece of land, Aboriginals of the present day have the right to demand ownership of it. There is the question whether establishing the principle that Aboriginals who can show some association with a piece of land and want to have it should be entitled to it as of right, is a help or hindrance in achieving the best possible future for the Aboriginals and for

all Australians. The Government believes that it would be a hindrance and no help.³⁷

For Nixon, it was not a matter of legal or moral entitlement, but rather a matter of social consequences determining the issue of land rights. Imagine if this test were applied to other landholders with the government saying that you could not hold title to land unless you could show that it would do you some good, given the government's presumption that it would probably do you harm. The government was adamant that Aborigines could secure land ownership in the same way as other Australians and that government would continue to provide encouragement, economic opportunities, and social and educational measures so that Aborigines might 'move from the fringes of society to enjoy on equal terms the mainstream of Australian life'. Referring to Papua New Guinea and Canada, Nixon told Parliament that land rights 'does not of itself solve problems of social, economic and cultural change, and sometimes hinders solutions'. In Papua New Guinea he found that land rights precluded younger progressive people from being able to plant commercial crops, and on a visit to Canada he found that land rights 'had the effect, in practice, of encouraging divisions between the Indian people and the wider Canadian community'. He was insistent that 'measures which are based on racial qualification are divisive in any community … It is important for Australia's future that we work towards minimising race consciousness and avoid steps which tend to emphasise divisions on a racial basis.'

Nixon was very wary about the CAA's suggestion that land be excised from pastoral leases to provide an Aboriginal group with a sub-lease from the pastoralist. The excised portion was often described as a living area. Nixon was adamant that you could not provide more than one living area on most cattle properties. The smallest cattle properties in the region were 1000 to 1500 square miles (2600 to 3900 square kilometres) and provided such a low return as to support only one owner-operator and one full-time employee. He saw little point in providing an excision of 500 square miles (1300 square kilometres) for a community that consisted of 15 to 20 men and their wives and children, with some of the men being beyond working age. 'It is quite fanciful to think that a cattle property of 500 square miles in that country could support an Aboriginal community at Wattie Creek at a reasonable standard of living.'[38] Nixon challenged the impression in the media that the people at Wattie Creek were 'a vigorous group with capacity and determination, needing only land and finance to prosper by their efforts'.

Conceding that many Australians supported compensation and recognition of land rights for Aborigines who had suffered dispossession and past injustices, Nixon said that compensation should take the form of measures 'which are related to the best future we can see for the Aboriginal people'.[39] He espoused direct government action and increasing assistance to church missionary bodies. He boasted that Aboriginal enrolments in Northern Territory primary schools had risen from 3200 to 4100 in the past five years with 'more than 90% of the children of primary school age ... now attending school regularly'. Post-primary education had been introduced only in 1965 with 600 students enrolled in transitional courses. There were 63 Aboriginal students in secondary school.

Nixon thanked the mining companies working on Aboriginal reserve lands in the Northern Territory because they were contributing royalties that assisted with the provision of welfare assistance to Aborigines and because they were able to provide some employment and training opportunities. He hailed the recent amendments to the legislation governing the Aborigines Benefits Trust Fund, which was the fund for receipt of royalties from mining on Aboriginal reserves. The government had set up an advisory committee with a majority of Aboriginal members to advise the minister on its expenditure. In theory, Aborigines could now obtain leases to land on Aboriginal reserves, but no significant leases had been granted. He sounded one last warning against land rights legislation:

> Let us not, by recognising so-called tribal land claims, encourage groups and families to attach themselves more firmly to isolated and inadequate plots of land, so that those whose future by inclination and aptitude ought to be away from the land are impeded and hindered in realising the best that they can achieve in a single Australian community. Let us rather concentrate on making equality of opportunity in a single Australian community a reality for the Aboriginal people.[40]

The Yirrkala court proceedings recommenced in Canberra, where all the remaining evidence, including that of the anthropologists, was heard on and off between 7 September and 25 November 1970. Ellicott spoke about one weekend during the Canberra hearings when, knowing most of the plaintiffs were Methodist, he enquired of their barrister, Ted Woodward, if he could ask them to join him at the service in the National Methodist Church and then take them to his Canberra home for lunch. Woodward agreed and they came. After lunch they sat around the open fire and started chanting traditional songs in their own language. Galarrwuy had a fine voice and joined in singing old Methodist hymns as well. Ellicott delights in the observation, 'It's not every Solicitor-General who appeared for a defendant Commonwealth would be able to say that he sat down and sang hymns with Aboriginal plaintiffs after taking them to Church and inviting them to his home, or that Galarrwuy as interpreter was there singing gospel songs as well as his own traditional songs.'[41]

Back in court, Woodward tried to convince the judge that he could accept the evidence of the anthropologists about which Aboriginal groups were related to which areas of land. That would have avoided the painstaking task of calling evidence from Aborigines who would have needed to give their evidence with the use of translators, risking long cross-examination by the government barristers who might have confused the witnesses. Ellicott would not concede that there was any shortcut for the plaintiffs being able to provide the historical 'hearsay' evidence of landholdings through the anthropologists. He was particularly stringent in his cross-examination of Stanner, thinking him 'like a lot of academics, not quite realistic in their thinking'.[42] Stanner was very dismissive of the Methodist missionary Chaseling, who provided evidence for the Commonwealth 'that within living memory violent battles had taken place, the result in each case being a migration of many miles'. Stanner thought Chaseling was a well-meaning missionary who did not have a sufficiently deep understanding of anthropology. Perhaps Stanner was also aware of just how devastating Chaseling could have been to the Aboriginal case if the judge, Sir Richard Blackburn, had believed him. Chaseling had been the founder of the mission in 1935. He remained there until 1941 and had written a book of recollections about what the Aborigines had told him. He had been quoted approvingly by the joint parliamentary committee in 1963. Ellicott on the other hand had a high regard for Chaseling. Ellicott recalls, 'When Chaseling arrived at the new court building in Darwin, Roy Marika, one of the plaintiffs and a clan elder, spotted him and ran down the hall crying, "*Bapa, Bapa!*"' Ellicott thought missionaries like Chaseling did a lot of good by not suppressing the Aboriginal culture and providing a necessary link between the two cultures.

There was a critical divide between the evidence of Chaseling and Stanner. Chaseling's observations and listenings at Yirrkala between 1935 and 1941 convinced him that there was a lot of coming and going by Aborigines on reserve lands, often with pitched battles followed by changes in land use and land entitlements. There was no way Chaseling was going to gild the lily so as to make it easier for his Aboriginal friends to establish their land claim. Stanner, working mainly from his more detailed researches at Daly River on the other side of the Northern Territory, was convinced that Aboriginal landholding arrangements were much more stable. Ellicott put it to Stanner: 'Would it be fair to say that you are not completely impartial as far as the Aborigines' position is concerned? I mean by that that your view is that you would like to see the Aborigines winning this case. Would that be a fair statement?'

Stanner answered, 'Hardly. My sole wish has been to see that they had their day in court to say what could be said on their own behalf and I have not tried to go beyond that stage. I think I could probably add that I have considerable sympathy for their point of view.'[43]

Stanner said that he had not read Chaseling's book *Yulengor*, published in 1957 and detailing his observations of the Yolngu from 1935 to 1941. Ellicott suggested that he might have read it if only to complete his knowledge of the written material available. Stanner was dismissive, saying, 'I appear to have presumed it was a non-scientific work and I had no great impulse to read it.'[44] Trying to establish the mobility and changeability of Aboriginal tenure arrangements, Ellicott got Stanner to focus more on the Daly River tribes who were better known to Stanner, and this exchange occurred:

Q: It is a fact, is it not, that European settlement appears to have affected the life and organisation of aborigines long before the aborigines came into physical contact with the European?

A: I can think of a number of instances where that took place.

Q: I think you pointed out, in relation to the Daly River tribes, that they voluntarily left the land even though white settlement had not come there?

A: Yes.

Q: And when they left the land they really had no burning desire to come back?

A: I do not know that.

Q: Are you quite sure of that?

A: What happened was that for reasons which can only be speculated upon some left their territories to visit the settlement and after they had been there some time some did not go back and some did, but the tendency was for them to dwindle away to the point where none went back. Whether there was no burning desire is something which I cannot hope to answer.

Q: It was quite clear, was it not, that they had lost their enthusiasm for going back and preferred to stay where they found themselves closer to tobacco and tea and other items which became part of their lives?

A: This, at all events, was the decision they made.[45]

Later, Ellicott extracted a critical concession from Stanner:

Q: Do you not agree that having seen the passage in Mr Chaseling's book and what I have shown you from Dr Warner's, that you place a reservation on your answer to this effect, that you want the situation to be explained before you would be prepared to say that it is more probable than not that the particular clans that now claim the area held the area in 1788?

A: I would have to admit the reservation.[46]

Justice Blackburn found Chaseling to be 'a witness of unquestionable honesty' though he often found him to be less reliable on historical land matters than the Aboriginal witnesses.[47] Blackburn did accept some of Chaseling's reporting of battles and displacement of ownership groups. He was more doubtful about Stanner's opinion that 'links between clans and land proved to have existed in 1935 were probably the same in 1788'.[48] Years later, Sir Edward Woodward reflected on the sad irony that Chaseling 'came back to give evidence against the claims of the people whom he had done so much to assist thirty and more years earlier'.[49]

When Stanner had concluded his evidence, he travelled overseas while the case continued. Staying at the Mexico Sheraton, he drafted a letter on hotel letterhead to Ted Woodward on 12 October 1970, but he never sent it. He kept it as a reminder of his thoughts at that time.[50] Woodward had once said that he was seeing Aborigines at their best in the Yirrkala proceedings. Stanner opined that the Yirrkala people well illustrated the 'veracity and integrity' of many Aborigines he had known and that 'they would have given the same evidence in 1870 or 1770 had they been required or allowed and encouraged to do so'. Stanner was deeply troubled by the Crown's 'whole cloth' argument and found 'their argument of linear continuity intellectually incredible':

> They appear to argue that the Crown's intention and policy were made of whole cloth from the start – 'no recognition' and 'inconsistent administration' from 1788. This is historically untrue, or at least contestable. From 1788 to, say, 1830 'intention' had not clarified; there had been no true debate, no contrary assertion, no rejection of alternative, no express declaration: we are in the realm of attribution, and in my opinion no inference of necessary force can be drawn. The state of affairs was at best one of 'unrecognition' and I think it unwarranted to try by retrospective attribution to give 'unrecognition' the positive force of 'no recognition'. The somewhat more explicit 'no recognition' after say 1830 was not of one piece with – indeed, was of a different kind from – the 'unrecognition' before that time. The whole cloth argument is just not sound.

Stanner then posited three stages of development:

1. 1788–1825 – no clear 'intention'; no discernible 'policy'; a do-as-you-go empiricism; the facts unknown; no one speaks any Aboriginal dialect (Thelkeld seems to be the first); the collapse of the Noble Savage idealism and the growth of the Comic Savage and the Ignoble Savage ideas; and importantly, the beginning of the insight (see Commissioner Bigge 1819) that eventually the Aborigines will withdraw from contact and diminish in numbers, which is the start of the thinking that it will probably not be necessary for the Government to face up to the question of Aboriginal rights in a thoroughgoing way.
2. 1825–1840? – a period of transition; a new growth of pro-Aboriginal sentiment (coming from Exeter Hall and the Colonial Secretaries); the spread of the settlement; the problem of the orderly disposal of

the wastelands; the increase of violence to and by the Aborigines; the first 'Aboriginal reserves'; the structured character of the colony takes shape. It is only now that 'intention' and 'policy' become palpable and start to run together. Pro-Aboriginal sentiment is strong enough to compel Government to extend the protection of the criminal law equally to the Aborigines but not strong enough to compel the equal protection of the civil law. All you get is a token inclusion in legislation of ambiguous references to Aboriginal 'possessions' and 'property' and 'interests', which can now be read down conveniently to their goods and chattels and hunting rights, but again this is not a necessary implication. Surely men of law in 1842 would not have said 'property' if they had meant only 'goods and chattels'.

3. 1840 and afterwards; as you said in Darwin, the 'men of affairs' win the day. What the Solicitor General and Harris appear to me to be arguing – and in my view illicitly – is that the mentality and purposes of this period can be used retrospectively to make necessary and positive inferences from the hesitancies and ambiguities of the second period and the negative or undeveloped intentions and policies of the first. The alleged 'consistency' (or as they put it in the weaker form of 'inconsistency' with any continuation of Aboriginal rights) is supplied *ex post*. It seems to be thoroughly fallacious as well as factually mistaken.

Stanner then put this proposition: 'the Crown cannot demonstrate – at least has not demonstrated – that it never has had any active intention to recognise; maybe it reached that intention, in a process of history, by the 1840s, but even then there were elements of ambiguity sufficient to weaken the absolutely necessary character of legal implication.' No matter what the outcome of the case, he thought that it would be 'but a prelude to large developments of policy, and is likely to have a cathartic effect'. Stanner then presciently spoke of a most curious inversion of history:

> Just as after the 1840s the decimation of the Aborigines and the collapse of their society allowed Governments to condone – and draw a decorous veil of legality over – the self-interested actions of the 'men of affairs', so now the remarkable increase in Aboriginal numbers and the very obvious growth of a new kind of Aboriginal society based on a strong self-identification (ie contra – 'Assimilation') is going to face Governments with a choice between their own political fortunes and the convenience of 'men of affairs'. If a veil of legality can be drawn it will hardly seem 'decorous' to modern opinion. The legal argument of 'inconsistency', if politically considered, is the proof of the indictment which the whole chorus of liberals, radicals and anarchists is singing, together with the not inconsiderable number of ordinary people who think the Aborigines are having a rather rough deal. If it turns out to be the case that 'the Law' is what the Commonwealth says (and, to me, incomprehensibly hopes) it is, then there will be intense pressure to change the Law, in other words, to adopt – at least in part – the Labor Party policy. Very difficult!

As the hearings continued in Canberra, members of parliament started to raise directly the question of land rights. Labor senator Jim Keeffe from Queensland put questions on notice to those representing both the minister for the interior and the minister-in-charge of Aboriginal affairs, asking why they were ignoring the advice of anthropologists that land rights were essential for the economic and social independence of Aboriginal communities. The minister for the interior replied, 'I have never put the view that Aborigines should not be granted title to land,' and he referred back to his lengthy September statement. The minister-in-charge of Aboriginal affairs replied, 'While this matter is *sub judice* I do not feel it proper to express an opinion on the issue.'[51]

When the Commonwealth concluded its submissions to Justice Blackburn, Bill Priestley, the barrister appearing for Nabalco, commenced 'by expressing an unfeigned admiration for the extraordinarily thorough and complete submissions that have been put to the court by Counsel for the Commonwealth and might I respectfully put to Your Honour that they are, one and all, submissions of a very great force'.[52] Edward Woodward, appearing for the Aboriginal plaintiffs, recalled that the solicitor-general had said that the Commonwealth 'puts its case on the basis of what it says to be the strict legal position, freed from any question of emotion or any question of a political nature'.[53] Woodward said, 'We, of course, shall do the same. But in doing so we will be asserting that there are questions of high moral principle involved and that the law is not so sterile that it must ignore such questions.'[54] Woodward was flying high, conceding that a decision in favour of his clients 'would obviously run contrary to the mainstream of Australia's treatment of its Aboriginal people over 180 years', but that such a decision would 'satisfy the requirements of natural justice and fair dealing as they would be seen by most people today'. He told the judge, 'This is one of those cases which occur rarely but which, when they do occur, test the genius of the British common law. It is one of those cases which lead the court along seldom trodden paths, with few recognisable signposts in the form of relevant authority.' He proffered his own signposts: 'Because authority is comparatively sparse and uncertain, the Court should have regard to fundamental considerations of natural justice, fair dealing, the preservation of the peace, respect for property and for deeply held spiritual convictions.'[55]

Speaking at an Aboriginal Graduation Dinner after the final hearing and before delivery of the judgment, Stanner said, 'In my opinion the general public is quite strongly moved to listen to what I might call the Four Good Voices – the Voice of Knowledge, the Voice of Conscience, the Voice of Reason, and the Voice of Justice, where Aboriginal affairs are concerned.'[56] Six weeks later, he addressed the Congregation at the Australian National University:

> The mass and weight of antipathetic interest are still too great for the leverage we have. This or that would cost too much; such and such would be against the policy of assimilation; something else would give

in to sentimentalism; one measure would look too much like apartheid; another would hold back national development; yet another, something that only an unworldly academic could ever think possible. Somehow, still too often, still too widely, it seems to end in the proposition that it would be wiser, more realistic, more statesmanlike, to keep the Aborigines, here, with less than the full right of free movement and control of their property; there, in captive employment and quasi-peonage; somewhere else, in a multipurpose institution with no apparent future but to go on being its soul-destroying self; and, almost everywhere, unable to be themselves, except in terms we set.[57]

Just four days before Justice Blackburn delivered his decision, a conference of Commonwealth and state ministers responsible for Aboriginal affairs was to take place in Cairns. There had been much ferment in the governing coalition of the Liberal Party and Country Party, which had been on the treasury benches for too long. The Labor Opposition had been rejuvenated by the charismatic leadership of Gough Whitlam, who was making Aboriginal affairs a distinguishing policy area between the major parties. Malcolm Fraser led a revolt against Gorton as prime minister. John McEwen, who had long vetoed the possibility of William McMahon ever leading the Coalition, had retired as leader of the Country Party. When Gorton stepped down after a vote of no confidence in his leadership was tied in the party room, McMahon saw his long-awaited chance and stood successfully for the leadership. Distinguishing himself from Gorton and trying to keep the Whitlam-led Labor Opposition at bay, the newly elected prime minister took the opportunity to spell out his government's Aboriginal affairs policy and to announce the appointment of a special ministerial committee presided over by the minister responsible for Aboriginal affairs. There were to be many chefs tending this broth – at Commonwealth and state levels – and with the minister for the interior still maintaining responsibility in the Northern Territory. McMahon said that he was taking steps to clarify and restate the role of the CAA. He had decided to move the Office of Aboriginal Affairs (which was effectively the secretariat for the CAA as well as the key public service link to the minister-in-charge of Aboriginal affairs) out of the prime minister's department. He hinted at some movement away from any simplistic notion of assimilation:

> I do not like attempts to embody complex policies in single words like assimilation or integration, capable as they are of varied interpretations and acquiring often irrational associations. We believe that Aboriginal Australians should be assisted as individuals and, if they wish, as groups to hold effective and respected places within one Australian society with equal access to the rights and opportunities it provides and accepting responsibilities towards it. At the same time they should be encouraged and assisted to preserve and develop their culture – their languages, traditions and arts – so that these can become living elements in the diverse culture of the Australian society.

But he dared not mention land rights. The closest he could come was:

> Consideration will be given to an appropriate policy for Aborigines and the land, ensuring to continuing aboriginal groups effective access to land for recreational and ceremonial purposes as well as for the development of enterprises.[58]

After considerable delay, Blackburn handed down his decision while sitting in Alice Springs on 27 April 1971. The delay was perfectly understandable given the complexity of the evidence and law that His Honour had to consider, and given the length of his written judgment. He ruled against the Aboriginal claim. He found against the Aboriginal plaintiffs on the law and on the facts. On the law: Blackburn ruled that the common law did not recognise communal native title and that any pre-existing rights to land would have been extinguished by the assertion of sovereignty by the British crown. Blackburn could find no case of the principle of communal native title being put into practice other than 'by statute or by executive policy'. He did not consider that there was enough material before him to warrant a lower court, like a single judge of the Northern Territory Supreme Court, concluding that communal native title existed.[59] That would be a matter for the High Court. Also, he could not be convinced that the clans' relationship with land was a recognisable and proprietary interest. To be proprietary, it would need to carry 'the right to use or enjoy, the right to exclude others, and the right to alienate' — being the right to sell, lease or give away one's interest in land.[60]

The Aboriginal plaintiffs had expressly repudiated the right to alienate because under their law and culture they could not give away their land; they belonged to the land, rather than the land belonging to them. Blackburn was convinced that the clan's main right to use and occupy land was for the purposes of ritual and ceremonies. The clan had no right to exclude other groups from using the land for hunting purposes. So, 'by this standard I do not think that I can characterise the relationship of the clan to the land as proprietary'.[61] Nonetheless Blackburn was very sympathetic to the Aboriginal view of their relationship with their traditional country. He observed, 'The evidence shows a subtle and elaborate system highly adapted to the country in which the people led their lives, which provided a stable order of society and was remarkably free from the vagaries of personal whim or influence. If ever a system could be called "a government of laws, and not of men", it is that shown in the evidence before me.'[62] However, he felt compelled to rule that the British common law did not recognise communal interests in land as described in the evidence in court. Even if it did, he ruled that all such interests would have been nullified by the assertion of sovereignty by the British crown.

The lawyers for the traditional owners had then to consider whether it would be worth appealing Blackburn's judgment to the High Court. Woodward saw little point in appealing the case. Admittedly, the judge had made rulings of law about Aboriginal land title, which had never been tested in the courts before and which might be more favourably decided in favour of the Aboriginal plaintiffs by an appeal court. The problem was that the judge had not only ruled against the Aborigines on the law, he had also ruled against them on the facts. On the facts, he found, 'I am not satisfied, on the balance of probabilities, that the plaintiffs' predecessors had in 1788 the same links to the same areas of land as those which the plaintiffs now claim.'[63] An appeal court was much less likely to interfere with the trial judge's interpretation of the facts than with his interpretation of the law. There was little prospect that any appeal court would do anything other than show great deference to Blackburn's interpretation of the facts, given that he had been so respectful and considered towards the Aboriginal evidence presented to him. Years later Woodward gave some indication of his thinking when, in 1989, he told a Darwin audience:

> I took the view that the finding of close identification between particular groups of people and particular land was sufficient to mount a claim for recognition of Aboriginal title at a political level. I had no confidence that the High Court, as it was then constituted, would produce any better result for the Aboriginal people than had already been achieved. Indeed, I was afraid that doubts might be cast on Blackburn J's findings about Aboriginal law. I therefore advised against an appeal.[64]

In his autobiography, Woodward revealed that he had ruled out instituting the proceedings in the first place in the High Court – as later happened with the *Mabo* case. He was confident that he would receive a patient and fair hearing from Blackburn, the resident Supreme Court judge in the Northern Territory. Of the seven High Court judges, he thought he would get the same from justices Victor Windeyer and Douglas Menzies but he was 'very doubtful about the other five'.[65] Deciding then not to appeal to the High Court, he 'took the view that what we had achieved before Justice Blackburn was sufficient to provide a basis for land rights legislation'. He feared not only that they might lose the appeal, 'but might also have cold water poured on Blackburn's finding that there was a coherent system of Aboriginal law relating to land'. He was confirmed in this view when he was told some months later that 'Chief Justice Barwick had been heard to say that our native title claim was "a lot of nonsense" or words to that effect'.[66]

There had been considerable dissension within the legal team appearing for the Aboriginal plaintiffs before Justice Blackburn. John Little had been the most junior barrister in the three-member team. He was the first barrister to be involved in the case in its infancy when the Methodist missionaries were wondering what might be possible to assist the Yirrkala people in their quandaries about the proposed Nabalco development. Once the case was fully underway, he was then led by the more senior barristers, Edward Woodward and John Fogarty. On the second-last day of the hearing, in the absence of Edward Woodward, who had finished his submissions and flown back home to commence other work, John Fogarty, the next most senior counsel for the Aboriginal plaintiffs, had told the court:

> As indicated by Mr Woodward yesterday, the submissions on behalf of the plaintiffs are now completed. I understand that Mr Little desires to make an application of some kind but I am instructed both by my instructing solicitors and Mr Woodward to say there are no further matters which we desire to put on behalf of the plaintiffs and, in particular, that Mr Little has no authority or instructions to add anything to the submissions already made on behalf of the plaintiffs.[67]

John Little told the court that he would need a day to put his submissions, conceding that the plaintiff's solicitors had phoned him that morning telling him that he had no instructions to so act. Justice Blackburn ruled that it would be inappropriate in these circumstances for him to hear anything further from Mr Little.

After Blackburn had delivered his judgment, a detailed correspondence commenced in the letters section of the *Australian Law Journal*. Phillip Jeffrey, the editor of the journal, had adopted a very positive line on Blackburn's judgment. Geoffrey Lester, a legal academic who later moved to Canada to pursue the jurisprudence of native title, expressed his dissatisfaction in the correspondence column of the journal: 'One would have expected that the major organ of professional opinion in Australia would have been a little more critical of the judgment of Mr Justice Blackburn.' He thought the judge had 'failed to come to grips with a number of issues which cast grave doubts on the correctness of his finding', and that the solution was simple: 'the Crown was obliged to respect aboriginal occupation and enjoyment of their traditional tribal lands according to customary native tenure.'[68] Writing under the nom de plume CA Fryer, another barrister joined the correspondence defending Blackburn and the editor: 'If you are not going to defend yourself against Mr Lester's charge that you were insufficiently critical of the decision of Blackburn J in the Nabalco case, it seems that a correspondent must do it for you.' The unidentified barrister defended the soundness of Blackburn's reasoning, saying that 'a moral judgment would start from different premises and apply different criteria', concluding, 'Mr Lester may well have sound moral grounds for regretting Blackburn J's conclusion but not any legal ones.'[69]

John Little then joined the fray, claiming that 'Fryer's reply hinges on two errors, one of fact, the other of law'. Little claimed that the key argument for the ongoing recognition of communal native title had not been put to the court and that when he had risen to put the argument 'the other members of the plaintiff's legal team – but not the plaintiffs themselves – objected or were said to object to him being heard, and the court refused to hear him'. Little challenged those lawyers who would draw too ready a distinction between law and morality:

> Ever since black people first confronted it, the common law has been in tension between those advocating racial discrimination and those favouring racial equality. Mr Fryer, I suggest, has talked himself into the former camp and is heir to those who, until Lord Mansfield's [1772] decision in *Somerset* v *Stewart*, argued that the law upheld the institution of slavery and that its immorality was no concern of lawyers. It is because the common law has come out against racial discrimination that it has created the doctrine of communal native title.[70]

Writing again in March 1973, Little asserted that the blame did not lie with the common law: 'The basic argument that the Commonwealth so patiently propounded and His Honour accepted in Milirrpum's case, namely, that the common law knew nothing of Aboriginal title and in the absence of legislation would not protect it, is simply false.' With a fine concluding flourish he declared, 'At least after the *Abolition of Slavery Act* of 1833 it was the sword, not the pen, that robbed the Aboriginal people of Australia.'[71]

With no further recourse in the courts, the Aborigines looked again to the politicians. The day after Justice Blackburn delivered his judgment, Commonwealth Solicitor-General Ellicott advised the government on Blackburn's ruling about the lack of continuous occupation and use of the same areas of land by the plaintiffs and their ancestors: 'This finding is of great significance in relation to any appeal. If the plaintiffs cannot upset it, it seems to me they cannot succeed and therefore the High Court could dismiss an appeal by accepting the Judge's finding of fact and without dealing with the significant questions of law.'[72] Ellicott did warn his political masters that some of the High Court judges were showing a propensity to butt into legal controversies when there was no need and thus there was the prospect that the High Court might comment on the legal issues even if the plaintiffs could not get to first base on the facts. He warned that the government could not be assured 'that if it pays the costs of an appeal, the High Court will, itself, decide the important questions of legal principle which are involved'. Ellicott was strongly of the view that the Aboriginal grievances were legitimate and that political action rather than further courtroom battles was the way to go. There was building public sympathy for the Aborigines at Yirrkala. The unions said they would stop all mining operations in the area.

That afternoon, Prime Minister McMahon was asked in Parliament about the proposed work ban by unions on mining operations at Gove. McMahon said that his government had been 'anxious to ensure that the Aboriginals had every conceivable opportunity to present their case in order to protect whatever legal rights they had' and that 'if the Aboriginals want to pursue their rights in the High Court they have every right to do so'. The Aborigines could appeal to the High Court if they wanted to, and the Commonwealth would fund their legal costs. McMahon, who had already discussed the matter with Coombs, wanted to emphasise 'that we should not confuse the legal approach, the moral approach and an approach based on justice for Australian Aboriginals'.[73]

Wentworth, who had only a month to run as minister-in-charge of Aboriginal affairs, put a submission to Cabinet, informing the ministry, 'The response of the press and other organs of public opinion to this judgment has practically without exception been to assert that since this is the law it should be changed by Parliamentary action to recognise or compensate for traditional rights of Aborigines to such land.'[74] He was in no doubt 'that there is widespread and deeply emotional support among the community for the claims of the Aborigines to land'. He wanted his colleagues to respond promptly lest the opposition, trade unions and militant protesters gain a political advantage. The government needed to act 'promptly and boldly', consistent with what the prime minister had told Parliament, with 'determination to act justly and morally towards the Aborigines'. Cabinet set up a Ministerial Committee on Aboriginal Affairs to consider policies appropriate for Aboriginal reserve lands in the Northern Territory, ensuring that 'continuing groups of Aborigines' would have use of these lands 'for ceremonial, religious and recreational purposes' and providing appropriate tenure for groups and individuals wanting to operate commercial enterprises.[75] The government was not leading on this issue; it was playing catch-up with community sentiment in favour of the Aborigines, a sentiment that was finding resonance with the Labor Opposition.

Reflecting back on all that happened at this time, Bob Ellicott wrote in 2014:

> I think it is important in telling the story of these early days to stress that in the *Milirrpum* case although the court did not find for the plaintiffs there was clear recognition that there was a recognisable relationship of immense importance between Aboriginal people and their land. By 'recognisable' I mean it was so obvious and deeply rooted that it could be recognised by statute. It changed Commonwealth thinking on the subject so much that within 5 years the *Northern Territory Land Rights Act* was passed by a parliament which was controlled by so called 'conservatives'.[76]

But for the persistence of Stanner, Dexter and Coombs, there would not have been such a rapid change in Commonwealth thinking. But for the 1967 referendum, these three wise men would not have been around the Canberra corridors to leverage that change in the wake of the failed *Milirrpum* litigation.

CHAPTER 4

AFTER THE 1971 GOVE LAND RIGHTS CASE

Confusion about land rights and life choices

Immediately after Justice Blackburn had delivered his judgment, three Yolngu elders – Roy Dadaynga Marika, Daymbalipu Mununggur and Wali Wulanybuma Wunungmurra – came to Canberra with solicitor Frank Purcell and met with Prime Minister McMahon, who was accompanied by Ralph Hunt, the minister for the interior, Sir John Bunting, the secretary of the Department of Prime Minister and Cabinet, Dr Coombs, and John Ballard, the new deputy secretary of Interior. The time had come for moral rather than legal analysis, for political action rather than litigation. The three elders presented the prime minister with a signed statement expressing their deep shock at the court decision. Their claims were clear: 'We cannot be satisfied with anything less than ownership of the land. The land and law, sacred places, songs, dance and language were given to our ancestors.' They listed five demands: 'title to our land; a direct share of all royalties paid by Nabalco; royalties from other business on Aboriginal reserves; no other industries to be started without consent of the Yirrkala Council; and land to be included in our title after mining is finished.'[1] Having handed their list of demands to the prime minister, Marika went on to say that they wanted the law changed to give them a fair chance and to recognise their ownership of the land. He asked the government to help the people of Yirrkala. The prime minister undertook to fund any appeal to the High Court and proffered the view that 'until they had tested their rights in the High Court it was perhaps premature to say that they had lost the case'.[2]

Stanner presented the Council for Aboriginal Affairs with a statement on land policy.[3] He told his fellow council members that Woodward had insisted that it was 'most important to counter any assertion that Aborigines as a whole, or even those at Yirrkala, did not have proprietary rights: all that was found was the particular clans did not meet the burden of proof in this instance'. According to Stanner, 'When the spiritual interest of the clans is added to the economic interest of the bands, the product is a kind of interest enjoyed by the aboriginal community generally which could be regarded as just as worthy of protection and recognition as a European "proprietary" interest. This approach would be well worth a leading place in a Cabinet submission.' He would not have been aware at this stage that he and Solicitor-General Ellicott were on the same page, and that the government would have been receiving the same advice from their lawyers. Stanner recommended:

> ... the need for land granted under lease to be granted wherever possible to the groups or communities which can demonstrate the two points made in the judgment – the 'spiritual relationship' and the 'duty of care' for it. Even in regions (eg. NSW and Qld) where the old communities are broken up it would be worth searching for land, for acquisition under the Land Fund, where old associations could still be made out. The idea would be, wherever possible, to make leases appear to relate to old rights than to be merely acts of charity or compensation.

On the fourth anniversary of the 1967 referendum, Peter Howson replaced WC Wentworth as minister for Aboriginal affairs. The CAA were very happy to see the last of Wentworth. Dexter found 'he had been difficult to work with, had frustrated most of the Council's more important initiatives without substituting anything relevant for them and had failed in Cabinet'.⁴ The next day, Howson took HC Coombs to lunch at the Melbourne Club and asked about the future of the CAA. Having consulted the other council members, Coombs penned him a note that afternoon, suggesting the council would need to operate for another two or three years, by which time the various functions would be performed by 'the several departments and agencies, Commonwealth and State, whose responsibilities bear upon the welfare and advancement of Aborigines'.⁵ After that he foresaw only the need for a non-departmental advisory council, which might meet a couple of times a year. Howson then met with Bunting, the head of the Prime Minister's Department, to see how best to position Coombs within the bureaucracy for the next couple of years, by which time he would hopefully have retired. Howson later suggested to Coombs 'that this might be an opportunity for him to be a little franker with me as his Minister, rather than always hopping off to the Prime Minister when he got into trouble. I think Nugget realised that he had erred.'⁶

The Liberal Howson had long discussions with Country Party Interior Minister Ralph Hunt about land rights and found Hunt agreeable to his ideas. Whatever the ongoing tension between the CAA and Interior, Howson was hopeful that he could avoid the antipathy that had existed between Wentworth and Nixon. In one of his early meetings with the CAA, Howson thought them delighted with his views on Aboriginal family planning, which he had been sharing with all comers, including the Anglican Primate, Frank Woods, who thought the World Council of Churches might even come on board. Howson thought a lot of Aboriginal social problems could be solved or alleviated if their young women had fewer babies, and had them after their teenage years. The federal–state meeting of the Council for Ministers of Aboriginal Affairs took place on 3 August 1971. Howson, in the chair, 'hadn't realised that the other ministers have never really sat down to think about our basic objective concerning the Aboriginal people. We therefore had to spend more time on fundamental objectives, rather than on matters on the agenda.'⁷ He continued to pursue his family planning agenda with Frank Engel, the secretary of the World Council of Churches, but could not find any common ground with the churches on land rights. By this time, the churches were strongly supportive of some legal recognition of land rights. Howson wrote in his diary:

> [Engel] feels that to an extent we would be expiating the sins of our ancestors by providing free rights to land for Aborigines, whereas I feel that our main task is not to look to the past but to the future and gradually to use land in the way in which it's going to be exploited. For instance, where the Aborigines are going to use it for the same purposes of farming as we are they should have the same form of legal organisation.⁸

Howson spent a week in Queensland with Sir Joh Bjelke-Petersen and Pat Killoran, the seasoned director of the Queensland Department of Aboriginal and Islander Affairs. Bjelke-Petersen and Killoran had become very wary of the CAA and its land rights and self-determination agenda. The CAA continued to receive good co-operation from the Queensland state departments, delivering services such as health and education, but they found Killoran quite obstructionist when it came to trying to deliver these services to the Aborigines and Torres Strait Islanders living on reserves in Queensland. The Torres Strait was a Queensland fiefdom where 'the feds' were not welcome. Howson discussed proposals for the protection and use of ceremonial grounds 'and also possibly what we should do concerning land rights for Aborigines'.⁹

Charles Perkins, having been a senior research officer with the Office of Aboriginal Affairs for two years, was growing impatient with the slow changes to policy in the Northern Territory, largely because of the stranglehold by the Department of the Interior. He wrote to Prime Minister McMahon, reminding him that the 1967 referendum was not simply an exercise conferring power on the Commonwealth Government. People had an expectation that the Commonwealth would act. It was first necessary that the Commonwealth get its own house in order and lead by example in the Northern Territory. He urged a separation of education, housing and health from the Welfare Branch of Interior, arguing that the existing arrangements 'perpetuate a welfare complex among Aborigines, thus sustaining the feeling that they are "problem people" in the community. This results, as can easily be witnessed, in the development of an inferiority complex, a lack of dignity and initiative, and eventual disrespect for Australian society.'[10]

The CAA met with Minister Howson, trying to reshape the distribution of responsibilities between Commonwealth ministers and departments in relation to Aboriginal welfare in the Northern Territory. The Country Party was insisting that the minister for the interior maintain 'substantially independent policy-making powers in the Northern Territory'.[11] On 3 August 1971, Ralph Hunt, the minister for the interior, and Peter Howson, the minister for the environment, Aborigines and the arts, signed an agreement setting out their respective responsibilities. It was a win for the Country Party. Howson had responsibility for national Aboriginal policies and for co-ordinating these policies between the states and the Commonwealth. In the Northern Territory, Hunt was to maintain policy and administrative responsibilities 'in the same way as the Government of a State'. Should there be disagreement between the ministers on the application of a national policy in the Northern Territory, either minister would be free to take the matter to the ministerial committee or to Cabinet. All communications from the CAA to the Northern Territory Administration were to be through the Department of the Interior. CAA members and officers would travel to the Northern Territory only once they had advised Interior, 'so that proper arrangements can be made for appropriate officers' to accompany them. Appointing Howson to the diverse portfolios of environment, arts and Aborigines, McMahon took the opportunity to move the Office of Aboriginal Affairs out of the Prime Minister's Department and into the new department responsible for these discrete policy areas.

Having received a bureaucratic response to his prime ministerial approach, Perkins wrote again suggesting that present policies were having 'a serious detrimental effect on Aboriginal affairs generally'.[12] He wanted McMahon to sit down and meet with him and two other Aboriginal leaders – Phillip Roberts from the Northern Territory and Pastor Doug Nicholls from South Australia. McMahon took advice from the public service and told Perkins to put his concerns through the relevant department, as he was a public servant.[13] Perkins was already doing so, having previously provided the CAA with a 23-page memorandum. He was convinced that the council and the Office of Aboriginal Affairs had 'failed to live up to the high expectations implicit on the wave of optimism which followed' the referendum, and that claims of benign influence on the states was 'just so much hogwash': 'The Commonwealth has no real intention of dominating policy trends as expected and uses only the avenue of cash handouts to obtain partial influence over the States.' Perkins identified 'the inherent prejudice of the Country Party interests in the Government and Cabinet', and 'the absolutely disgraceful influence and manipulation of Aboriginal Affairs within and outside the Northern Territory by Mr Harry Giese and certain State directors'.[14] Giese was one of Hasluck's great disciples of assimilation and he had stayed on as the senior public servant responsible for Aboriginal welfare in the Northern Territory. Perkins opposed the appointment of further Aboriginal liaison officers within the Office of Aboriginal Affairs until their role could be clarified, thinking they should be more out in the field, not in Canberra.

The mode of Aboriginal consultation was proving very problematic. Perkins recommended a nationally elected Aboriginal council should sit with the CAA every three months to give the CAA policy directions, with two members of the Aboriginal council being eligible to serve on the CAA. He was opposed to the CAA's ready funding of church missions, arguing that no funds should go to church bodies that suppress Aborigines, such as the Aborigines Inland Mission, 'plus some of the more established churches for crude sectarian reasons'. He wanted to set preconditions for church funding, including guarantees of eventual Aboriginal land ownership and control, and encouragement of Aboriginal languages and culture. In a conciliatory tone, he concluded his memo noting that Coombs and Dexter 'are the best white men ever to become involved in Aboriginal affairs' and that the council and its small Office of Aboriginal Affairs 'should not carry the burden for the current and possibly future disasters in policy and administration'.[15]

Dexter confided to Coombs that he shared Perkins' natural impatience but he was disappointed that Perkins understood so little of the council's approach of working constructively within present constraints. Dexter acknowledged that most Aborigines would never benefit directly from the fund that had been established for Aboriginal enterprises because 'the original intention never was that the mass of the people should benefit directly, but only that (as in white society) the competent, entrepreneurial minority should be assisted by it'.[16] Dexter would have welcomed Aboriginal membership of the CAA but Minister Howson regarded it as premature. Dexter thought Perkins was wrong in claiming that churches received favoured treatment. Churches received grants, rather than loans, for the delivery of welfare services that, in their absence, would have been provided by the state.

At this time, articles were appearing in the press venting the CAA's dissatisfaction with government and suggesting that the members might resign. Dexter maintained a close working relationship with Bruce Juddery from *The Canberra Times*, which published an article by him on 20 August 1971, pointing out that the Office of Aboriginal Affairs had submitted a budget request for $30 million and come away with less than half that, and that Minister Howson had instructed Dexter to stop making public statements. Juddery spelled out the divisions between the CAA and Interior – the CAA being 'integrationist' and 'all in favour of land rights', having done all they could in the *Milirrpum* case to assist the Yirrkala people 'in a sort of guerrilla defiance' of the Commonwealth

Government; and Interior being 'assimilationist', considering that 'Aboriginal culture has deteriorated so far that Aborigines must rule off their past, starting again as committed members of the majority community'. The CAA was minded to resign en masse but were 'dissuaded by the thought that their battling on is the only real guarantee that Aboriginal affairs will have a friend at court'.

Howson called the CAA to Parliament House for an explanation. They assured the minister that they were not contemplating resignation. They had too much work to do. Coombs told him that Juddery had provided 'a fairly penetrating analysis of differing approaches as between various Departments involved in Aboriginal advancement'.[17] Howson professed his own belief in McMahon's Cairns doctrine, which was a significant departure from the 1965 assimilation policy, but said that there was a need to bring other departments and ministers along to embrace the change.

Stanner penned a paper, preparing for the CAA to ask government formally to abandon all reference to 'assimilation': 'The time has come to stop talking about the "assimilation" of the Aborigines as if it were an intelligent, a moral, or a politically possible policy.'[18] In the short term, he thought it inadvisable to drop the word 'assimilation' or to substitute another one-line policy descriptor like 'integration'. Rather it would be best to highlight in government statements how the notion had evolved both before and after the 1968 Cabinet decision, which had reaffirmed the policy:

> There is, in fact, a good deal of technical evidence which, soberly interpreted, tends to support the interpretations which Mr Holt, Mr Gorton and Mr McMahon have put forward. Experience indicates that the pace of Aboriginal assimilation cannot be forced; that they do not respond to things which do not attract them; that their will to retain parts of their culture, whether we like it or not, is strong and in some areas may be growing rather than diminishing; and that while not rejecting outright,

and even favouring in a realistic way, some sort of union of their lives with
us, they are insistent on retaining an identity of their own.

Stanner thought it inappropriate in the Australian context to be juxtaposing assimilation and apartheid, or assimilation and separate development. There was no need for such 'hard line sloganistic thinking'. In Australia, it was more a matter of timing and choice: 'the terms of Aboriginal entry into the life of the "single Australian community" – at what speed, with full or restricted choice, by volition or compulsion, with or without an identity of their own based on their own traditions, with or without special compensation for the deprivals they have sustained at our hands.'

On 16 September, Howson had a long chat with Governor-General Sir Paul Hasluck. It was almost three years since Hasluck had left the fray of politics and taken up residence at Yarralumla. Howson had the opportunity to get some further insights into Coombs, who had been at university with Hasluck. Howson thought Hasluck 'was also particularly interested in views I have about land rights for Aborigines which, of course, differ from those of Coombs, but he feels my ideas make a lot of sense. I will try to develop them a bit over the next few weeks'.[19]

Howson was convinced that Coombs had many imaginative ideas but that his administrative procedures were lamentable. Howson saw his role as hosing down the divisions between Interior and the CAA. On 1 October, he discussed the matter further with the secretary of his department, Len Hewitt. Hewitt was a very seasoned Canberra mandarin, having watched Coombs in action for a couple of decades. After the meeting, Howson wrote in his diary:

> It's obvious that there are grave fundamental differences between the council on the one hand and Interior on the other, particularly concerning the title that should be given to Aborigines, either in the reserves or off the reserves. Every time he thinks that he has got agreement, Coombs

increases his demands and, in fact, appears as if he really wants to hand over the whole of Arnhem Land to the Aborigines, giving them, in effect, title to all the land that they believe they own by historical association.[20]

Around this time, Stanner gave a talk to a community discussion group named the Third Monday Group. Typical of him, he had 33 octavo pages of typed notes. He looked back to the time when he was asked to join the CAA. He 'was reluctant to have any part of it. I thought the Commonwealth's policy deplorable. I had, to my regret, fallen out publicly with Hasluck over it as early as 1958.' Four years after receiving the letter of appointment from Prime Minister Holt, he said he was 'still waiting, four years later, for a letter from someone telling me what my position, powers and functions, if any, are'. He took this as being illustrative 'that the Referendum very soon began to lose force'. With Holt's death, he thought the Liberal Party had made a backward step to the Hasluck policy: 'Hasluck seems to have thought that Aboriginality was finished and that there was no sense in trying to keep it alive. I think this was wrong on several counts. New conditions changed the whole picture. Aboriginality was not finished; Yirrkala alone proves that.'[21]

For Stanner, Dexter and Coombs, the law determined by Blackburn was not the end of the matter; it was the beginning. The judgment simply moved the forum for resolution of the issue from the courts back to Parliament, which needed to respond to public sympathy and notions of public morality. The CAA had prepared a very detailed submission on land issues for Howson to present to the Cabinet Committee for Aborigines in light of the *Milirrpum* decision. They submitted: 'The Court's findings, where favourable to the Commonwealth and Nabalco, express an established legal doctrine, but one which rests on a philosophical justification of imperial colonisation of which modern public sentiment disapproves.'[22] They saw a need for land rights legislation that would enjoy strong community support. They noted, 'Opinion is strongest in Aboriginal advancement organisations and church bodies but representations have also been received from university groups and from branches of the Liberal and Labor parties.' They were aware of concerns, particularly in the Country Party and in Interior, that land rights could mean separate development, something akin to apartheid. They noted:

> The Aborigines' future perforce lies in an association with the rest of the Australian community. It is therefore important that whatever may be done in relation to Aboriginal land claims: (a) should not call in question rights and title to land established under the Crown since 1788; (b) should be in terms of the existing Australian legal system; and (c) should further the ability of the Aborigines to take an effective and respected place in Australian society.

The CAA suggested that any law or policy start with the Northern Territory reserves, aiming to satisfy the Aborigines' desires for land, which includes it being a symbol of identity and a link with the past, a source of recreation, rest and privacy, a base for religious and ceremonial life, and a source of livelihood and economic independence. The CAA had already succeeded in having the government move away from assimilation accelerated by *terra nullius*. They were still prepared to acknowledge voluntary assimilation as a desired social outcome but thought the granting of some form of title over reserves could provide a haven or a stopover, especially for those not too keen to make a change of lifestyle, as well as an economic incentive or asset for those willing to make the move. Their submission stated:

> Since Aboriginal Australians will need real help to become part of the general community, reserves can be seen also as providing resources to ensure that Aborigines do not enter the economic system in a state of poverty and dependence. For this, the land will need to be supplemented with capital, with training and with managerial expertise.

> The Prime Minister has stated that Aborigines should be assisted and encouraged to maintain their traditional culture and to choose to what degree and at what pace they wish to accept our way of life. Accordingly reserves can be seen also as a base for the continuity of Aboriginal life and as a refuge for those unwilling or unable wholly to accept our way of life.

The CAA suggested 99-year leases for Aborigines resident on reserve land 'with which they are identified by traditional claim or long occupancy'. They recommended that communities be able to sub-lease land to entrepreneurs but on terms subject to ministerial approval. The crown ought be able to acquire reserve land for public purposes with reasonable compensation. They suggested a ten-year moratorium on mining but thought it was 'probably in the long-term interests of Aborigines that technically sophisticated enterprises (other than mining) using non-Aboriginal capital should, with due regard to the wishes of resident Aborigines, be established when opportunity offers'.

The CAA at this time was amenable to reserves being opened up for economic development, which would entail non-Aborigines residing on the lands. They said, 'Townships and villages could develop on the traditional Australian patterns but remain predominantly, though not wholly, Aboriginal in population.' They also put recommendations about pastoral leases and Aboriginal economic enterprises outside reserves.

Howson took their submission to the Cabinet committee and suggested that it be referred to an interdepartmental committee (IDC) of public servants that had been set up to assist the Cabinet committee. Thus began the process of the federal bureaucracy and the Coalition Government considering its response to the unfinished business of the *Milirrpum* case. The CAA had put forward a comprehensive agenda for change but one that could not be seen as a blueprint for separatist development. The IDC set about three months' work analysing various policy proposals. The CAA thought the IDC report was satisfactory, 'in that it set out the issues clearly and, notwithstanding Interior's quibbles and reservations, recommended or implied the constructive approaches put forward by the Council'.[23]

The IDC presented its report on land and mining issues to the ministers on 11 October 1971. The report dealt with enhancing the security of Aboriginal reserves, proposed leases on Aboriginal reserve lands, arrangements for exploration and mining on reserves, and access to the Aboriginal Advancement Trust Account for economic enterprises. The tensions between the CAA and Interior were as obvious as ever. The CAA wanted to discuss the report with Howson but at first he was not available. Howson saw himself as the committee chairman and not as an advocate for the policy preferences of the CAA, even though he was their minister. Howson met briefly with Dexter and Stanner on 13 October. Dexter was critical as ever of Interior's approach, 'which is to stand pat on existing policies' that 'would not meet the needs of the situation, would satisfy neither the Aborigines nor concerned public opinion and would be likely to attract international criticism'.[24]

Howson found it difficult to pin down the CAA on the specific recommendations they were making about land title and access to lands for Aborigines in Arnhem Land. He noted, 'It seems at the moment that the Department of Interior would give a tribe or clan approx. 1,000 square miles [2600 square kilometres] for a cattle station, whereas the council would want to give them 2,500 square miles [6500 square kilometres], partly for pastoral activities and partly for hunting and recreation.'[25] He saw one real issue: 'to what extent do we give Aboriginals title or long leases for land use other than for economic purposes? All the Ministers, except Bill Wentworth, felt that we should go along with Interior and not accept the council's recommendations.'[26]

Coombs wrote to the prime minister expressing strong concerns about how the ministry was lining up, siding more with Interior and its Country Party minister. McMahon agreed to attend part of the Cabinet committee meeting. Both Coombs and Howson claimed the credit and advantage for getting McMahon to attend. McMahon sided with the majority of his ministers in making two fateful decisions. The CAA had convinced the IDC to recommend that traditional association with land be accepted as a criterion in the granting of a lease to an Aboriginal community. The Cabinet committee rejected this idea. Interior and the Country Party won the day with Howson's support. The CAA had no advocate at the table. The Cabinet committee agreed to leases being granted but primarily for economic purposes. They decided that 'leases of land on reserves should be made available to Aboriginal communities, groups or individuals with the intention of providing them with an effective base for their economic future. Before granting a lease there should be an investigation to test the economic prospects of the area but the criteria should be interpreted liberally.'

The CAA's second major loss was in relation to mining. Though prepared to have decision-makers consider the needs and concerns of a local Aboriginal community before granting a mining interest on an Aboriginal reserve, the Cabinet committee rejected the CAA's proposal that 'the welfare of Aboriginal communities likely to be affected should be the dominant consideration in policy and administration decisions in relation to prospecting for minerals and the development of mining enterprises within reserves'. These decisions, then ultimately endorsed by the full Cabinet with some fine tuning following Coombs' further direct appeals to the prime minister, cast the die for the confused land rights policy that was to be announced by McMahon on Australia Day 1972, providing the opportunity for the opposition Labor Party to capitalise on public support for land rights in the lead-up to the election at which Gough Whitlam would become prime minister.

Coombs wrote again to McMahon on 18 October 1971, expressing the CAA's shock and disappointment, especially in relation to the Cabinet committee's decision 'that traditional association with a specific area of land should not be used as a criterion for the granting of a lease to an Aboriginal community'. Coombs said this was:

> ... a denial of the assurance contained in your Cairns statement and in the subsequent re-statement of Commonwealth policy that Aborigines would be encouraged and assisted to preserve and develop their traditions and culture. We believe that this decision, which could have mobilised behind the Government the advocates in all sections of the community of humane and forward-looking policies towards Aboriginal Australians, will be seen as another expression of outmoded prejudice and discrimination.

Howson wrote in his diary, 'The council, however, have sent me a paper today indicating their dissatisfaction with the decisions we made last week, and it seems that they might even be prepared to resign.'[27] McMahon rang Coombs, suggesting that the provision of $5 million for land purchases would go a long way towards meeting the CAA's recommendations. He did not realise that the money was for the purchase of land off reserves. Coombs insisted on the need to recognise traditional ownership, especially of land that was presently reserved for Aborigines. Coombs told McMahon:

> The Council is really serious about this. We think that if you write to the Yirrkala people and tell them that they can apply for individual or community leases for solely economic purposes and that they will be allotted only land sufficient for specific purposes – a farm here, a garden there, a cattle property perhaps, land for a brickworks somewhere else – this will appear to them to be a continuation of the present position. Frankly, we have to tell you that this proposal is not going to bring the confrontation to an end. Aborigines are going to believe that they have been denied reasonable recognition of the importance of traditional association with the land.[28]

Recognition of traditional ownership was essential. According to Dexter, 'The Council believed not only that it was the only just basis, but also that it was the only basis which would have a chance of acceptance by the Aboriginals and therefore of resolving the present confrontation.'[29]

On 19 October, Howson went off to the Melbourne Club for lunch as he often did, this time with Malcolm Fraser. 'I warned him that Coombs had been talking with the PM, and that we might have to revise our views on traditional land rights. Malcolm indicated very firmly that he would not change his mind or the views he expressed in Cabinet last week.'[30] Within five years, Malcolm Fraser would be the prime minister trumpeting the passage of land rights legislation in the Northern Territory. There was still a considerable distance to run in the political stakes and in the public discernment of what morality required of the law and public policy on land rights. Fraser and his colleagues were stuck on leases for economic purposes. There was no way that they were open to inalienable freehold for traditional owners regardless of their lack of plans for economic development. An inalienable freehold title would guarantee the owners all the rights of land ownership and use, except that there would be restrictions on giving away any interest in the land, whether by gift, sale, lease or mortgage.

Stanner and Dexter were fed up and thought they would resign when McMahon announced the land policy. The wily Coombs made McMahon's agreement to the CAA's proposed addition to the ministerial committee's recommendations a precondition for his joining McMahon on an overseas trip to discuss economic questions. Howson was getting very frustrated, saying that he could not trust anyone. Howson's departmental head, Hewitt, and Coombs were at war. Gorton was 'wanting to fight us all'.[31] Howson conceded that Coombs might be the best adviser available to McMahon on economic questions, but then again McMahon may have just been 'worried about Coombs's threat of resignation on the Aboriginal land rights issue and wishes to get him so attached that he is unable to put in a resignation'.[32]

Overseas, Coombs was working his magic on McMahon. On 30 October, McMahon called Howson from New York, questioning Coombs' loyalty but obviously affected by his advocacy. McMahon told Howson that he had to be careful with the Country Party on the land rights issue. Howson thought McMahon was waking up to the problems in following the Coombs path and that the prime minister was starting to realise that Howson was taking the right approach. A week later, McMahon called Howson again from New York, having prepared a paper on land rights. Howson wrote in his diary on 7 November, 'It's obvious that Coombs has been getting at him while he's been away, and we'll have problems to solve when he gets back.'[33] McMahon phoned Howson again on 19 November. Howson noted:

> First, talking about the land rights issues, he's firmly convinced that he must go along with Nugget Coombs in favour of traditional association for the granting of land rights to Aborigines. I explained some of the problems, and he got annoyed; but I pointed out to him that I was only indicating the fact that I was chairman of a committee in which most of the Ministers were taking the opposite point of view from his own, and that it was wiser for me to give him the views of the committee, rather than trying to go along with everything that he was recommending. He's firmly convinced that this is an election winner and that we're just a lot of reactionary Ministers who can't see the problem as clearly as he can.[34]

The ministerial committee reviewing its October decisions about leases received a range of materials, including papers by Sir Richard Blackburn, the judge in the *Milirrpum* proceedings, and Robert Ellicott, the solicitor-general who had appeared for the Commonwealth. After he concluded the *Milirrpum* litigation, Sir Richard Blackburn prepared a brief paper on Aboriginal land matters and sent it to friends, including Dexter and Coombs. Coombs provided Prime Minister McMahon with a copy and so Blackburn then provided a copy to Gough Whitlam, the leader of the opposition. Blackburn thought that 'no one should take it for granted that the introduction of a system of aboriginal title is either morally right, or socially expedient. It may be both: personally I think it probably is; but I am out of sympathy with demands for "aboriginal land rights" which assume that the need for such a system is self-evident, and its morality beyond question.' He put forward 'tentative' suggestions that Aboriginal title be vested in tribes by means of trusts or corporations. He was adamant that any title be leasehold rather than freehold: 'A leasehold system would imply that the aboriginals had certain obligations, both positive and negative, in using the land, and the sanction for breach of these obligations would, ultimately, be the termination of their interest in the land.' He pointed out that, but for small town blocks, leasehold was the usual form of tenure in the Northern Territory and the only form of tenure for large landholdings. He would 'apply to all landholders, black or white, the same principle that ownership of land carries responsibility for its socially acceptable use'. When Ian Viner finally introduced land rights legislation in the Commonwealth Parliament for the Fraser Government, Blackburn resurrected his paper and sent it to Viner with a covering letter acknowledging that Woodward had provided comprehensive reports on land rights and deferring to his views, still insisting that 'aboriginal land should be perpetual leasehold, with terms making the aboriginals responsible for proper care of the land'.[35]

Blackburn wanted to avoid any 'false impression of my own certainty'. He acknowledged that much of the public discussion of the issue revolved around two propositions, each of which had some appeal while also being somewhat problematic. First, 'the land belonged to the aboriginals in the first place, and the whites took it away from them'. Second, 'our duty therefore is to give some land back to them and let them do what they like with it'. He opined, 'There can be no moral justification for giving back to the aboriginals only some, but not all, of the land taken from them,' and asked if Aboriginal land owners would be 'allowed to sell their land to white men who want to buy it? To prevent them from doing so is inconsistent with the moral principle upon which the land is restored to them.' Having agitated the moral issues without resolution or limitation, Blackburn said:

> My personal opinion, for what it is worth, is that the establishment of a system of aboriginal title, integrated within the framework of Australian law, and providing proper machinery for its own practical application and development, is desirable in order to give, to some groups of aboriginals who want it, a sense of responsibility for their own future, and in order to satisfy the aspirations of aboriginal people generally.

He insisted, 'It must not be assumed that the Commonwealth can contemplate only one basis of land allotment to aboriginals – either economic or tribal.' If a new form of statutory title for tribes was not to be instituted, Blackburn urged a consideration of trusts or incorporation to allow the vesting of land title in an entity committed to acting in the interests of the tribe. As for the form of tenure, he ruled out freehold whether alienable, inalienable, or alienable only to other Aborigines. As leaseholders, they would be responsible to some authority for the proper care of the land. He also envisaged that the authority would need to grant approval to any proposed alienation of the tribal interest in the land. Furthermore, Blackburn saw that leasehold would allow some flexibility as government came to terms with this 'new and experimental idea' of Aboriginal ownership and control of large land areas. Yet he accurately foresaw problems with the lease idea:

> Journalists and propagandists would probably seize on the word 'lease' and cultivate the idea that it is ungenerous to aboriginals to give them less than full control of the land. Names are unimportant; however the system is described, in my view it is essential that aboriginals be held responsible for their land. Without such responsibility, I do not believe that either aboriginals or the whole Australian community would benefit from the scheme. I would apply to all landholders, black or white, the same principle that ownership of land carries responsibility for its socially acceptable use.

Blackburn wrote just a five-page paper; Ellicott provided a 28-page advice. Ellicott set out to provide a practical way in which 'claims made by aboriginal people to land situated within the Northern Territory should be recognised'. He said, 'The problem we ought to be facing is not should we recognise but – what is the method of recognition most likely to be in the interests of the Australian community.' When he first came to the *Milirrpum* case as counsel, he 'was sceptical as to whether recognition was in the interests of the Australian community as a whole'. But on acquaintance with the issues he was strongly convinced of the need for recognition. And he was satisfied that some form of recognition was necessary for the Aborigines at Gove, 'to maintain their own culture and way of life and thereby retain self-respect and dignity within the Australian community … Elementary justice would seem to require it.' He did not think they could develop as part of the Australian community with their own culture and way of life without such recognition: 'We might as well expect fish to live without water.'

Ellicott was aware of the intrusive effect of mining: 'The magnitude of change at Gove can only really be understood by those who have witnessed it.' He appreciated the Aboriginal perceptions that governments were untrustworthy unless they were prepared to guarantee legal title to land, which would lead to an acknowledgment of their entitlements to a share in economic development of their lands rather than the receipt of welfare assistance from a paternalistic government. He conceded that this was a difficult human problem which did not admit of ready solution: 'I think we are more likely to find the wise answer if we seek to apply to it our basic notions of justice, rather than if we allow fear or expedience or similar criteria to determine our judgment.'

He had carefully considered the IDC report provided to the Cabinet committee in October, taking 'a different view on recognition to that adopted by the Department of Interior' and 'a different approach on the manner of recognition to that expressed by the Council for Aboriginal Affairs'. Ellicott was firmly of the view that the Aboriginal interest in land was 'not in the nature of a proprietary right', but was inalienable, and that 'the basic relationship is spiritual in nature and finds its origin in a firmly held and traditional belief that areas of land were given to particular groups by their mythological ancestors'. From his experience as counsel in the *Milirrpum* case, Ellicott was convinced that Aborigines on reserves were people in transition and that any legal arrangements for land should reflect both the reality of past traditional and spiritual association as well as future economic prospects. He thought that outside contact and education would lead to a weakening of spiritual ties with land. The challenge was to find how best to protect the past interest and to foster the future interest. He proposed that reserve lands be divided into tribal zones, where the relevant clans would maintain their rights to hunt and forage and to tend spiritual sites. Within the tribal zone, Aborigines resident in the area would be able to apply for a lease of land for particular purposes, including economic development, while clan members would maintain the right of access for tribal purposes.

Ellicott found himself seeking a compromise between the Department of the Interior and the CAA. Unlike Interior, he was unfazed by the prospect that some recognition on reserves would entail some recognition of Aboriginal access rights off reserves and that similar arrangements might then be sought beyond the Northern Territory. Unlike the CAA, and in agreement with Interior, he thought that 'if leases are to be granted to aboriginals, they should be for specific projects which direct the aboriginal to a positive economic use of land'.[36] Ellicott thought that his proposal would have 'the advantage that if economic use is not made of the land and if, in time, the aboriginal ties with it weaken and the rights to hunt, fish and forage and use sacred sites fall into disuse, a future government will be better able to deal with the land, than it would, if it was the subject of long term leases'. He was in no doubt that younger Aborigines would be more individualistic and would thus seek individual leases within tribal zones. This proposal could be equally workable on pastoral leases, because the clan rights for hunting and foraging and accessing sacred sites would not be that much different from the ongoing access rights provided on Northern Territory pastoral leases. Pastoral leases issued before 1964 even included the right to erect wurlies and other dwellings. Those issued after 1964 included ongoing protection of the Aboriginal right to enter and use natural waters and springs and to kill and use birds and animals *ferae naturae* for food.

As solicitor-general, Ellicott had to give thought to what limits there might be on Aboriginal claims to public land. For example, some Aborigines had made a claim to the Darwin post office. He thought that Aborigines living in towns and cities had lost their close relationship to the land: 'For this reason it does not seem to me that the recognition of claims on reserves necessarily creates a precedent for acknowledgment of claims to town and city areas.' Some urban dwellers might want to have a tribal zone declared over their traditional country on a reserve or pastoral lease. Ellicott had no answer to this difficulty, noting, 'A question of policy could arise as to whether these groups should be given the right to have their lands declared in the manner proposed, and if so, whether they should be required to return there.' Ellicott made no claim to having all the answers and he was 'clear that legal recognition will not provide the complete answer to the aboriginal problem'. He was adamant about one thing: legal recognition was 'one of the bases on which our future aboriginal policy should be structured'.

Coombs was very impressed that both the judge and senior counsel for the Commonwealth after the case had gone to the trouble of formulating ideas about how Aboriginal aspirations to land might be met. He wrote, 'It is difficult to imagine more powerful evidence of the emotional impact which the Yirrkala land rights issue has exerted on the conscience of thoughtful Australians.'[37] But at this stage, no one, not even the CAA, was proposing inalienable freehold.

Howson was prepared to consider an appeal tribunal from decisions of the Northern Territory Land Board but he still thought that the land board should make decisions on lease applications informed by the criterion of economic development. He was confident that he could carry the majority of the ministerial council with him. By 25 November he was very frustrated with the CAA: 'So far they feel that they can have complete irresponsibility in carrying out the decision and just say, "Well, we advise you this way, and if you don't take our advice – well, we're not going to help".'[38]

Having returned from overseas, Coombs wrote to McMahon on 29 November 1971:

> I understand that the Ministerial Committee on Aboriginal Affairs is likely to meet this week. I think it is imperative that a decision should be reached about leases to Aboriginal communities on reserved lands which leaves no room for differing interpretations and which goes far enough towards meeting the expressed wishes of the Aborigines to have a reasonable chance of acceptance by them and to command the support of those responsible sections of the Australian community concerned with Aboriginal welfare.
>
> The papers by Mr Justice Blackburn and the Solicitor-General more than justify the course of action the Council has recommended to you. It is of immense significance that both the trial judge and the Commonwealth senior counsel should have been impelled to urge legislative action to remedy the social injustice being done to the Yirrkala and other Aborigines. Council considers Judge Blackburn's paper the more persuasive and the more likely to yield true advantages to the Aborigines. It urges a course of action very similar to that put forward by the Council.
>
> Mr Ellicott's concrete proposals, despite his sympathetic introduction, appear to us to be less satisfactory. The idea of formally establishing 'tribal zones' is interesting and at first sight could appear to go some way to meet the Aboriginal requests. However, in fact, it does little more than formalise the situation in Aboriginal use of reserved lands which has caused the existing problems. His proposals for subsequent leases for economic purposes follow closely on those of the Department of the Interior, and are subject to the same disadvantages.

We believe it important politically that a decision should be followed promptly by a reply from yourself as Prime Minister to the Yirrkala Aborigines' requests. This would have the further advantage of demonstrating by clear example to the public and administrators alike the intention underlying the policy decision. Last week we sought Mr Howson's concurrence in the circulation to the Ministerial Committee of Council's submission entitled 'Unresolved Issues of Aboriginal Policy (Mr Bailey's Draft)' suggesting a paragraph for this section of your reply to the Yirrkala requests. I suggest that you show this paragraph to the Ministerial Committee. It runs:

> In relation specifically to the request from Yirrkala for title to land, it is agreed that the Prime Minister might inform the Yirrkala Council that:
> a. the Government is prepared to grant the community a 99-year lease of approximately 2,500 square miles [6500 square kilometres] in north-east Arnhem Land, to be used for general economic and social purposes;
> b. the precise limits of the area would be determined after consultation with the Yirrkala community as well as with other communities to ensure that it does not encroach on their interests;
> c. the lease would exclude all areas leased; and
> d. the lease might include offshore islands and, subject to the consent of the applicants, all those areas between Arnhem Bay in the west, Blue Mud Bay in the south and Bremer Island in the north where leases have already been applied for by groups at Yirrkala.

The CAA then wrote to Minister Howson on 1 December, indicating their general disappointment with the approach of the ministerial committee, which was too much in the grip of Interior. The three members were insistent that Aboriginal communities be able to apply for leases over large areas of land with which 'they are and have been associated'. Once again, the council was prepared to resign en masse if they did not win this concession. They were becoming like the boy who cried, 'Wolf!'

The next day, Howson circulated a submission to the ministerial committee, setting out the conflicting views of Interior and the CAA. The CAA favoured the grant of leases on reserves where Aborigines could demonstrate a long association. Interior was opposed as this 'will lead to claims to land not on reserves that it will be difficult if not impossible to resist'.[39] Interior thought that the 1970 legislation providing for limited leases to Aborigines for pastoral, agricultural and miscellaneous purposes was adequate. They were opposed to the grant of leases over 'consolidated areas', which could include land for commercial purposes as well as for hunting and foraging. Such areas could include 'traditionally claimed land' and 'would lead to the land remaining under-developed for years, and could lead to claims for similar treatment on other and smaller reserves, on pastoral properties and in the States'.[40] Neither side was in any doubt that whatever was done on Aboriginal reserves in the Northern Territory would eventually be done on other lands throughout Australia. The CAA thought 'multi-purpose leases of large areas would best meet Aboriginal mentality and needs'.[41] Howson outlined the decision at hand:

> A decision is required whether an Aboriginal community can be given a lease of major areas that will allow not only recognised economic activities (the Council agrees that these are essential) but also, to help sustain the whole community and provide a base for the maintenance and development of traditional ways of life, such activities as hunting and foraging which require 'broad acres' (and which the Department would not wish to grant).

The Department of the Interior thought that 'the only special criterion to adopt in granting a lease to Aborigines is that it will provide a base for an economic enterprise'.[42] Interior would concede that a lower threshold would apply to assessment of economic prospects on a reserve than off a reserve, and that the economic criteria would be 'liberally interpreted'. Given that Aborigines enjoyed hunting and foraging rights on vast areas of the Northern Territory, including pastoral leases, Interior saw no need for the grant of leases for only these traditional purposes. The CAA argued that the grant of a large consolidated lease to a community would lead to 'a state of economic independence more rapidly than would a number of separate individual leases, which inevitably mean that a substantial portion of a community not involved in the projects on the individual leases could remain dependent indefinitely on training allowances, social service payments, and other forms of government intervention'.[43]

Interior was opposed to granting leases to Aborigines even within existing reserves on the basis of 'long association'. There had already been claims made by Darwin Aborigines and the department feared 'the development of a feeling that Aborigines are being given preferred treatment in the Territory', and that there could be 'implications for the States in adopting a policy having a reference to long association'.[44] According to Howson, the CAA believed 'its solution acknowledges no rights and establishes no principles, but would give to incorporated Aboriginal communities (multi-clan groups) leases over land in which they are interested'.

On 6 December 1971, it was time to make the key decisions about land rights. Howson asked Coombs and Warwick Smith, the secretary of the Department of the Interior, to be in attendance. The ministerial committee decided that Aboriginal communities on reserves should be able to apply to the Northern Territory Land Board for multi-purpose leases and that legislative provision be made for hunting and foraging on reserves as was already provided on pastoral leases. The ministers asked that the IDC consider whether 'lease' was the appropriate term to use and whether there might be different durations and qualities of any interest granted in land. They did not think it necessary that all leases be for 99 years. They insisted on the need for supervision of land use and that any supervising authority 'might have power to withdraw the whole or part of a multi-purpose grant when there was a failure adequately to comply with the conditions'.⁴⁵

The CAA was devastated. Howson wrote in his diary:

> It was quite clear that no Minister present this afternoon was prepared to acknowledge traditional association as a criterion for granting land rights to Aboriginal communities. The whole discussion was much more satisfactory than I had expected. I had even got Ralph Hunt to be prepared to come closer to the view of the CAA than was actually necessary, and the final statement tonight is more towards Interior's views than the Council's, but generally I think it's the right answer, the best solution we can get at this stage of Australia's history.⁴⁶

The details were to be worked through by the IDC while everyone prepared the prime ministerial statement for the new year. Meanwhile, the Northern Territory Land Board was being urged by the Northern Territory Administration to hurry up the hearings for lease applications on reserves so that they might demonstrate how the existing regime was equal to the task.

After this flurry of bureaucratic and political activity, Stanner was back at his university chairing a regular anthropology seminar with his academic colleagues, who were to discuss a paper on matters completely unrelated to Aboriginal land issues in the Northern Territory. Stanner craved the indulgence of his colleagues to make a statement at the beginning of the seminar. His colleague Diane Barwick recalled that he was 'deeply disturbed' about the goings-on in government. He thought he had reached an historic watershed. He told his colleagues, 'My professional knowledge of Aboriginal affairs has developed over a period of more than forty years. It has proven to be entirely useless over the last four years.' He recalled how Harold Holt had appointed him four years previously, telling him that 'he thought my long experience would be very useful'. Stanner told the academy, 'I can but report that during the four following years I was not personally asked a single question concerning Aborigines by anyone connected with the Northern Territory Administration or with the Department of Interior.' He said:

> I think it is a simple inference from the dominant mental and social structure of Australians that the prescription for Aboriginal policy for some years forward will come in an old bottle, with a new, good looking, high sounding label, but containing essentially the mixture as before, possibly with some saccharine added. I made a good try for four years to get the prescription changed. I have no reason to believe that I have succeeded.[47]

In Canberra, people worked until 11 pm on Christmas Eve to finalise the fine print of the policy. Tensions were running high. The Commonwealth police had reported militant action being planned by the National Tribal Council. Howson was put under police guard. Howson writes that at a social event four nights before, 'I was attacked by Mrs Dexter, who tells me that I did not appreciate the fine qualities of her husband, and how he had been specifically asked by Harold Holt to undertake this task, and how difficult we'd all made it for him ever since. Not an easy wife to have to deal with.'[48] The CAA made one last attempt to include a more comprehensive allowance for land claims on the basis of traditional association. Howson insisted that the ministerial decision had been made and that there were to be no back-door changes. 'Dexter puts on the look of a pained spaniel who's just been kicked in the guts and says they never tried to be difficult,'[49] Howson noted. He then went to talk with Ralph Hunt to seek final agreement to all details of the policy. Hunt told him that 'the communists are going to use the Aboriginal issue as one of the main matters with which to attack the government in 1972, and we can expect more problems'.

In the lead-up to Christmas, the CAA had been getting a caning from all sides. Charles Perkins had followed up his August memo, calling for the CAA to be more militant, taking on the forces of darkness.[50] Stanner was very hurt. He thought Perkins was naively asking that the CAA be more confrontational in dealing with the states, the Country Party and the Department of the Interior. After the Christmas break, Stanner told Dexter, 'If it had been possible simply to go out and "beat" Interior and to "force" the Government or Public Service Board to do things we have recommended, this would have been done long ago. Mr Perkins is simply being romantic and rhetorical. Things don't happen that way. He apparently has not yet grasped what sort of machine Government is and how it works.'[51] Stanner gave vent to what has often been the frustration of competent whites wanting to enhance Aboriginal prospects:

> It is up to individual Aborigines and organisations to decide for themselves how militant they want to be, and what exactly they mean by militancy. If they ever ask my advice, which is unlikely, it will be that in my opinion they will be wasting their time and will lose support they really need. I think he is completely mistaken in his view that Aborigines are 'the only great force that will bring change in Australian society to suit their needs'. By themselves the Aborigines are not 'a great force' and doubtfully a force at all. By themselves they cannot exert a sufficient influence. They will be able to do so only by alliance with Europeans. Mr Perkins had better clear his mind on this matter. He might consider, for example, what the Aboriginal situation would be like if all European reformist elements (Council, Office, church organisations, academics and other well-wishers), plus the grants, subsidies, loans and so on which their influence has largely helped to obtain, were suddenly and permanently removed from the scene.

Stanner thought 'militancy' was a matter of horses for courses. He saw Perkins falling into the same class as many of his own 'half-baked academic associates', who thought it was just a matter of either explaining a policy to government and results would follow or else turning militant.

For Stanner, 'this is stuff for children, unless Mr Perkins is prepared to regard persistence, patience, manoeuvre, and constant renewal of effort as "militancy"'.⁵² He thought Perkins' theory of what was needed was 'largely wrong':

> The Government machine does not respond to emotional submissions or to vague programmes in uncontrolled words. It is embarrassed and held up by them until they are translated into forms the machine can handle. The only Aborigines who will be of any use on the Council or in 'high administrative positions' in the Office are those who, while retaining real links with and understanding of their own people, can learn to accept the natural limits of the Government machine and how to make the machine work in their interests ... I think it romantic nonsense to suggest that whether an official is an Aboriginal or a European will make much difference at that level of the machine.

Perkins had also alleged that the CAA was 'more concerned with its image amongst tribal than amongst part-Aboriginal groups'. Stanner told Dexter, 'I believe it has been right to give a lot of attention to e.g. the Yirrkala and Gurindji questions. These are strategic issues, and both more urgent and more consequential than others.'

Howson was on a beach holiday at Barwon Heads in Victoria for two weeks over Christmas and he wrote a reflection on his past year: 'My own feeling is that we have given too much attention to this problem of land rights over the last few months, and not enough to thinking of how to assimilate the fringe dwellers, particularly in the big cities, and how to find employment for the increasing number of Aborigines who wish to adopt a European mode of life.'⁵³ William McMahon decided that Australia Day, 26 January 1972, would be the appropriate day to announce his new land policy of 'general purpose leases' for Aborigines living on reserves in the Northern Territory. The CAA tried to dissuade him as they thought the policy proposals were niggardly and likely to occasion adverse reaction on the anniversary of Aboriginal dispossession. McMahon was convinced that his statement constituted a major turning point in government–Aboriginal relations in Australia. The CAA had some wins over the announcement but, as Barrie Dexter later wrote, 'We had, through persistence, won some important points; but overall the new policies were a disappointment for us.'[54] The day before the release of the government document, *The Australian* ran a front-page story by journalist Paul Kelly, saying that Coombs had threatened to resign as chair of the CAA and that the fear of adverse publicity had caused the government to make some improvements to the package. The prime ministerial statement described the government's 'New Decisions':

> The Government understands fully the desire of the Aboriginal people to have their affinity with the land with which they have been associated recognised by law.
>
> We are deeply concerned to assist them to feel it has, in fact, been recognised and to enable them, in the current circumstances, to have some security in their relationship with the land, and, in particular, to give continuing Aboriginal groups and communities the opportunity of obtaining an appropriate title under Australian law over lands on Reserves which they are interested in to use and develop for economic and social purposes.
>
> The Government believes that the changing needs of the Aboriginal people themselves will require that they make more use of land to which they obtain title for these purposes.
>
> Accordingly, the Government has decided to create a new form of lease for land on Aboriginal Reserves in its territories which may be applied for by Aborigines as individuals, groups or communities; such leases to provide for economic and social purposes including those which arise from Aboriginal educational, recreational, cultural and religious activities.

Wanting to distance the CAA from the outcome while at the same time expressing some hope for improvements, Coombs had prepared a one-page statement for the media, 'in reply to requests for comments on the Prime Minister's announcement on Aboriginal Affairs'. It stated:

> The Council had the opportunity to place before the Cabinet Committee a wide range of proposals concerning land for Aborigines and related matters. Some of these were rejected, others were adopted either wholly or in part. The Council is disappointed about some aspects of the outcome. However, the decision reached could, if Aborigines are able effectively to take advantage of them, provide the basis for an improvement in their economic and social condition and for the preservation and development of their culture.[55]

The Age's editorial was cautiously optimistic, acknowledging that the statement 'falls short of an absolute guarantee that public policies have caught up with public attitudes and conscience. It is, however, a great advance … Administered with good will and sincerity it could be good policy.'[56] *The Canberra Times*' editorial was less complimentary: 'In formulating its policy the Government has not taken full advantage of the powers it was given in the referendum of 1967.' The editors thought:

> the Prime Minister must be chided for his not wholly accurate description of the outcome of the referendum 'through which the Australian people recognised Aborigines as members of one Australian society'. The effect of the referendum was to authorise an amendment of the Constitution giving the Commonwealth power to make laws affecting Aborigines in the States.[57]

The Canberra Times took objection that the states were left undisturbed in their right to dispose of lands used by Aborigines.

The Australian's editorial nailed the key issue: 'No amount of fringe improvements on paper in the new programme changes the fact that the central issue was and remains the specific one of Yirrkala land, whether occupation rights would pass irrevocably from white men to black – either by outright transfer of ownership or perpetual lease – for the first time since Phillip's landing.' The editorial also noted, 'The whole weight of advice from the Government's appointed Council for Aboriginal Affairs was that the transfer could and should be made out of respect for that people's sense of identification with the land.' McMahon's proposals were not considered very remarkable 'when considered as the fruit and culmination of the massive expression of public opinion in the 1967 referendum'.[58]

Aboriginal activists around Redfern were very unimpressed with the prime minister's announcement. Four of them drove down to Canberra on Australia Day and planted an umbrella adorned with the sign 'Aboriginal Embassy' on the lawns in front of Parliament House. The police came by and were told that the Aborigines were protesting until the government granted land rights. The police remarked that this 'could be forever'. Michael Anderson, one of the Aboriginal leaders of the protest, told *The Canberra Times*, 'As soon as they start tearing up Arnhem Land we're going to start tearing up bits of Australia … the land was taken from us by force … we shouldn't have to lease it … our spiritual beliefs are connected with the land.'[59] These remarks resonated with what the CAA had been saying for months. Howson received criticism from both sides, with Joh Bjelke-Petersen claiming that he had not been adequately consulted. US Ambassador Walter Rice provided Howson with some solace, telling him about 'the land rights problems they've had with the Eskimos in Alaska, which has cost the American government $1000 million and indicated to me that our policy on land rights at the moment was extremely wise'.[60]

The CAA viewed the statement as a rejection of land rights, though it was at the same time the final nail in the coffin for forced assimilation.

There was continuing media speculation that the council members would resign. The Labor Opposition saw an opportunity to curry some electoral favour. Shadow Minister Gordon Bryant said the government announcement was 'a cynical exercise based on false values'. Taking the high moral ground, he declared, 'Land rights for Aborigines is not a question of economics but a spiritual, even a religious, matter. The Australian Aborigines are the least materialistic people and to them the land is fundamental.'[61] Bryant said that the only hope was to make land rights a major issue in the 1972 federal election. Labor premier Don Dunstan from South Australia also weighed in, adversely comparing the McMahon offer with the South Australian *Pitjantjatjara Land Rights Act*.

The federal proposal did not accord land rights: the government retained most reserves as government property and could repossess or dispose of them as it wished. The Australian people were to be provided with a choice as the parliament was now divided on land rights as it had never been before. The great national moral quandary was to be an election issue. McMahon and Howson had misread the public mindset. Whitlam and Coombs were on the money.

CHAPTER 5
AUSTRALIA DAY 1972
New prospects for land rights and better life choices

With the politicians returning to Canberra after the summer break, Stanner published an opinion piece in *The Canberra Times* entitled 'Aborigines and the Language Barrier'. He wrote, 'The recent statement of Commonwealth policy towards the Aborigines was not based on direct consultation with them, was directed as much towards a European as an Aboriginal public, and was couched in words that to a considerable extent must have passed over the heads even of English-speaking Aborigines.' He quoted this 94-word sentence in the statement, which was incomprehensible:

> We decided to create this new form of lease rather than attempt simply to translate the Aboriginal affinity with the land into some form of legal right under the Australian system, such as that claimed before the decision of the Supreme Court of the Northern Territory because we concluded that to do so would introduce a new and probably confusing component, the implications of which could not clearly be foreseen and which could lead to uncertainty and possible challenge in relation to land titles elsewhere in Australia which are at present unquestioned and secure.

He proffered an alternative, more comprehensible rendition of the sentence:

> The Yirrkala people asked the court to say they own land. The court said, 'No, that is not the law.' The people asked the Government to change the law. The Government thought about that idea for a long time. Now it understands. This is what it says: 'No, we will not change the law. If we did the law might not be clear. We might not know what would happen tomorrow or next year. Some white people might be frightened for their land. Some Aborigines might try to take some white people's land from them. The Government does not want trouble like that. So we will go another way. We will give some Aborigines some land by a new kind of lease. ….'

He then highlighted the hypocrisy of it all:

> The Yirrkala people can now get a lease of part of Arnhem Land to serve all their passions of life (provided we first approve) for up to 50 years. Nabalco, in the same area, already has a lease for a particular purpose for up to 84 years. Why the difference? The Yirrkala people simply cannot understand this kind of thing. They have also heard talk of further expansion by Nabalco. No wonder then if they say 'the thoughts are deep'.[1]

The protesters at the tent embassy, where tents now replaced the founding umbrella, received a great boost that day. Gough Whitlam, the leader of the opposition, came across from Parliament House and visited them. Aboriginal lawyer Paul Coe was able to subject him to close questioning. Stanner's piece was later reprinted elsewhere, including in *Smoke Signals*, the publication of the Aborigines Advancement League in Melbourne. Howson was undaunted. He was feeling emboldened by the publication of the land rights policy. He met with Dexter the day after Stanner published his critique, discussing the need to focus more on issues like employment rather than land: 'I feel the council spends far too much time in dealing with a mass of minor problems all over Australia rather shallowly, without getting down in depth to the really critical matters.'[2] The council declined to assist with his forthcoming ministerial statement to Parliament on land rights. Don Chipp, the leader of the Democrats in the Senate, had written to William McMahon suggesting that the government 'should completely change' their policy on land rights. Howson said there was no chance of change 'after getting a unanimous Cabinet decision on the subject after 6 months' hard work'.[3]

On the day before Parliament resumed, Aboriginal protesters demonstrated at the tent embassy. Whitlam came and spoke at the protest rally, pledging the Labor Party to land rights legislation if elected later in the year. His presence was welcomed, but the caution of his words caused some of the protesters to be a little equivocal. Scott Robinson and Gary Foley later noted that Whitlam was 'being careful to commit his party to land rights where "there is a historical connection between a tribe or clan and land" and made no mention of compensation for lands alienated'.[4] Peter Howson made his ministerial statement to the House of Representatives the next day. The parliamentary debate set the contours for the policy differences that were to play out in the federal election campaign later that year. The government was hopeful that McMahon's Australia Day statement would provide a basis for a uniform approach to land rights by the Commonwealth and the states. But this was not to be. Howson commenced his remarks with an assimilationist tone, informing the House of the government's intentions for the advancement of Aborigines:

> Fundamentally, the Government's aim is to have one Australian society in which all Australians – including Aboriginal Australians – will have equal rights, responsibilities and opportunities. We seek in this that Aborigines will achieve effective and respected places in a single Australian society. But at the same time they will be encouraged to preserve and develop their own

culture, languages, traditions and arts, which will become living elements in the diverse culture of our society.[5]

Howson's vision was similar to that espoused by the Country Party minister Peter Nixon when he had been trying to talk some sense into his Liberal colleague Bill Wentworth. Later, in his autobiography, Nixon recalled organising a dinner party that included Coombs and Bob Swift from Interior. During the dinner Coombs asked how one could expect Aborigines to fit in to one Australian society. Nixon reports, 'I said they should be like the Scots, wear their kilts as much as they like and be proud of it, but also be members of the broader community. This was obviously not to Coombs' liking. He complained about Aborigines driving bulldozers and trucks at some mines.'[6] To Nixon, Coombs' vision was separatism, 'apartheid in reverse'. Thus, the tension in Howson's parliamentary declaration. He went on to say:

> The Government recognises that individual Aborigines have a right to decide for themselves at what pace and to what extent they come to identify themselves with that society. We believe that they will do this more readily and more happily when they are drawn to it voluntarily and when their membership of it encourages them to maintain and take pride in their identity, their traditions and their culture.[7]

Having opened the door on self-determination, which might result in Aborigines putting on the long finger any assimilation with mainstream Australian society, Howson was anxious to reaffirm the evil of separate development: 'The thought of separate development of Aborigines as a long-term aim is completely alien to the Government's objectives.'[8] He outlined five new initiatives. The law would guarantee the right of Aborigines to hunt and forage on Aboriginal reserves in the Northern Territory, just as the law already provided such rights on pastoral leases. The government would delineate and protect lands on and off reserves for Aboriginal religious and ceremonial purposes. The government would consult with local Aboriginal communities before granting exploration and mining development rights, guaranteeing that such rights would not be granted if 'in the Government's view, they would be detrimental to the interests and wellbeing of an Aboriginal community in the area'.[9] Existing Aboriginal reserves would not be dedicated to other purposes 'without an effective opportunity for a review of such proposals' by both the Northern Territory Legislative Council and the Australian Parliament. The government would introduce legislation providing for renewable 50-year 'general-purpose leases' on Aboriginal reserve lands in the Northern Territory.

Howson described the general-purpose leases as 'an imaginative attempt to adapt Australian legal forms to fit in with Aboriginal ideas in relation to land'. He said that freehold was 'alien to Aboriginal thought and custom'. Conceding that a lease was too, he thought it capable of greater adaptation in line with 'Aboriginal ideas and aspirations'. Seeing the ongoing case for change, he told Parliament:

> It is likely that within the next 50 years further changes are going to take place, and the generation that is now young or as yet unborn may have very different ideas of land use from their parents now living. The idea of a lease provides flexibility in regard to future generations, which we believe to be wise. On the other hand, the granting of a freehold title to a community provides a degree of inflexibility which may not be in the best interests of future generations.[10]

Howson then overplayed his hand by referring to a meeting that the Yirrkala leaders, including Roy Marika, had held with the prime minister a few days before. Howson told Parliament that the Aboriginal leaders 'intimated that they were contemplating applying for a general-purpose lease in the Gove area. This shows that already there are Aboriginal communities that are prepared to endorse the new policy and participate in it.'[11] Marika was promptly on the national airwaves proclaiming, 'We will not be satisfied until we get our land rights.'

The CAA's disaffection with the government position was clear to the opposition. Gough Whitlam lamented, 'I believe that the House is handicapped by not having the advice of the Commonwealth Council for Aboriginal Affairs and the Office of Aboriginal Affairs on this matter. It is asserted that both these bodies recommended that full title to land should be given to Aborigines on the basis of traditional occupancy.'[12] Whitlam identified the series of Country Party ministers responsible for Interior and the Country Party government in Queensland as the chief obstacles to necessary reform. He labelled the government's measures as 'patronising'. He advocated that the parliament legislate for communal title similar to arrangements in Canada and the United States. He espoused the virtue of the International Labour Organization's *Indigenous and Tribal Populations Convention, 1957 (No. 107)*, which called for the recognition of 'the right of ownership, collective or individual, of the members of the populations concerned over the land which these populations traditionally occupy'.

In preparation for the 1972 election, Labor had formulated its new policy on Aboriginal land rights, which met with the full approval of the CAA:

> All Aboriginal lands to be vested in a public trust or trusts composed of Aborigines or Islanders as appropriate. That exclusive corporate land rights be granted to Aboriginal communities which retain a strong tribal structure or demonstrate a potential for corporate action in regard to land at present reserved for the use of Aborigines, or where traditional occupancy according to tribal custom can be established from anthropological or other evidence. No Aboriginal lands shall be alienated except with the approval both of the trust and of Parliament. Aboriginal land rights shall carry with them full rights to minerals in those lands. The sacred sites of the Aborigines will be mapped and protected.

Whitlam was able to claim strong endorsement from the Australian Council of Churches. He saw a need for Aboriginal title being created by legislation, to be drafted after a royal commission had been established to report on national possibilities, including determining which 'tribes are to be recognised as still in existence as such and as having some foreseeable future existence', and 'what land is linked with each tribe and what system or systems of law must be adopted or invented to regulate the holding of land by Aborigines'.[13] He committed Labor to ensuring that 'Australia pays as much attention and gives as much assistance to the Aboriginal population as comparable countries do and as international standards require'.[14]

Ralph Hunt, the minister for the interior, put the Country Party line, warning against great change in policy and repeating his prediction that the Aborigines would be used as a political football in the year ahead. Conceding that Aborigines had suffered continued injustices and disability, he said it would be 'tragic if for the first time they are to be used for political motives and purposes by Communist elements and left-wing union leaders'. Hunt was convinced that well-meaning Australians were tied up in the campaign for land rights, just as they had been involved in the Vietnam moratorium movement: 'It was forecast in all the various Communist media that land rights would become the big issue in 1972 in view of the fact that Australia was withdrawing its troops from Vietnam.'[15] While espousing equal rights and the aim of achieving for Aborigines 'an efficient and respected place in the single Australian society, preserving their own cultures, languages, traditions and arts if they so desire', he abhorred separate development or apartheid, 'whether it is voluntary or enforced'. The government had already received 135 applications for the general-purpose leases on Aboriginal reserves, ranging from 33 acres (13 hectares) for tourist purposes to 800 acres (325 hectares) for ceremonial and religious purposes and up to 2100 square miles (5500 square kilometres) for pastoral purposes. These leases were 'tailor made for Aboriginal economic and social needs on reserves'.[16]

The Country Party was concerned about the precedential value of granting any land rights. Hunt told Parliament, 'The claim for $6 billion compensation for dispossession of land in the past which has been made by some groups flows quite naturally from the argument that Aborigines anywhere in Australia have a moral, if not a legal, right to land based on ancestral association with that land.'[17] Hunt asked, 'If traditional rights are to be accepted for the Yirrkala at Gove by what logic can they be denied to the Larrakeah people in Darwin?' He also put the long-held position of Interior that the existing or remaining Aboriginal reserve lands were not intended for the exclusive use only of those Aborigines living on the land or whose traditional country it was. For instance, 'the Arnhem Land reserve of over 34,000 square miles [88,000 square kilometres] was never intended to meet the requirements of only the people resident in Arnhem Land'. The government remained convinced that the existing reserve lands were sufficient to meet the land needs of 'a great percentage' of Aborigines 'provided title to large areas is not held by relatively few communities which cannot possibly use that land'. Special land rights laws would tend to divide the Australian community and would cause a white backlash.

The government wanted to know where the grant of Aboriginal freehold would end once it started. What would Labor do if Aborigines claimed land in North Sydney, South Yarra, Torrens Park or South Brisbane? Manfred Cross, the Queensland Labor member who had worked long and hard on Aboriginal issues, told Parliament that a system of Aboriginal land trusts would not result in land being available for sale to overseas investors but that 'presumably they could sell out to other Aborigines, but it would be a corporate trust'.[18] Labor wanted to avoid the situation in the United States, 'where generations of chiefs lived it up and their descendants have remained paupers to this day'.[19]

Another aspirant for the ministry in a future Labor government, Les Johnson, ruled out any possibility of Aborigines claiming areas like Martin Place in downtown Sydney. But he considered it quite sensible to say to Aborigines on reserves in the Northern Territory, 'You can have corporate rights if you have the capacity to run your Aboriginal reserve, to own it and to utilise it.'[20] He went further than Whitlam in publicising the CAA's reaction to McMahon's Australia Day statement: 'The speech sent shockwaves even through the Council for Aboriginal Affairs and brought the Chairman, Dr Coombs, who takes a very capable and inspired interest in these matters, within an ace of resignation.'[21]

A week after the parliamentary debate, Stanner wrote a personal letter to Sister Marita, a nun in Darwin whom he knew well from her work with Aborigines at the East Arm Settlement. He was clearly not satisfied with the lack of progress in policy:

> You have not seen much of me in recent years because I have been giving all my time to the job which I share with Dr Coombs and Mr Dexter on the Council for Aboriginal Affairs. We have to travel all over Australia and are terribly burdened with the tasks in Canberra itself. Another reason why I have not returned to Port Keats or thought it prudent to see too much of my friends in the Territory is that I have been unwilling to let them think that I have been in any way in support of the existing policy towards Aborigines. The members of my Council have been fighting a very sustained and vigorous battle to bring about many improvements and I wanted to wait until we were very sure there were to be improvements, as we understand them, before appearing amongst them. I am not too sure even now that the time is right for my return.[22]

On 15 April 1972, Coombs was heading overseas for two months. He wrote a letter marked 'Personal' to Prime Minister McMahon, expressing strong concern about the lack of implementation of the land policy, regardless of its deficiencies. He wrote:

> I continue to feel grave concern, however, about the General Purpose Leases which were a major element in the Government's decisions. No such

> leases have been granted and we have no information about the progress of the necessary legislation being presented to the Legislative Council of the Northern Territory. We doubt whether the decision about General Purpose Leases is being adequately presented or explained to communities and in the meantime we believe the Administration is pressing on with the granting of smaller Special Purpose Leases the effect of which may be to deny to Aborigines the choice of the benefits which the General Purpose Leases were intended to offer them. It would be a pity if the really distinctive components in the Government's decisions of December were without effect before the end of the year.

By the end of the year, the government would be gone. Community agitation about land rights continued to increase. In July 1972, violence erupted when the ACT police removed the tent embassy with government authorisation. The CAA had constantly opposed the removal of the tent embassy because any police action 'would create martyrs and was unnecessary'. Ralph Hunt had proposed to the Federal Council for the Advancement of Aborigines and Torres Strait Islanders (FCAATSI) that the government make available some land in Canberra for a national Aboriginal centre. The CAA had advised Minister Howson that 'the "Embassy" stands for Aboriginal land rights and that therefore no compromise seeking to buy the Aborigines off with some other proposal is proper or would be acceptable to the bulk of the Aborigines'.[23] Coombs was in Perth the day the police moved in to close the embassy. He told the ABC, 'I have no comment to make on the closing of the "Embassy". This is a Government decision and it is a matter for them.' Having noted his regret that violence had occurred, he then went on to say, 'The only comment I would make is that the closing of the "Embassy" has cut off one channel of protest open to Aborigines and others interested in their cause. But Aborigines and others have a right to protest about these matters and there remain other avenues for protest which I hope they will continue to use.' Back in Canberra, Dexter's office distributed these remarks to the major newspapers.

Coombs then went overseas again, this time to London on Reserve Bank business. He took the opportunity to meet with Lord Vestey, who said he was willing to relinquish 1500 square miles (3900 square kilometres) of his Wave Hill lease for the Aborigines camped at Wattie Creek. Back home, the Cabinet committee 'accepted the suggestion for the acquisition of an area of 1500 square miles from Vestey's Wave Hill lease as a pastoral project for the Gurindji was not practicable and should not proceed'.[24]

Stanner delivered his presidential address to the Anthropology section of the Australian and New Zealand Association for the Advancement of Science. He spoke of 'Fictions, Nettles and Freedoms', lamenting that the five years of the CAA since the 1967 referendum was hard labour, yet to bear the fruit to be expected from the 'strong moral imperative' of the 1967 referendum. He could not claim that it had become any easier to make 'scholarly and scientific information closely relevant to social policy': 'All I will say is that we were prepared to question every part of the received or conventional wisdom about what Aborigines want and do not want, or can and cannot do.'[25] He dropped his earlier haughty tone in relation to McMahon's Australia Day statement. He saw it as an attempt to articulate 'a doctrine of four Aboriginal freedoms':

> First, they may decide for themselves to what *degree* they will identify with what the Prime Minister called 'one Australian society'. Second, they may decide for themselves at what *rate* they will so identify. Thirdly, they have the right to *preserve* their own culture and, fourth, the right to *develop* their own culture.

He made the case for land rights and self-determination in terms of choice and options being offered Aboriginal communities:

> Up to and through the Hasluck era of policy, when we were not pushing the Aborigines out of European society, we were requiring them to un-be what they had been as the price of possible entry to it. Now, at least on the formal plane of policy statements, we have replaced requirements by options.[26]

He offered an insightful glimpse of the desired outcomes from the new policies being contemplated, 'that something had to change decisively, and that we too had to change':

> That we should not deliberately put (Aborigines) in situations which foreclose their power to choose, as at Yirrkala. That people learn about choice by choosing; about management by managing; about being responsible by having responsibility. That if some Aboriginal people turn their backs on our kind of life the inference should be 'it does not attract them, so let us find out why', not 'how stupid and backward they are, let them stew.' That there is already much evidence to suggest that what makes many of them turn away is the absence, or scarcity, or mock-availability of elementary good things – real property which is veritably theirs, simple freedoms, civil liberties, health, fair wages, unimpeded education, the chance to get working capital, decent homes, real standing in the courts, basic knowledge of how to handle bureaucracy – which are part of our breadth of life. That the truth may be that many of them turn away, not so much from our way of life, as from the terms of life within it we have so far offered them. That there has to be a significant degree of change in all those terms, and a quick end to what I have summarised as absence, scarcity and mock-availability.[27]

In September 1972, the government gave permission for the CAA to meet with the ALP Parliamentary Committee on Aboriginal Affairs. The opposition's committee gave notice that it wished to discuss a range of issues, including land rights, the attitude to national Aboriginal organisations (including FCAATSI), the Torres Strait boundary, Aboriginal co-operatives, health and education. The CAA 'confirmed its policy of having functional departments assume responsibility with, if necessary, an Aboriginal affairs section created within the functional department'.[28] Since the 1969 party conference, the ALP was committed to establishing a federal department of Aboriginal affairs.

With an approaching federal election, Sir Joh Bjelke-Petersen wrote to Howson, complaining that the Commonwealth authorities were giving material and other support to militant Aboriginal groups in his state. Howson sought clarification from the CAA. While offering to co-operate with the Queensland Department of Aboriginal and Islander Affairs in consulting with Brisbane Aboriginal groups so that their problems might be eased and their energies better directed, Coombs took the opportunity to drive home a few political points. Responding to Howson's query about how the prime minister should respond to the premier, Coombs wrote:

> We believe that 'militancy' in Aborigines can best be dealt with by: (a) showing obvious willingness to hear and consider grievances, (b) a policy obviously directed to greater social justice for Aborigines, (c) the promotion of communication between Aboriginal groups of all kinds and between them, the rest of the community, and the Government, and (d) providing outlets for 'militant' zeal by involving Aborigines in the conduct of their own affairs and in organisations promoting the welfare of their own people.[29]

On 10 October 1972, Prime Minister McMahon announced that the election would be held on 2 December 1972. During the election campaign, Stanner delivered an address to the Royal Australasian College of Surgeons entitled 'After the Dreaming – Whither?' He concluded the address with a scathing attack on McMahon's timorous Australia Day statement about Aboriginal land issues in the Northern Territory. He returned to the incomprehensible 94-word sentence:

> It was recently said (by Prime Minister McMahon) that we could not give the Aborigines there what they are asking for because of some 'new and probably confusing component, the implications of which could not clearly be foreseen and which could lead to uncertainty and possible challenge in relation to land titles elsewhere in Australia which are at present unquestioned and secure'. Count up the fears in that statement: fear of the unknown, fear of confusion, fear of the unforeseeable, fear of implications, fear of uncertainty, fear of challenge, fear of insecurity, fear of loss. It is a tale told to frighten children.[30]

Stanner clearly had no fear of the re-election of a McMahon government. Change was in the air. The ALP's fresh approach to Aboriginal affairs featured strongly at Whitlam's 1972 campaign launch two weeks later. Whitlam proclaimed, 'Let us never forget this: Australia's real test as far as the rest of the world, and particularly our region, is concerned is the role we create for our own Aborigines.' Having committed to the withdrawal of all Australian forces from Vietnam, he boldly asserted that Australia's role in that war would be long forgotten, but that the world would not let Australians forget their one unique responsibility: 'The Aborigines are a responsibility we cannot escape, cannot share, cannot shuffle off; the world will not let us forget that.' He declared:

> We will legislate to give Aborigines land rights – not just because their case is beyond argument, but because all of us as Australians are diminished while the Aborigines are denied their rightful place in this nation ...
>
> All of us as Australians have to insist that we can do so much better as a nation. We ought to be angry, with a deep determined anger, that a country as rich and skilled as ours should be producing so much inequality, so much poverty, so much that is shoddy and sub-standard. We ought to be angry – with an unrelenting anger – that our Aborigines have the world's highest infant mortality rate. We ought to be angry at

the way our so-called leaders have kept us in the dark – Parliament itself as much as the people – to hide their own incapacity and ignorance.

The CAA was directly involved in formulating the ALP's policy for the election. The CAA members remained of the view that the creation of a separate department would reduce the quality of services that functional departments like Health and Education had the expertise to deliver, provided only that government insisted on their giving priority to Aboriginal needs. Except for the ALP's insistence on a separate department, the CAA and the ALP were on the same page. The CAA, rather than Labor speechwriter Graham Freudenberg, could claim credit for this part of the policy speech. Whitlam told the men and women of Australia:

> There is one group of Australians who have been denied their basic rights to the pursuit of happiness, to liberty and indeed to life itself for 180 years – since the very time when Europeans in the New World first proclaimed those rights as inalienable for all mankind. In 1967 we, the people of Australia, by an overwhelming majority imposed upon the Commonwealth the constitutional responsibility for aborigines and Torres Strait Islanders. The Commonwealth Parliament has still not passed a single law which it could not have passed before and without that referendum. Mr McMahon has side-stepped Mr Gorton's solemn undertaking of 1969 to abolish discriminatory legislation against aborigines and Torres Strait Islanders. A Labor Government will over-ride Queensland's discriminatory laws. To ensure that aborigines are made equal before the law, the Commonwealth will pay all legal costs for aborigines in all proceedings in all courts. We will establish once and for all aborigines' rights to land and insist that, whatever the law of George III says, a tribe and a race with an identity of centuries – of millennia – is as much entitled to own land as even a proprietary company. There will be a separate Ministry for Aboriginal Affairs; it will have offices in each State to give the Commonwealth a genuine presence in the States.

Specifically, we will:
- Legislate to establish for land in Commonwealth territories which is reserved for aboriginal use and benefit a system of aboriginal tenure based on the traditional rights of clans and other tribal groups and, under this legislation, vest such land in aboriginal communities;
- Invite the Governments of Western Australia and South Australia to join with the Commonwealth in establishing a Central Australian Aboriginal Reserve (including Ayers Rock and Mount Olga) under the control of aboriginal trustees;
- Establish an Aboriginal Land Fund to purchase or acquire land for significant continuing aboriginal communities and to appropriate $5 million per year to this fund for the next ten years;
- Legislate to prohibit discrimination on grounds of race, ratify all the relevant United Nations and ILO Conventions for this purpose, and set up conciliation procedures to promote understanding and co-operation between aboriginal and other Australians;
- Legislate to enable aboriginal communities to be incorporated for their own social and economic purposes.[31]

For the Liberal–Country Party Coalition Government, Prime Minister McMahon made almost no mention of Aboriginal issues in his campaign speech. He said:

We have announced programmes for urban and regional development, the protection of the environment, the promotion of the arts, and the welfare and advancement of our Aboriginal fellow citizens.

This has been done in the last 20 months – and it is only the beginning. We promise you that the return of this Government will guarantee further constructive and, above all, responsible changes – not for the few, but for the benefit of all.[32]

By the time Labor came to office, 'not a single "general purpose" lease had been approved'.[33] The Coalition had failed to deliver any of their promised land reform. McMahon's 1972 Australia Day address had effected no real change in land policy. But it had mobilised the Labor Party inside the parliament and the tent embassy protesters on the lawns outside. It had contributed to a change of government. During the brief two-week 'Whitnard Government', when Whitlam and his deputy Lance Barnard held all portfolios, the CAA kick-started major reforms. Dexter had been living in the United States during JF Kennedy's first 100 days as president and knew that resolute action was possible with a new government rightly focused. Dexter thought the ministry of two had turned policy around 180 degrees in just ten days. They recommended the appointment of Edward Woodward, who had been the barrister for the Aborigines in the *Milirrpum* case, to conduct the promised royal commission on Aboriginal land rights. They settled the commission's terms of reference, having to accommodate the ALP's abandonment of an Aboriginal veto on mining activity on Aboriginal land.

The old Department of the Interior with its assimilationist culture was abolished. Dexter was appointed secretary of the new Department of Aboriginal Affairs (DAA), which had to absorb many of the old Interior personnel. He fostered good working relations with most Commonwealth and state departments. The old managers on remote Aboriginal communities in the Northern Territory were recast as community advisers. Universal alcohol restrictions were lifted. Aboriginal residents were told they were free to return to country; there was no need for them to remain within the town areas of communities. This was the beginning of the outstation movement. The CAA recommended the establishment of a Bureau of Advice and Aid for Aborigines.[34] Cabinet was told that 'the local autonomy or self-determination of Aboriginal communities, as sought by the Government, cannot properly be fostered where all advice, community services, and development must be dependent on a department or departments'.[35]

In his three years as prime minister, Whitlam had three ministers for Aboriginal affairs: Gordon Bryant, Jim Cavanagh and Les Johnson. Only Cavanagh had a good working relationship with his senior bureaucrats. The CAA had expected Manfred Cross to be the initial minister, but Bryant scored the position, in part because of his long-standing involvement with FCAATSI, which included many left-wing union members and politically active urban Aborigines. Bryant never saw a need to develop close working relations with Aboriginal leaders in remote communities or with the newly emerging Aboriginal leaders in the cities. Bryant did not trust the public service. He even appointed Gareth Evans briefly to second-guess the riding instructions for the Woodward Commission.

The new department abandoned all talk of assimilation, using the new terminology of self-determination and self-management interchangeably. Bryant invested much energy in establishing the National Aboriginal Consultative Council (NACC). He invited 80 Indigenous persons to Canberra to constitute the first council. They had no democratic mandate, nor necessarily any traditional authority in their home communities. The council's 1973 election had to be funded by and conducted by the DAA because the Australian Electoral Commission refused to be involved. The NACC met seven times during the life of the Whitlam Government. It did not work well with the bureaucracy or with the CAA.

Dexter and his family were often under police guard, having received threats from some of the more militant Aboriginal activists. Dexter was always trying to make better provision for Aborigines in the senior ranks of the new department. The most senior Aboriginal public servant was Charles Perkins, who considered himself having licence beyond that of other public servants to make public political statements, often critical of the Commonwealth or state governments. Having been charged with public service breaches in 1974, he was granted a year's leave without pay to write his autobiography, *A Bastard like Me*. Senator Cavanagh had written to Whitlam expressing total opposition 'to rewarding this individual for his continual outbursts against the Department'. Cavanagh would oppose any request for a university fellowship funded by the department. Noting that Perkins might receive a grant from the Council for the Arts, Cavanagh expressed his opposition and added that 'Mr Perkins has displayed no literary capabilities and I think the only writing he could do would be a condemnation of the department for which he is now employed'.[36] In his autobiography Perkins recalls being asked by the CAA members, early during Labor's time in government, whether they should resign. He answered, 'Absolutely ... definitely go. You have no further role to play. The Council has outlived its usefulness.'[37] His relations with Dexter were always tense. He was ultimately suspended for publicly 'criticising the racist Country Party', after making a series of stands 'naturally that led to all sorts of repercussions'. He wrote, 'I just could not, in all clear conscience, condone the behaviour of the Department of Aboriginal Affairs, nor the activities of its senior ministers.'[38]

The new government was anxious to transfer all Aboriginal affairs functions from the states to the Commonwealth. South Australia was willing from the outset, and the other states (except Queensland) gradually came aboard. Sir Joh Bjelke-Petersen held out. The negotiations for the Torres Strait border allowed Bjelke-Petersen to portray himself as the defender of Torres Strait Islanders in the wake of Canberra's initial willingness to agree to a border that would have placed some Torres Strait islands on the PNG side of the border. Ultimately, Torres Strait Islanders were assured they could maintain the benefits of Australian citizenship. Whitlam adopted Coombs' suggestion of a maritime protected zone, which would allow the joint sharing of resources without the need for a dividing border. It was difficult for the Canberra bureaucracy to break the Queensland Government's stranglehold on access and communications to the Torres Strait.

Ultimately, Whitlam abandoned all hope of having the Queensland Government transfer functions to the DAA, with the DAA setting up a handful of small branch offices around Queensland. Pat Killoran, the long-time head of the Queensland department, was very critical of Commonwealth invitations to Aborigines to establish outstations with no ready access to health and education services. He was also mistrustful of Commonwealth consultation mechanisms, which favoured urban Aborigines over those living on reserve communities. The Queensland Government wanted to maintain its privileged relationships with the elected leaders of reserve communities. For its part, the Commonwealth was suspicious that the Queensland officials went to great lengths to isolate these reserve leaders from outside political influences. Whitlam also maintained that Queensland needed to amend its discriminatory laws relating to Aboriginal reserves so that the Commonwealth could ratify the *Convention on the Elimination of Racial Discrimination* and *ILO Convention 107*. Ultimately, the Commonwealth Parliament enacted the *Aboriginal and Torres Strait Islanders (Queensland Discriminatory Laws) Act 1975*.

In July 1974, the Whitlam Cabinet accepted the recommendations of the Woodward Commission on land rights and issued drafting instructions for legislation affecting Aboriginal land claims in the Northern Territory. Traditional owners of land would be able to make a claim over any vacant crown land. If successful, the government would issue an inalienable freehold title over the land to a land trust that would be administered by a land council, which could not deal with the land without first obtaining the consent of the traditional owners. The government's hope was that the states would then follow suit legislating similar laws in their jurisdictions. The Woodward recommendations had been discussed at the Premiers Conference in June 1974. But when Senator Cavanagh sought to discuss the matter with his Queensland counterpart, Cavanagh was told 'that he had raised the matter with the Queensland Cabinet and that the Premier and he believed the whole question of Aboriginal land rights need no longer be discussed'.[39] On 20 October 1974, Whitlam wrote to Bjelke-Petersen seeking co-operation, having received no response to three earlier letters. Bjelke-Petersen continued to ignore Whitlam, calling his bluff. The Commonwealth *Aboriginal Land Fund Act 1974* was passed, setting up a fund for the purchase of land on the open market in the states and territories, which could then be held on behalf of local Aboriginal groups.

On 16 August 1975, Whitlam flew to Wattie Creek with his minister and members of the CAA to hand over lease documents for the land to Vincent Lingiari. Coombs, on advice from Stanner, suggested that Whitlam pour soil into Lingiari's hands. This he did with the declaration:

> Vincent Lingiari, I solemnly hand to you these deeds as proof, in Australian law, that these lands belong to the Gurindji people and I put into your hands this piece of the earth itself as a sign that we restore them to you and your children forever.[40]

Lingiari replied, 'They took our country away from us, now they have brought it back ceremonially. We are all mates now.'

The leaders of two peoples had met and the voice of each was heard. This was a novel development in the *terra nullius* of Australia. Each leader spoke with authority for the land. By the time of the 1975 dismissal of the Whitlam Government by the governor-general Sir John Kerr, the *Aboriginal Land Rights (Northern Territory) Bill* and the *Aboriginal Councils and Associations Bill* had passed the House of Representatives. With some amendment, the land rights legislation would ultimately be passed at the behest of the Fraser Government. The *Councils and Associations* legislation allowed for the ready incorporation of Aboriginal communities and entities, thereby permitting the federal department to fund and deal with them directly. The *Racial Discrimination Act 1975 (RDA)* was passed faithfully, implementing the key provisions of the *Convention on the Elimination of Racial Discrimination*. The *RDA* proved critical in later years in striking down Queensland's discriminatory policy against land transfers[41] and in buttressing fragile native title, thereby giving Aborigines a place at the Cabinet table negotiating the *Native Title Act 1993* after the High Court's *Mabo* decision.[42] Legislation was also passed for the establishment of the Aboriginal Enterprises Fund and the Aboriginal Housing and Personal Loans Fund.

Reflecting on these achievements, Whitlam observed, 'Advances, rather than solutions, hold the key to any realistic program of reform in Aboriginal affairs.'[43] Four decades on, the country is still coming to terms with the limits on land rights and self-determination, and wondering how best to close the gaps on Aboriginal disadvantage. When addressing the NACC in February 1973, Whitlam spoke of the ambition and achievement for which he hoped historians would salute his government: that it 'removed a stain from our national honour and brought back justice and equality to the Aboriginal people'.[44] His government changed the course from assimilation and the *terra nullius* mindset, setting the direction we are still following, sometimes with less optimism as we debate the demands of justice and equality for the first Australians. Bjelke-Petersen's obstinacy probably kept in check some of federal Labor's more romantic notions about land rights and self-determination, especially when it came to service delivery to remote outstations at taxpayer expense.

In just over three years, with a cumbersome bureaucracy and an emerging Aboriginal leadership not used to negotiating with government, Whitlam delivered on what he promised for Aboriginal Australia when he declared at Blacktown, 'It's time'. No member of Harold Holt's Cabinet, which had signed off on the 1967 referendum proposal, could have imagined this outcome just eight years later. After all, the referendum was not really meant to change anything. Without the referendum result, Stanner, Dexter and Coombs would never have been invited to the table of deliberation, shifting the country from *terra nullius* to land rights, and from assimilation to self-determination.

Looking back on the period since the referendum, Dr Coombs in the 1976 Murdoch Lecture acknowledged that the reasons behind the overwhelming vote of support in 1967 had never been systematically studied, 'but it is now widely believed that it reflected a shamed acknowledgment of past injustice and a recognition that humanity and justice demanded a New Deal as a matter of right for Aboriginal Australians.'[45] Reflecting on the intervening nine years, he said:

> I do not think it is to say too much if I remark that these years of work among Aboriginal Australians and in seeking to influence policies and attitudes towards them have led me to question whether we, the dominant white society, may not lack the spiritual qualities to resolve this problem quickly. Until the arrogance, the prejudice, the fear which still largely determine our attitude towards Aborigines gives way to humility, generosity and human warmth there can be little grounds for hope of a quick resolution. If there is a taste of ashes on the lips of white Australian civilisation, it is because while we have mastered a continent and subordinated a proud people, we have remained in spirit aliens and strangers to it and them.[46]

Stanner, Dexter and Coombs ultimately had the satisfaction of seeing the *Aboriginal Land Rights (Northern Territory) Act* passed into law by Malcolm Fraser's Coalition Government after the 1975 election. The minister for Aboriginal affairs was Ian Viner, who joined the illustrious company of Jim Cavanagh, they being the only two ministers for whom the CAA had a high regard. The Coalition did not agree to all the provisions in the bill prepared by the Whitlam Government before its dismissal by Sir John Kerr. But by 1976, both sides of the Australian Parliament were agreeable to the propositions about land rights that had been agitated by the CAA since the *Milirrpum* case in 1971. Leases were unacceptable. It was essential that title be 'communal and inalienable', as Justice Woodward had recommended in his royal commission report.

The council dissolved at Christmas time 1976. They had performed the herculean task of helping to move the federal bureaucracy and the major political parties along the path to land rights and a modicum of self-determination. This would not have occurred but for the overwhelming vote in the 1967 referendum. The referendum's expansion of Commonwealth power, permitting intervention in the states, had been exercised more sparingly than they would have hoped. Bjelke-Petersen was able to continue on his own path as an outrider on land rights. On his last day as departmental head of DAA, Dexter wrote to Viner offering some reflections on the nine years' work of the CAA. He looked back to the immediate post-referendum time, observing:

> When the Council and Office of Aboriginal Affairs were set up in November 1967 following the Referendum of May of that year, the Aboriginal people throughout Australia were generally in a depressed situation and in despair. In its early assessments the Council for Aboriginal Affairs was impressed by the general lack of ability of the Aboriginal people to make their voice heard; by the extent to which their affairs were directed by others; by the inadequacies of the Federal and State agencies for Aboriginal affairs; by the lack of adequate financial provision; by the disadvantage suffered by Aboriginals in housing, health, education, employment, civil liberties and by the general lack of involvement of departments responsible for those aspects for the community as a whole; and by the denial, except in South Australia, of the land rights which they regarded as of such paramount importance to the preservation of their heritage and way of life.[47]

He was satisfied that Aborigines now thought change was possible and were now vocal and able to make representations on their own behalf. The era of the three white wise men had passed. He thought self-management was now an accepted principle though in need of greater development. And the principle of land rights had been 'accepted federally and to a varying degree in all States except Queensland'. He identified two of the key social objectives in land rights measures: 'many tradition-oriented Aboriginals have prospect of living in security and retaining their culture and traditions to the extent they desire, and many non-traditional communities have prospect of a more stable land base.' Looking to the future, he wanted to see 'tradition-oriented Aboriginals' being free to set up outstations on their traditional country. But there were limits to what was affordable and practicable. Government needed to work with Aborigines helping to determine realistic options. The holding of land tenure did not carry an entitlement to the delivery of all government services on that land. He told Viner:

> In my view, it is essential that we should not pre-empt the options of such Aboriginals. To the extent that we build, or facilitate the building of, houses, hospitals, schools, stores and so on in their areas, we tend to fix the people to particular areas and circumstances. Of course, there have to be some material facilities and services in the tradition-oriented areas. But we need, I believe, to keep these from spawning *ad infinitum*, and rather to think in terms of providing and maintaining a limited number of major centres, serving not only their immediate inhabitants but decentralised groups in a much wider area. The Council for Aboriginal Affairs over a period drew attention to the profound significance of the decentralisation movement, including the need to preserve for tradition-oriented communities the option to move out from the main centres if they so desire. Partly, what I am saying is that the decentralised groups cannot expect the same level of provision of material facilities as applies at the centres – and indeed the provision of such facilities would destroy much of the essence of the decentralisation movement.

He ended on a very cautionary note, which almost four decades on reads as an indictment of so much that has been left undone and unchallenged:

> But I believe it is not putting it too high to say that all the efforts of the Commonwealth over the last nine years could be brought to nothing unless the abuse of alcohol can be controlled. Its control will not be an

easy task. I have indeed only one suggestion to make, namely that it will be controlled only by the Aboriginals themselves, and they will be able to control it only to the extent that life has a purpose for them in terms of the preservation and development of their society and culture, the opportunity for employment not too inconsistent with their environment, and the encouragement and respect of the whole Australian community.

Viner replied, thanking Dexter for his insights and assistance, having come to his position 'as a "new chum" in Aboriginal Affairs as well as to the Ministry'. He confided:

It seemed to me that we had a common approach through a simple philosophy and fundamental truth – all men and women are equal in the sight of God and deserve to be accorded the dignity of that status within the Australian community. Where it has been diminished by disadvantage or discrimination or inadequacy on the part of Governments, then that is where the resources of the Department of Aboriginal Affairs should be directed.[48]

In 1981, Coombs delivered the eulogy at Stanner's funeral. He spoke of Stanner's role on the CAA, 'in which Bill was the source of the intellectual and emotional energy behind the Council's effort to change, not merely the policies of Governments in relation to Aborigines, but the very conception of Aboriginal Australians held by the great majority of their countrymen'. He spoke of Stanner's 'comprehension of the spiritual and poetic qualities which lent [Aboriginal society] coherence and gave meaning to the universe of which it was a part'. In all this, Coombs detected something new, 'something which provided the basis for a view of Aborigines and their traditional way which was at once humane, respectful and compassionate'. Ten years after Stanner's death, reflecting on the outcomes from the 1967 referendum when speaking at the National Press Club in 1991, Coombs was less than enthusiastic about the changes 'on the white side' but very upbeat about the changes for Aboriginal Australians:

> Until that Referendum in 1967 the prevailing tone of Aboriginal attitudes towards Australian society was one of despair. If you cast your mind back to that period and to the occasional conference held to deal with their problems you will remember that Aborigines were so downcast that they didn't even feel that it was worthwhile protesting: there seemed no prospect even of somebody listening. That sense of despair was I believe almost universal throughout Aboriginal society at that time. Now that has changed dramatically. Aborigines today are articulate and literate; they are producing leaders, who think coherently and practically about the problems that face them. They are no longer a dispersed group incapable of commanding the attention of the community. The time when Aborigines could be dismissed as politically and socially unimportant has gone. Australians have to live with the fact the Aborigines believe themselves to be the inheritors of a tradition important, not merely to them, but to the world.

At Coombs' funeral in 1997, Governor-General Sir William Deane delivered a eulogy. Speaking of Coombs' role on the CAA, Deane highlighted his capacity to argue passionately for the welfare of Aborigines and their right to be different:

> ... different in their human, material and spiritual relationships – to each other and to the land and its resources. To be part of and have equal access to non-Aboriginal society if they chose; but also, as he put it, 'to be able to conduct their society in accordance with their ways of thinking, educate their children in relation to that and to conduct their own ceremonies'.

Whatever the legal shortcomings of the 1967 referendum, whatever the political shortcomings of the prime ministers dealing with the immediate aftermath of the vote, the referendum was the great catalyst for change in Aboriginal rights and in their relations with other Australians. The next referendum, even if the wording is as modest, and even if the government as unresponsive, will be the next great catalyst for all Australians to work towards better solutions for Indigenous Australians, many of whom now have a secure land base and a sense of choice about life options. From here, the focus will move from land rights to land use, from the abstract right to choose a way of life to the entitlement to make life choices which are practical, resourced and life-fulfilling. Noel Pearson put it memorably at the 2014 Garma Festival in Arnhem Land when speaking on the ABC's *Q&A* program about his vision for Aboriginal children on the Cape York communities: 'Our vision is that we should have a strong home base, but we should go out into the world in orbits and come back home. We say Cape York to New York. We want our children to have a strong home base but also have the facility to go out into the world in pursuit of art, sport, education, careers but always be anchored back home.'[49]

For years I have used one simple test. We need the laws, policies and public attitudes in place so that when an Indigenous child at the end of a difficult day in the privacy of their own home or community complains to parents that life is hard, and choices difficult, the response is: 'We know that. But give it a go. Because this is your country, the country where you get a fair go, the country where there is respect and due acknowledgment of our history and our future.' That is not about choosing whether Hasluck or Coombs was right, the other being wrong. It is about Aborigines being free to choose, within fair and practical parameters, but with their land rights assured. It is about moral entitlements and realistic choices being assured by Australia to all Australians, especially the first Australians. It is the national task to be achieved by a successful referendum for the first time putting Aborigines and Torres Strait Islanders in the Constitution in a positive light.

CHAPTER 6

THE NEED FOR CONSTITUTIONAL CHANGE
Enhancing land rights and life choices

Neville Bonner was the first Aborigine to sit in the Australian Parliament. Bonner wanted the nation to own its lamentable past, draw the line and move on together, recognising everyone as equal and according special treatment only when it was sought and justified. He wanted to see his people at the table when their futures were being determined. Though conservative on all manner of issues, he sat in Parliament as a thorn in the side of his own Liberal Party, as well as of the Labor Party when it was in government. On 11 July 1974 he placed a motion on the Senate notice paper:

> That the Senate accepts the fact that the indigenous people of Australia, now known as Aborigines and Torres Strait Islanders, were in possession of this entire nation prior to the 1788 First Fleet landing at Botany Bay, urges the Australian Government to admit prior ownership by the said indigenous people, and introduce legislation to compensate the people now known as Aborigines and Torres Strait Islanders for dispossession of their land.[1]

He sought to speak to his motion on 19 September 1974. Senator Jim Cavanagh, minister for Aboriginal affairs, immediately sought to delay consideration of the motion, urging the president of the Senate to rule that the matter was *sub judice* because Aboriginal lawyer Paul Coe had commenced an action in the ACT Supreme Court claiming rights to land. Not even Attorney-General Lionel Murphy saw this as a problem. Seasoned Senate debater Robert Rae joined Murphy in urging that Bonner be allowed to speak. Eventually the Senate president disallowed Cavanagh's objection, observing, 'I am not altogether satisfied that this matter is not *sub judice*. However, I will allow the debate to continue and will bear very closely in mind the points made by Senator Cavanagh.'[2] Having spent so much time debating whether the motion could be debated, the Senate then had time to hear only from Bonner before adjourning debate on the motion. Bonner told the Senate:

> We, the indigenous people, for far too long have been the recipients of charity – the charity of the government of the day; charity, with its modern day connotations implying a handout mentality. What I am seeking is true and due entitlement for dispossession.[3]

He urged the establishment of an Aboriginal trust which would receive an annual payment in compensation for past dispossession. He concluded with this plea to his fellow senators:

> In the final analysis, Mr President and honourable senators, should I be deserted and sit here alone on one side of the chamber, one lone senator, one lone Aborigine, I will mind not at all, I will understand. But honourable senators, where, I ask, stand you in history? Mr President and honourable senators, today you will judge me. Australia, and particularly my State of Queensland, may judge me tomorrow. But history, I assure you, will judge us all. I pray that history will not render a verdict of guilty.[4]

On 17 February 1975, the Whitlam Cabinet decided that the government would not oppose the Bonner motion were it to be brought on again for debate and that, if put to the vote, the government would support it.⁵ Cavanagh told Cabinet that the government's various programs for land rights, the setting up of land councils, and a proposed home purchase grants scheme were appropriate means of compensation. Consistent with recommendations made by Edward Woodward's royal commission on land rights, the government saw the provision of land title and funds for the development of Aboriginal lands as the best form of compensation. Except for obstruction from Queensland, the states were moving, if gradually, towards providing recognition of land rights. Cavanagh warned Cabinet, 'Explicit rejection of the idea of cash compensation would certainly attract strong criticism from some Aboriginal spokesmen, especially the urban activists.'

Three days later Senator Cavanagh told the Senate, 'The Government will support this expression of the Senate.'⁶ Bonner thought Cavanagh's speech so full of qualifications and waffle that he was left in doubt about whether the government supported the motion in its entirety. He was also disappointed that there were so few people in the chamber. No one else spoke for or against the motion. Before moving that the motion be put, Bonner expressed the hope 'that when the motion is passed there will be rejoicing in the Aboriginal community'.⁷ There was not likely to be much rejoicing by those Aboriginal leaders who had been running the Aboriginal tent embassy; they thought Bonner altogether too conciliatory and appeasing. Those senators present in the chamber passed the motion on the voices and immediately proceeded to the next item of business. Through this motion, Bonner had planted a seed: now, there was a need to recognise the past with a symbolic gesture and move on.

From time to time, an idea takes root in the Australian public discourse that owning our past, drawing the line and moving on together as a nation would be assisted by amending the Constitution. It is only in recent years that Aboriginal advocates have come to express dissatisfaction with the 1967 amendment to the race power, section 51(26). No one has objected to the repeal of section 127 back in 1967. There were amendments passed to the Constitution in 1977 but they related to Senate casual vacancies, the retirement age of federal judges and the procedure for amending the Constitution.

Just before Christmas 1985, when Prime Minister Bob Hawke was overseas, Attorney-General Lionel Bowen was acting prime minister. Bowen announced the establishment of a high-powered six-member Constitutional Commission to carry out a fundamental review of the Australian Constitution in time for the 1988 bicentenary. The attorney-general also announced the appointment of five advisory committees to provide input to the commission. The Advisory Committee on Individual and Democratic Rights under the Constitution (the Rights Committee) conducted broad-ranging inquiries on Indigenous rights and on the desirability of a constitutional bill of rights. There was also a Distribution of Powers Committee (the Powers Committee), which offered opinions on some proposals relating to Indigenous rights.

The Constitutional Commission was chaired by Sir Maurice Byers, who had been the Commonwealth solicitor-general after Bob Ellicott. He was joined by two retired politicians from opposite sides of the political fence, Gough Whitlam and Sir Rupert Hamer, who had been the Liberal premier of Victoria. There were also two highly esteemed legal scholars, Enid Campbell and Leslie Zines, each of whom had published leading works on constitutional law. Justice John Toohey served as a member for one year but resigned when appointed to the High Court. He was ultimately one of the judges in the *Mabo* case.

The eight-member Rights Committee included Ron Castan, who later became a leading barrister in many Aboriginal cases in the High Court, including *Mabo*; Aboriginal academic Eric Willmot; author Thomas Keneally; and Peter Garrett, a songwriter, lead singer of the band Midnight Oil and later a politician. They thought there should be some acknowledgment of Aborigines in the Constitution and a more complete statement of the history that led to Federation. Presently, the Australian Constitution is an attachment to the UK Parliament's

Commonwealth of Australia Constitution Act 1900. That piece of imperial legislation commences with a preamble:

> Whereas the people of New South Wales, Victoria, South Australia, Queensland, and Tasmania, humbly relying on the blessing of Almighty God, have agreed to unite in one indissoluble Federal Commonwealth under the Crown of the United Kingdom of Great Britain and Ireland, and under the Constitution hereby established:
>
> And whereas it is expedient to provide for the admission into the Commonwealth of other Australasian Colonies and possessions of the Queen:
>
> Be it therefore enacted by the Queen's most Excellent Majesty, by and with the advice and consent of the Lords Spiritual and Temporal, and Commons, in this present Parliament assembled, and by the authority of the same, as follows ...

The Rights Committee was concerned that this preamble did not tell enough of the pre-Federation story of this land. The Constitution, as distinct from the imperial act to which it is attached, does not contain any preamble. No doubt prompted by the 1975 Bonner motion, the committee wanted a preamble which would recognise that 'prior to the arrival of European settlers, Australia was owned by the Aboriginal people' and which would 'acknowledge the historical truth of the settlement of Australia by Europeans in 1788'. They thought this would be a symbolic act of good faith, furthering reconciliation between Aboriginal and non-Aboriginal Australians.[8] The committee recommended this preamble:

> Whereas the People are drawn from a rich diversity of cultures yet are one in their devotion to the Australian traditions of equality, the freedom of the person and the dignity of the individual
>
> Whereas Australia is an ancient land previously owned and occupied by Aboriginal peoples who never ceded ownership

Whereas the Australian people look to share fairly in the plenty of our Commonwealth

Whereas Australia is a continent of immense extent and unique in the world demanding as our homeland our respect, devotion and wise management.[9]

The Constitutional Commission noted that any proposed preamble would not confer any substantive rights and could not be used to interpret other provisions of the Constitution. It could be used as an aid for interpretation 'only in the event of ambiguity in the substantive provisions of the Constitution'.[10]

The commission received a range of criticisms and concerns about the proposed preamble. For example, some asked why sexual equality had not been mentioned as one of the national aspirations, or our triumph over war and adversity as one of our significant achievements, or a common language, democratic institutions, and British legal and political heritage as constitutive elements of the nation. The commission saw that the wording would excite community passion and debate and this could be 'a significant distraction from other substantive and more important proposals submitted to the electors'.[11]

The ever-hopeful commission thought there might be a real prospect of significant constitutional change following their report, but they were wary about trying to graft on a new preamble to a 90-year-old Constitution when there might be substantive change just around the corner. Some expected that Australians would consider the move to becoming a republic within the next generation or two, so any substantial rewriting of constitutional provisions – especially any preamble that purported to set out the key elements of national identity – would be forthcoming at that time. If there were to be a substantial rewrite of the preamble when Australia became a republic, why bother with an interim preamble being put to the Australian people at referendum now? When the Constitutional Commission distanced themselves completely from the preamble proposed by the Rights Committee, the commissioners said, 'Had we been writing a new Constitution we may have been concerned to prepare an opening statement, though not in the terms suggested by the Rights Committee.'[12]

The next matter of historical oversight or anomaly considered by the Rights Committee was section 25 of the Constitution, which they labelled 'odious and outdated' in that it permitted a state parliament 'so minded to create "white only" or "black only" electorates'. Section 25 provides:

> For the purposes of the last section, if by the law of any State all persons of any race are disqualified from voting at elections for the more numerous House of the Parliament of the State, then, in reckoning the number of the people of the State or of the Commonwealth, persons of the race resident in that State shall not be counted.

Calling for the section's repeal, the committee said:

> It is a leftover from the racial intolerance of the nineteenth century and is a standing temptation to a State to discriminate on the grounds of race. Although the provision is not being used by any State at the present time, it is unacceptable and dangerous to democracy to retain such a provision in the Australian Constitution.[13]

The commission was a little more sanguine. The members acknowledged it was an outmoded provision that might be considered objectionable.[14] The section had been based on part of the fourteenth amendment in the US Constitution, which had the purpose of encouraging the states 'to enfranchise the emancipated negroes after the Civil War by reducing the federal representation of the States if they failed to do so'. The commission recommended that section 25 be repealed 'because it is no longer appropriate to include in the Constitution a provision that contemplates the disqualification of members of a race from voting'.[15]

The Rights Committee then considered the 'race power', section 51(26) of the Constitution, which as amended in 1967 provides:

> The Parliament shall, subject to this Constitution, have power to make laws for the peace, order, and good government of the Commonwealth with respect to the people of any race, for whom it is deemed necessary to make special laws.

The Rights Committee recommended the repeal of this section because it could be used to make laws discriminating against Aborigines and not just laws for their benefit. Also, the committee thought the provision offensive in its operation, 'turning as it does upon a concept of race, which is not a valid physical or scientific concept'.[16] They proposed a new paragraph for section 51(26), providing the parliament to have the power to make laws for 'the benefit of the Aboriginal people and of the Torres Strait Island people; and the making of compacts deemed necessary by the Parliament in order to recognise ownership of Australia prior to acquisition of sovereignty by the Crown'. The commission, though, showed no interest in the proposal for the making of compacts. That was put on the very long finger.

The Powers Committee, which included Don Dunstan, who as South Australian premier had led the way legislating for land rights in Australia, was not persuaded that any new power should be qualified so that only laws for the benefit of Aborigines could be made. The committee thought the concept of benefit might prove difficult to interpret 'since there can be frequent disagreement on whether legislation benefits or adversely affects the interests of particular groups in a community'.[17] Benefit was seen to be more a political matter to be judged by politicians and their electors, rather than judges. The commission agreed with the Powers Committee and rejected the recommendation of the Rights Committee.

Recommending a power for the Commonwealth Parliament to make laws with respect to 'Aborigines and Torres Strait Islanders', the commission noted that 'the nation as a whole has a responsibility for Aborigines and Torres Strait Islanders' and 'the new power would avoid some of the uncertainty arising from, and concern about, the wording of the existing power'.[18] The commission was particularly pleased to be able to make recommendations (repealing section 25 and amending section 51(26)) omitting the word 'race' entirely from the Constitution. They saw no need to define Aboriginality in the Constitution as the courts were already well equipped to determine contested cases.

The Rights Committee had also proposed a constitutional bill of rights. The commission, rather surprisingly, supported the idea, reintroducing the word 'race' into the Constitution. Included in the package was a general equality right. The commission recommended:

- Everyone has the right to freedom from discrimination on the ground of race, colour, ethnic or national origin, sex, marital status, or political, religious, or ethical belief.
- Subsection (1) is not infringed by measures taken to overcome disadvantages arising from race, colour, ethnic or national origin, sex, marital status, or political, religious or ethical belief.

The Australian Parliament had absolutely no interest in a constitutional bill of rights. The Constitutional Commission was seen to have overreached itself.

The government decided to go ahead with just a handful of proposals for constitutional change without even waiting for the final report of the commission. During the bicentenary year, the Hawke Government badly mishandled the process for putting referenda proposals to the people with the result that no constitutional changes occurred. The cause of constitutional reform was put back.

The first item of substantive business in the new Parliament House opened by Queen Elizabeth during the bicentenary year was a motion in the House of Representatives moved by Prime Minister Bob Hawke, acknowledging Aboriginal prior occupation of Australia and affirming the importance of Aboriginal and Torres Strait Islander culture and heritage, as well as the 'the entitlement of Aborigines and Torres Strait Islanders to self-management and self-determination subject to the Constitution and the laws of the Commonwealth of Australia'. The motion failed to win the support of the opposition led by John Howard. The Liberal and National parties thought the words 'self-management and self-determination' should be further qualified by the words 'in common with all other Australians'. The Coalition would then have been prepared to acknowledge 'the entitlement of Aborigines and Torres Strait Islanders to self-management and self-determination in common with all other Australians subject to the Constitution and the laws of the Commonwealth of Australia'. Church leaders who had proposed the motion as a gesture of national reconciliation and key Aboriginal leaders like Patrick Dodson thought that these additional words of qualification carried an assimilationist overtone and thus were unacceptable.

Those considering a future constitutional referendum on Aboriginal entitlements need to acknowledge that the concepts of self-management and self-determination have not been sufficiently qualified in the past for them to win unconditional acceptance by the Liberal and National parties. In the 1988 parliamentary debate, John Howard said, 'We are concerned that the motion in its present form, and without the addition of those words, can create the perception of separate development and the impression of divisions in the Australian community.' He wanted 'to remove any doubt at all that the passage of this motion will build a case for separate development, because that is repugnant to our notions of a united nation'.[19] Ian Sinclair, the leader of the National Party (the new name for the Country Party), spoke of 'the possibility of setting up a separate apartheid state'.[20] Any constitutional referendum supported by an Abbott Coalition Government of the Liberal and National parties today will be sure to avoid all such doubt and possibility in its wording, its intent and its likely outcomes.

On the issue of Indigenous rights, the parliament became focused on greater Aboriginal self-management with the establishment of the Aboriginal and Torres Strait Islander Commission (ATSIC) in 1989, and on reconciliation with the establishment of the Council for Aboriginal Reconciliation in 1991. The parliamentary debate on the ATSIC legislation was protracted and divisive. The legislation setting up the Council for Aboriginal Reconciliation was passed unanimously. The latter act included a preamble stating:

Because:
 a. Australia was occupied by Aborigines and Torres Strait Islanders who had settled for thousands of years, before British settlement at Sydney Cove on 26 January 1788; and
 b. many Aborigines and Torres Strait Islanders suffered dispossession and dispersal from their traditional lands by the British Crown; and
 c. to date, there has been no formal process of reconciliation between Aborigines and Torres Strait Islanders and other Australians; and
 d. by the year 2001, the centenary of Federation, it is most desirable that there be such a reconciliation; and
 e. as a part of the reconciliation process, the Commonwealth will seek an ongoing national commitment from governments at all levels to co-operate and to co-ordinate with the Aboriginal and Torres Strait Islander Commission as appropriate to address progressively Aboriginal disadvantage and aspirations in relation to land, housing, law and justice, cultural heritage, education, employment, health, infrastructure, economic development and any other relevant matters in the decade leading to the centenary of Federation, 2001.

The Council for Aboriginal Reconciliation existed for ten years, during which time it hosted two national reconciliation conventions in 1997 and 2000. The rhetoric of reconciliation was sorely tested with the parliament having to legislate for native title in 1993 after the *Mabo* decision, and again in 1998 after the *Wik* decision. Constitutional recognition and constitutional change were the last things on anyone's mind in Canberra. There was a desperate need to negotiate outcomes on native title for the wellbeing of all landholders and developers.

When Paul Keating became prime minister in December 1991, he put the republic issue on the table even before the *Mabo* decision was handed down in June 1992. He told the Queen that it was time for change. After winning the 1993 election, he appointed a Republican Advisory Committee headed by Malcolm Turnbull. With the election of the Howard Government in 1996, there was ongoing agitation about the issue and division within the Coalition ranks. To put the matter to rest, John Howard sensibly agreed to the 1998 Constitutional Convention to consider different models of republic and to determine which model would be put to the Australian public by referendum in 1999.

Neville Bonner was one of the more fervent monarchists to attend the convention. He was upset that a change to a republic might be contemplated. At the convention he sang his Jagera Sorry Chant and lamented there were only six Indigenous Australians participating in the convention. His heart was heavy: 'I worry for my children and my grandchildren. I worry that what has proven to be a stable society, which now recognises my people as equals, is about to be replaced.'[21] Earlier, he had recalled historic grievances: 'You came to my country. You invaded my land. You took our Earth (our everything). You poisoned my waterholes. You killed my people. You gave away my land. You imposed your law on my people. You ignored the instructions of liberal colonial secretaries to deal with us and respect us.'[22] His old friend, fellow monarchist and Liberal Party colleague Sir James Killen, thanked him for his 'gracious indictment' of the chamber and the country, saying that if need be, 'then you and I will adjourn to the Condamine of old where I had, years ago, swum in a certain state of disrobe with your people'.[23]

Aboriginal representatives at the convention agitated Indigenous issues, including a need to revisit the question of a preamble for the Constitution. Early in the convention, Lowitja O'Donoghue, who had been the first chair of ATSIC, convened a working group favouring the recognition of Indigenous Australians in the preamble. She was joined by Neville Bonner and Gatjil Djerrkura, who had also been the chair of ATSIC. Also on board were Julian Leeser and Dame Leonie Kramer. Kramer was a senior fellow of the conservative think tank the Institute of Public Affairs. Leeser later went on to become executive director of the Menzies Research Centre, the Liberal Party's think tank. This meant that a broad cross-section of the delegates had the opportunity to give some thought to the likely shape of any new constitutional preamble. While there was no agreement about Australia becoming a republic, there was unanimity about the need to better recognise Aborigines in the Constitution, whether or not Australia was ever to become a republic.

Professor Greg Craven, a constitutional lawyer whose opinion is sure to be sought by the Abbott Government on any proposal for Indigenous recognition in the Constitution, moved a motion at the convention, setting out the principles applicable to any preamble. These included:

- any preamble should build upon the existing preamble;
- the preamble should recognise prior occupancy of Australia's indigenous peoples;
- the preamble should acknowledge the past contribution of the Crown;
- the preamble should contain appropriate statements of acknowledged historical fact;
- the preamble should not contain statements of abstract values or rights such as equality or democracy.[24]

Craven explained that his motion was:

> ... designed to put into the Constitution – or at least to set a framework for putting into the Constitution – a preamble that does nothing more than to reflect the realities of a republican Constitution, to provide an appropriate opening to that Constitution, to recognise the position of Aboriginal people, not to insert inappropriately vague values that could be the subject of inappropriately vague judicial determination and, in particular, to prevent any chance of a political scare campaign based upon a suicidal preamble as part of a republican amendment.

Julian Leeser, who later went on to assist with the 2009 national campaign against a charter of rights, acknowledged that there was much bipartisan support for a preamble that said the correct things. He told the convention:

> I think that there is broad based support in this place for the fact that recognition of the existence of indigenous people is long overdue in our Constitution. It has been long overdue in our legal system. It was a great shame and a great black mark on Australian history that it was only in 1992, with the *Mabo* judgment, that the notion of *terra nullius* was finally put to bed. Even now we do not see it completely put to bed with the question over the *Wik* legislation and the *Wik* decision. But, that aside, I think we have to take positive steps at this Convention and show that on certain issues we as an Australian community can unite. I believe that on recognition of indigenous people in the Constitution we can unite.[25]

He went on to say:

> I think this is the one issue and the one point in this debate where we can come together and present a unified approach and say, 'Yes, indigenous recognition in the Constitution is important, indigenous recognition is

long overdue,' so let us work together and support that working group's recommendations.[26]

Leeser later moved that there be 'a separate question to ask the Australian people if the Preamble should be amended to recognise the original occupancy and custodianship of Australia by the Aboriginal people and Torres Strait Islanders'.[27] Dame Leonie Kramer was even more blunt and to the point: 'I want to appeal for you all to agree unanimously, as we did the other day, to the inclusion of Aboriginal people and Torres Strait Islanders in the preamble.'[28] Nova Peris, who is now a senator chairing the Joint Select Committee on Constitutional Recognition of Aboriginal and Torres Strait Islander Peoples with Ken Wyatt, said, 'I am pleased that there has been a wide range of support for including some form of recognition for indigenous Australians in the preamble. We are the original Australians, and it is a matter of justice that we be recognised as such.'[29]

In the final Communique of the convention, delegates agreed to certain principles about a preamble. Some of those are relevant to a new preamble even without Australia becoming a republic. In part, they resolved:

> That the Constitution include a Preamble, noting that the existing Preamble before the Covering Clauses of the Imperial Act which enacted the Australian Constitution (and which is not itself part of our Constitution) would remain intact.
>
> The Preamble to the Constitution should contain the following elements:
> 1. Introductory language in the form 'We the people of Australia';
> 2. Reference to 'Almighty God';
> 3. Reference to the origins of the Constitution, and acknowledgment that the Commonwealth has evolved into an independent, democratic and sovereign nation under the Crown;

4. Recognition of our federal system of representative democracy and responsible government;
5. Affirmation of the rule of law;
6. Acknowledgment of the original occupancy and custodianship of Australia by Aboriginal peoples and Torres Strait Islanders;
7. Recognition of Australia's cultural diversity;
8. Affirmation of respect for our unique land and the environment;
9. Concluding language to the effect that '[We the people of Australia] asserting our sovereignty, commit ourselves to this Constitution'; and
10. A provision allowing ongoing consideration of constitutional change.

The delegates suggested that there be some consideration given to 'recognition that Aboriginal people and Torres Strait Islanders have continuing rights by virtue of their status as Australia's indigenous peoples'. They wanted the preamble to be drafted in such a way that it could not have implications for the interpretation of the Constitution.

For now, the republic is well off the agenda, at least while Tony Abbott is prime minister. Like his three predecessors – John Howard, Kevin Rudd and Julia Gillard – Abbott is convinced that the time is ripe for appropriate recognition of Aborigines and Torres Strait Islanders in the Constitution. Understandably, many people now think first about a revision of the Constitution's preamble when considering Aboriginal recognition. There is general agreement on the need to repeal the outdated section 25. There is an emerging consensus that section 51(26) needs to be amended also. There will certainly also be advocates and lobbyists agitating the need for greater constitutional protection of human rights in conjunction with any Indigenous recognition. This would be a serious mistake. The Liberal and National parties have long been opposed to a constitutional bill of rights and are very wary about the need for even a statutory charter of rights. The

Labor Party has become more reserved about both measures. The 2004 Party Platform of the ALP stated:

> As a means of building community confidence in the constitutional recognition of the rights enjoyed by all Australians, Labor will introduce a legislative Charter of Citizenship and Aspirations.
>
> Labor supports constitutional reform to achieve a comprehensive recognition of the rights enjoyed by all Australians. These inalienable rights also carry with them a responsibility to respect the individual and collective rights enjoyed by others and the need to protect and promote institutions and practices fundamental to an equal, just, democratic and tolerant society.[30]

The party platform was amended prior to the 2007 election. The 44th Party National Conference resolved, 'Labor will initiate a public inquiry about how best to recognise and protect the human rights and freedoms enjoyed by all Australians.' The platform went on to state:

> Labor will establish a process of consultation which will ensure that all Australians will be given the chance to have their say on this important question for our democracy ... Any proposal for legislative change in this area must maintain sovereignty of the Parliament and shall not be based on the United States Bill of Rights.[31]

When Prime Minister Kevin Rudd first came to power in 2007, the ALP had a commitment only to consultation about the enhanced protection of human rights. When the government appointed a National Human Rights Consultation, which I chaired, it specified in our terms of reference that any options we identified 'should preserve the sovereignty of the Parliament and not include a constitutionally entrenched bill of rights'. The government rejected out of hand our recommendation that 'Australia adopt a federal Human Rights Act'.[32] No major political party in Australia has taken any step towards the constitutional entrenchment of human rights since the tabling of the 1988 Constitutional Commission report. In any referendum campaign, a proposal to constitutionalise the right to equality or the existing legislative prohibitions on racial discrimination will be labelled a constitutional bill of rights by the back door. It would have no prospect of success. Its inclusion in the Constitution would contribute further anomalies.

A constitutional prohibition on racial discrimination would apply to the Commonwealth and the states. The existing constitutional prohibition on religious discrimination would be confined to the Commonwealth, with the state parliaments remaining free to legislate in a discriminatory way against people of a particular religion. Also, there would be no constitutional prohibition whatever on discrimination on the grounds of gender or sexual orientation. Many would say that assurances against sex discrimination are as constitutive of Australian identity in the twenty-first century as assurances against racial discrimination. We decide either in favour of a constitutional bill of rights or against it. We decide either in favour of a constitutional protection against all forms of discrimination or against it. There can be no half measures like a constitutional right of equality and non-discrimination only in relation to race, or only in relation to Aboriginality. If we were to constitutionalise a ban on racial discrimination only, we would need to ensure that such a ban was workable and capable of certain application by the High Court.

Whether or not there be constitutional change, there is an ongoing need to consider changes to laws and policies affecting land rights and realistic life choices so that contemporary Indigenous Australians might make the best of their lands, culture and heritage. The forthcoming referendum, like the 1967 referendum, should provide the stimulus for a deeper reassessment of major policy parameters about land, Indigenous participation in law and policy-making that affect Indigenous Australians uniquely, and realistic life choices aimed at maintaining culture and heritage while being able to share equitably in the delivery of government services. It might also lead to substantive changes that are not presently in the minds of key government decision-makers. The real change to the lives of Indigenous Australians is more likely to result from modest referendum proposals that are overwhelmingly endorsed than from extensive referendum proposals that could generate opposition and perhaps even defeat.

As Australians come to focus on Aboriginal aspirations before and after the referendum, we will find that land management and practical use of Aboriginal land are issues crying out for attention. These issues will not be specifically mentioned in any proposed constitutional amendment but they will underpin what many Aborigines will be hoping to gain from a successful referendum. The secure grant of land rights was the big tangible outcome from the 1967 referendum. The practical use of land rights should be the big tangible gain from the next referendum. Forty years after first granting land rights, the nation now needs to review how Aborigines and Torres Strait Islanders can go about using their land rights.

When Sir Edward Woodward concluded his royal commission into Aboriginal land rights over 40 years ago, he knew that he was not setting down propositions in stone. He wrote, 'I regard it as generally undesirable to try to find solutions today for a period as far ahead as forty years. I believe, as I have said elsewhere, that we should try to find solutions for today and the foreseeable future.'[33] One of the problems confronting us more than 40 years on is that many people take the view that Woodward's recommendations and the legislation that followed are unchangeable, especially given the centrality of the proposition that Aboriginal title be inalienable. But as Woodward said, 'We cannot now envisage what the social or economic climate may be like in forty years time and I believe it would be wrong to try to solve today's problems by entering into commitments which later generations would have to make good.'[34] He thought the best that could be done was to tell Aborigines what government was prepared to do for them in the next ten years. But he thought it important 'that there should be provision for a formal reconsideration of the situation at regular intervals in the future'.[35]

In the final stages of the drafting of the Northern Territory land rights legislation, Gerard Brennan, who had been the senior barrister for the Northern Land Council, had cause to write to Ian Viner, the minister for Aboriginal affairs in the Fraser Government. He restated the case for the grant of a fee simple title, a form of freehold ownership, rather than a lease or statutory title: 'The essential feature of any title sufficient to satisfy Aboriginal cultural and spiritual needs, and the expressed aspirations of the Aboriginal people, is perpetuity. The fee simple alone gives this title.'[36] With a leasehold, there was always the risk of termination for failure to perform a condition of the lease. With a statutory title, 'the rights which such a title may confer lie only within the continuing gift of the legislature'. But there was a further benefit of freehold: 'If, in the years to come, it is deemed desirable to withdraw the proposed legislative prohibition against alienation, the titleholders will be enabled to pass a title with recognised incidents.' Everyone was aware that this day could come, but that it should come only at the request of Aboriginal landholders, after due consideration for future generations.

An inalienable freehold title was the strongest protective husk the law could put around the complex array of relationships that Aborigines had with their lands as owners and users, as spiritual guardians, and as hunters and foragers. At the Woodward Commission in the 1970s, there was a difference of opinion between the two land councils about the appropriate titleholder for Aboriginal lands. In his first report, Woodward put forward three options for granting land title: to a council trust, a community or a clan. He tended to favour granting the title to a community even though most communities included a mixture of people from various clans and traditional landholding groups. That seemed also to be the clear consensus of Aboriginal opinion. As well, the larger communities had become used to electing their own councils. The

Central Land Council favoured this community approach. But Gerard Brennan put compelling submissions for title to be vested in a council or trust.

Initially Woodward was resistant to the Northern Land Council's approach. He thought that most Aborigines in the Northern Territory had two different loyalties: one to their traditional clan and one to their local community. Many would think it more sensible and more convenient that land ownership be exercised by the local community. He asked, 'To what extent are we white members of Australian society entitled to try to force solidity and stability on to an Aboriginal system and prevent or discourage change and development taking place? Do we have any more right to prevent those changes of thinking and changes in development than we have to try to force them?' Brennan replied, 'I think to develop any scheme which has about it the air of compulsion is undesirable. It seems to me that what is necessary is the creation of structures of choice, and one ought, in dealing with land as we would see it, create those structures of choice in such a way as will then permit the choice between the traditional land usage and the modern land usage.'[37]

Jack Elliott, the senior barrister appearing for the Central Land Council, was very strong in his attempted rebuttal of the Northern Land Council's position, favouring Woodward's initial position. He told Woodward:

> I think the fallacy ... is that (Mr Brennan) sees Your Honour's task as a restoration of a culture which is at the best surviving only in a most fragmentary form and which is in the process of changing. It is not static. It will gradually go through a degree of change varying, of course, in localities, but necessarily reflecting the impact of the European culture. It involves as well people who have lost all touch with their own culture and become, as it were, half assimilated but certainly divorced from their ancient traditions and the criteria such as we have roughed out, as it were, were intended to enable a detached and independent mind to arrive at a

just finding upon, of course, the evidence of Aborigines who would be asserting their, if I may say, Aboriginal claims to any piece of land or any area of land.'[38]

Elliott was particularly concerned that the Northern Land Council's suggested mode of tenure 'would dispossess or disentitle a great many Aborigines' for whom association with land was now 'only relative to what their association must have been 200 years ago but are still sufficiently alive and discernible to attract a recognition of some sort of title'.[39] This would be 'falling short of what is expected to result'.[40] Brennan responded, 'It has been put to us in one of the comments we have had upon our submission that that is going to exclude far too many people but on discussions with our observer as to how wide the net should be cast, once you depart from the criteria of the spiritual and cultural tie and go beyond that, you come to a well-meaning sloppiness of thought.'[41]

Elliott continued to agitate for a loose test for identification of traditional ownership, consistent with being able to vest title in a community group of mixed tribal and clan affiliations. Arguing that the eligibility for claims should be 'as wide as possible', he submitted, 'There has been so much mixture in Australia. It has been going on for so long that I think the definition under the South Australian *Aborigines Act* is the only one that should be used. It does not cut anybody out who has a touch of the tar brush, as they used to rashly say in the past.'[42] Brennan would not yield.

When the commission moved its hearings from Alice Springs to Darwin, the Northern Land Council members attended in large numbers. In their presence, Brennan submitted again that title needed to be grounded in traditional authority. There was no way around this, 'because if there be a necessity for control, whether of assets or of persons, there are only two possible sources of authority which can be used in Aboriginal society today. One is traditional and the other is imposed ... acquired or assimilated.' He submitted:

> Therefore it seems to us, with respect, that once one moves away from traditional forms of authority with respect to land use one is left foundering in a morass of uncertainty in relation to the control of land, in relation to the use to which land can be put, and with great respect to those who may think otherwise we can devise no method which is likely to succeed at all unless it has built into it a system which depends upon traditional Aboriginal authority for control and use of the land.[43]

Woodward ultimately accepted that the council or trust system would work best because 'it is in harmony with traditional Aboriginal social organisation'.[44] Land would be vested in a land trust administered by a land council, which would benefit traditional owners and be responsive to their desires. He acknowledged that in his first report he had undervalued the continuing importance of the clan structure. But he could see that things would change:

> Community councils now perform useful functions in areas other than land ownership. For many other purposes they are both necessary and desirable. And in cases where communities are living on land that is not theirs traditionally, or have otherwise lost touch with traditional values, the community council or its representatives may well be the best body to have land vested in it.
>
> Indeed I believe that the most likely development over the next fifty years or so will be a gradual weakening of links with specific areas and sites and the strengthening of community identity with larger tracts of land. If this occurs, community ownership would be appropriate.[45]

In 1999, John Herron, the minister for Aboriginal affairs in the Howard Government, instituted a major review of the Northern Territory land rights legislation. The review was conducted by Darwin barrister John Reeves, who had been a Labor member of the House of Representatives representing the Northern Territory. Reeves met with Woodward before completing his report. Reeves was keen to break down the influence of the major land councils and to move the focus of land ownership and control from traditional owners to local communities. Woodward insisted that he had got the principles right in his royal commission report and that the basic framework of the legislation was still correct. However, he did concede that there might be a case for change over time.

Woodward made a submission to the parliament's Joint Standing Committee on Aboriginal Affairs, which reviewed Reeves' report once it was tabled in Parliament. Woodward submitted that when he conducted his royal commission, 'I left it open for communities to make applications for land under a trust system and saw a time in the future when such community-based land ownership could become more appropriate than a trust system. Whether that time has yet arrived I am unable to say of my own knowledge, but I doubt it.'[46] He told the parliamentary committee:

> I maintain that the emphasis I placed on the local descent group was right at the time and that Mr Reeves is wrong to suggest otherwise. I believe that it is still right today, though I foresaw and now willingly concede that times are changing and, as true spiritualities weaken, it may be appropriate to put greater emphasis on communities.[47]

Appearing before the parliamentary committee in 1999, Woodward said, 'I did envisage in my original report that over time there would be a move of emphasis – and I wanted to allow it to happen – from traditional owners to communities.' He 'did envisage that over time, particularly as some of the spiritual connections with land become more attenuated and the community becomes a more natural Aboriginal construct and not just something which has in effect been organised by a mission station or a government settlement, that there would be a change'. He concluded:

I am not sure that that time has yet come and I am not really in a position to be able to advise you on that. I suspect that it has not yet come but this is something on which I am sure you will be listening to the voice of the Aboriginals themselves: if they tell you the time has come then clearly it has. As I see it, your problem will be if you get different messages from different Aboriginal groups, and that may be hard to determine.[48]

Against the backdrop of recent discussion about constitutional recognition of Aboriginal rights, key Aboriginal leaders have been agitating the need to recast laws and policies relating to land rights so that local Aboriginal communities and their members might be more able to use the land productively. At the 2014 Garma Festival in Arnhem Land, Galarrwuy Yunupingu pronounced that 'land rights is sleeping and that it is full of everything yet full of nothing'. He said:

> Land rights sleep because the system does not give life to the leadership that owns the land. It does not give life to that ownership – 'land rights' is a process of claim, not of use. It does not give the land the energy and power it needs to be useful to its owners and to enrich their lives. It does not unlock the wealth that belongs to the landowners.
>
> Decisions for use of our land should happen naturally and through clear pathways, always directed by local landowners, reflecting their priorities. In the 1970s, our leaders were not ready to take full responsibility in the new era of land rights, but now the time is right to move to a new model with political authority transferred to the regions.[49]

As Sir Edward Woodward surmised, 40 years on, the time has come to revisit the basis of land rights legislation at the request of the Aboriginal owners to ensure that they are not impeded from enjoying their land to the full, while at the same time providing some assurance that the land will be available for future generations. This will be one of the key tasks confronting governments and Aboriginal leaders as they build on the good faith and political momentum generated by any successful referendum aimed at providing due recognition of Aborigines in the life of the nation.

One of the legitimate Aboriginal claims that was not met by the Woodward Commission was the ongoing entitlement of traditional owners whose lands were subject to pastoral leases in the Northern Territory. They sought recognition of the reversionary interest they would have once any pastoral lease on their land had run its course. A reversionary interest is the owner's remaining interest in land once a lease granted to another occupier has expired. The Aborigines argued that pastoralists ought pay their annual lease fee to them as the true owners of the land, rather than to the Crown. They would be entitled to resume occupation of their lands once any pastoral lease had expired. Woodward could not bring himself to agree to either of these propositions.

Given that most pastoral leases were to expire between 2010 and 2020, Woodward did not want to create unnecessary uncertainty for the pastoralists or false expectations for the Aborigines; after all, the bulk of the Northern Territory's land mass was Aboriginal reserve, unalienated Crown land or pastoral lease. Most of the territory could have eventually reverted to Aboriginal ownership. Even if Aborigines could establish a traditional land claim over a pastoral lease, they would need to pay the cost of improvements. Despite the strong urging of the barristers for the land councils, Woodward remained 'very much concerned that Aborigines would be misled by being told that they are the owners of these lands subject only to existing leases'. He thought this could create 'a legacy of great trouble for both Aborigines and the wider Australian community in forty years time'.[50] It is now 40 years on, and I daresay there would be considerable commotion now in the Northern Territory if all pastoral leases were up for renegotiation, with traditional owners at the table being free to reject any application for lease renewal. Woodward's judicious, pragmatic judgment was correct. But the moral argument did not go away.

The matter of reversionary pastoral interests had to wait until another occasion. It was left unresolved by the royal commission back in the 1970s. Woodward knew that he had not provided any final resolution. In his autobiography, he disclosed that he had 'particularly asked' that Brennan be briefed in the royal commission as the senior barrister for the Northern Land Council.[51] He wrote that Brennan 'had some influence on my approach to the report' but that he had followed his cardinal principle of ensuring that any recommendations 'should be reasonably capable of implementation after taking into account financial and political realities'. Nonetheless he bore in mind Brennan's submission that 'this is a report which will for all time mark the high-water mark of possible Aboriginal aspirations. Whatever Your Honour does not recommend in favour of Aborigines, at this stage, will never be granted.'[52]

As governments and parliaments failed to act on reversionary pastoral interests, it was left to the High Court in the *Wik* decision to set down some parameters between Aboriginal and pastoral interests on the same areas of land. Brennan, as barrister for the Northern Land Council, had put the most detailed arguments to Woodward, seeking both Aboriginal title in the reversionary interest of pastoral leases and legislative recognition of ongoing Aboriginal rights of access to pastoral leases. Ironically, 22 years later Brennan was chief justice of the High Court and author of the dissenting judgment in *Wik*. He argued that it was not possible for a court to develop the common law recognising that native title could co-exist on a pastoral lease. Though he had no hesitation as a barrister in urging a royal commission to recommend that Parliament provide for just recognition of Aboriginal rights on a pastoral lease, he saw no role for a judge recognising such unlegislated rights which would conflict with the pastoralist's rights. This is what he wrote in his High Court judgment:

> The law can attribute priority to one right over another, but it cannot recognise the co-existence in different hands of two rights that cannot both be exercised at the same time. To postulate a test of inconsistency

not between the rights but between the manner of their exercise would be to deny the law's capacity to determine the priority of rights over or in respect of the same parcel of land. The law would be incapable of settling a dispute between the holders of the inconsistent rights prior to their exercise, to the prejudice of that peaceful resolution of disputes which reduces any tendency to self-help. To postulate extinguishment of native title as dependent on the exercise of the private right of the lessee (rather than on the creation or existence of the private right) would produce situations of uncertainty, perhaps of conflict. The question of extinguishment of native title by a grant of inconsistent rights is – and must be – resolved as a matter of law, not of fact. If the rights conferred on the lessee of a pastoral lease are, at the moment when those rights are conferred, inconsistent with a continued right to enjoy native title, native title is extinguished.[53]

Woodward had given one further practical, rather than legal, reason why such claims ought not be recognised by government:

Another possible reason for not granting this claim is that it might tend to be divisive amongst Aborigines. It promises much to those who can establish traditional claims and tends to mark them off from those who are unable to establish such claims. Although it is true that these people can be dealt with and provided for in other ways, I am still reluctant to make a recommendation which would draw such a clear dividing line between persons of the full blood who have had good fortune to retain close contact with their country and those who, because of their mixed descent or for other reasons, have lost touch with their traditional lands. I am concerned about the danger of creating, by implication, categories of first and second class Aborigines.[54]

When legislating for land rights in 1976, the Fraser Government agreed to Woodward's recommendations that land claims be permitted over existing Aboriginal reserves and over unoccupied Crown lands. It did not agree to claims on the basis of need rather than traditional association, even though many Aborigines had been long dispossessed of their lands without compensation. Neither did it agree to the setting aside of land in towns and on pastoral leases to satisfy traditional land claims. When Woodward conducted the royal commission on land rights he had visited Canada and the United States. He later wrote:

> The main lessons I learnt concerned the things we should not do in Australia because they had been tried and failed in Canada. The chief message I received from the Native Americans to whom I spoke was about the damage done to this people by welfare payments and the ready availability of alcohol. A major paradox that was brought home to me was that, because Australia had so far done nothing about native land rights, we were actually in a better position to act: we had a virtually clean slate to write upon.[55]

Speaking at the 1985 Australian Legal Convention, Woodward shared two basic conclusions he had drawn after his involvement over the years, including the equal wages case, the *Milirrpum* case and the royal commission. The first was:

> Given the historical and political difficulties, there could be no ideal solution to the land rights problem; there was not even a good solution available to reconcile conflicting interests; but somewhere, in each situation, there was a best solution waiting to be identified – one which had fewer defects than any other. This means, in my view that none of the interested parties should expect too much of the solution (or solutions) which will finally be adopted; it has to represent a compromise, a second-best, a disappointment in some degree for all concerned – Aboriginals, miners, graziers, governments, moralists and the general public.[56]

His second conclusion was somewhat counter-intuitive to what he had previously written about the need not to try and put in place solutions for the long term, given the uncertainty about future developments:

> Planning should essentially be for the longer term. We should be prepared to plan for years and even decades ahead and not expect to have all our solutions in place immediately or to see immediate benefits from those that are; this also requires some flexibility to be built into all proposals, as experience or attitudes may require amendments. In particular, it will be no bad thing if the short-term sees a continuation of the withdrawal by some tribal Aboriginals from large settlements, and from direct contact with European styles of living, which has occurred in recent decades.[57]

Forty years on from Woodward's recommendations for land rights in the Northern Territory, each jurisdiction with land rights legislation has of late been questioning whether they have struck the appropriate balance between security and utility of Aboriginal land titles. In 2012, the Queensland Government issued a discussion paper on 'providing freehold title in Aboriginal and Torres Strait Islander communities', noting the complexity of communal landholding arrangements that 'do not provide ordinary, individual freehold title as an option to Aboriginal people and Torres Strait Islanders wishing to own their own homes and pursue commercial interests in their communities'.[58] In 2013, Justice Trevor Morling conducted a review on Aboriginal landholding laws in New South Wales, in which I participated. We were commissioned by a handful of local Aboriginal land councils (LALCs) that wanted greater flexibility in land use. The Morling Review Panel recognised:

> There are cultural considerations affecting the development or sale of land owned by LALCs. One LALC CEO with whom we spoke expressed the view that land owned by a LALC should never be sold, essentially because (as he asserted), 'Having fought for over 200 years to get our land back,

why would we want to dispose of it.' However, this was not the view shared by the overwhelming majority of the LALCs' representatives with whom we met, who take the view that if the objects of the Act are to be achieved, it will be essential for LALCs to develop and sell some lands within their area. Indeed, the view that land, having been successfully claimed by a LALC, should under no circumstances be sold, is plainly in conflict with what is envisaged by the Act – specifically the sections which expressly provide for land dealings.[59]

Regardless of any constitutional referendum, the nation is now on the cusp of having to determine in response to Aboriginal demands whether to make some Aboriginal land titles more alienable, by gift, sale, lease or mortgage, so that they might be rendered more useful to the present generation of owners. The alternative is to maintain the lockup of Aboriginal lands for the benefit of future generations who, like the present generation, might find that their land base is not that useful, especially if the spiritual connection with land is less than it once was and if the desire for economic development is greater than what it once was.

It is difficult to predict what forum, event or group pressure will help build the momentum for change. Just as they would have obtained little traction in the Northern Territory but for the *Milirrpum* judgment, the advocates for a national response to Aboriginal land issues were to receive little traction until the High Court decisions in *Mabo* and *Wik*. On issues at the cutting edge of law and justice, it is not only politicians who carry a responsibility to shape law consistent with moral principles. Australian law is in better repair given the majority judgment of the High Court in *Mabo*. And yet, one can have the highest regard for the intellectual integrity of Justice Daryl Dawson, the sole dissentient, who wrote in *Mabo*:

> As I have said, any traditional land rights which the plaintiffs may have had were extinguished upon the assumption of sovereignty by the Crown

over the Murray Islands and any fiduciary or trust obligation that might otherwise have existed in relation to such rights is precluded by the terms of the relevant legislation. Accordingly, if traditional land rights (or at least rights akin to them) are to be afforded to the inhabitants of the Murray Islands, the responsibility, both legal and moral, lies with the legislature and not with the courts.[60]

When native title came on for debate in the Australian Parliament, as our elected politicians wrestled with how to make *Mabo* workable for all land users, including miners and developers, Tasmanian Brian Harradine held the balance of power in the Senate. He said:

> This parliament comes second place because it was the High Court that showed us the way. It was the *Mabo* decision that showed us the way. That really is to the shame of the parliament ... The parliament had to be almost dragged screaming to face reality because of the High Court decision. To me, that is shameful. To have acted sooner would have been the appropriate thing to do.[61]

Stanner, Dexter and Coombs would have agreed.

Over the years, there have been some warnings from the High Court bench that the complex law of native title, born of the admixture of High Court jurisprudence and the parliament's increasingly lengthy *Native Title Act* amendments, might not be quite what was intended when their honours delivered the *Mabo* decision. In *Fejo* v *The Northern Territory of Australia*,[62] Justice Michael McHugh, one of the majority in the *Mabo* decision and one of the dissentients in *Wik*, said during argument: 'My view was that native title would apply basically to only unalienated Crown land. If, for example, I thought it was going to apply to freehold, to leaseholds, I am by no means convinced that I would have not joined Justice Dawson [the sole dissentient in *Mabo*], and it may well be that that was also the view of other members of the Court.'[63] Late in his term on the High Court, Justice McHugh had cause to look back over the history of native title litigation:

> The dispossession of the Aboriginal peoples from their lands was a great wrong. Many people believe that those of us who are the beneficiaries of that wrong have a moral responsibility to redress it to the extent that it can be redressed. But it is becoming increasingly clear – to me, at all events – that redress cannot be achieved by a system that depends on evaluating the competing legal rights of landholders and native-title holders. The deck is stacked against the native-title holders whose fragile rights must give way to the superior rights of the landholders whenever the two classes of rights conflict. And it is a system that is costly and time-consuming. At present the chief beneficiaries of the system are the legal representatives of the parties. It may be that the time has come to think of abandoning the present system, a system that simply seeks to declare and enforce the legal rights of the parties, irrespective of their merits. A better system may be an arbitral system that declares what the rights of the parties ought to be according to the justice and circumstances of the individual case.[64]

Other High Court judges have voiced similar concerns. In *Wilson* v *Anderson*, Justice Michael Kirby said: 'The legal advance that commenced with *Mabo* v *Queensland (No 2)* or perhaps earlier, has now attracted such difficulties that the benefits intended for Australia's indigenous peoples in relation to native title to land and waters are being channelled into costs of administration and litigation that leave everyone dissatisfied and many disappointed.'[65] In *Western Australia* v *Ward*, Justice Ian Callinan said:

> I do not disparage the importance to the Aboriginal people of their native title rights, including those that have symbolic significance. I fear, however, that in many cases because of the chasm between the common law and native title rights, the latter, when recognised, will amount to little more

than symbols. It might have been better to redress the wrongs of dispossession by a true and unqualified settlement of lands or money than by an ultimately futile or unsatisfactory, in my respectful opinion, attempt to fold native title rights into the common law.[66]

The issue now is not the legitimacy of land rights but determining the cut-off point for recognising native title rights when other parties also have rights over the same land, and matching the remaining native title rights with the real, rather than imagined, Aboriginal and Torres Strait Islander aspirations. Noel Pearson says that 'native title is all about what is left over. And land rights have never been about the dispossession of the colonisers and their descendants. Whether it be statutory land rights or common law land rights – these land rights have always been focused on remnant lands.'[67]

The moral conscience of lawmakers, whether politicians or judges, has a place. It was the High Court that helped the nation face what justices William Deane and Mary Gaudron described as 'the conflagration of oppression and conflict which was ... to spread across the continent to dispossess, degrade and devastate the Aboriginal peoples and leave a national legacy of unutterable shame'.[68] There is a parallel need for public discussion about contested moral issues while the law takes shape in the courts and in our parliaments, determining the legitimate claims and realistic options for Indigenous Australians. There is no going back on land rights. The National Native Title Tribunal reports:

> The registered determinations of native title (that native title does or does not exist) cover some 1,394,956 sq km (or approximately 18.1 per cent) of the land mass of Australia, and registered indigenous land use agreements (ILUAs) cover about 1,398,127 sq km (or approximately 18.1 per cent) of the land mass, as well as approximately 5,753 sq km of sea (below the high water mark).[69]

Half the Northern Territory is now Aboriginal land with secure title, including 85 per cent of the coastline. The Indigenous Land Corporation, which now has a self-perpetuating fund for land acquisitions, has purchased 58,600 square kilometres of land since 1995, including some major projects such as the Yulara Resort at Uluru. Perhaps the time has come for an Indigenous Land Bank that can provide mortgages over Aboriginal land titles, allowing land to be used as security for loans while ensuring that the land will remain under Aboriginal control unless strict guidelines for sale are met.

There is a need for a new balance to be struck between security and utility of Aboriginal landholdings. We need to balance the need for security for future generations and utility for the present generation. Professor Marcia Langton, a long-time Aboriginal campaigner for her people's land rights, speaks about the revitalisation of the issue: 'People need the power to have a say about their land titles, what happens on their land, how many houses are built and where, what businesses are established, doing what, and where, and they need that power here in their own homeland.'[70] The law needs to take into account the decline in the spiritual connectedness with land of an increasing number of Aboriginal claimants who would like to use their traditional lands for economic enterprises whether conducted by themselves or others. Constitutional change is just a part of the mix in getting right the balance between security and utility of Aboriginal lands and maximising the realistic life choices for Indigenous Australians so that, like the descendants of Neville Bonner, they might live in a stable society, recognised as equals, and the proud custodians of their cultures and heritage, whether they live in a high-rise city apartment or out bush on their traditional country.

CHAPTER 7

ABORIGINAL CONCERNS ABOUT DISCRIMINATION AND ADVERSE TREATMENT

Disappointment with the 1967 constitutional change to the 'race power'

When Aboriginal groups are dissatisfied with the actions of politicians responding to issues unique to Aboriginal Australia, they sometimes have recourse to the courts. As the High Court has developed the jurisprudence of Aboriginal rights, recognised by the common law and created by Commonwealth statute, Aboriginal advocates have developed two strong concerns that have become the focus for arguments in favour of amendment to the Constitution.

In the absence of a constitutional bill of rights, Aborigines have to depend on the *Racial Discrimination Act 1975 (RDA)* to protect them from racially discriminatory acts by government. But they have learned that this act of the Commonwealth Parliament operates only to invalidate the legislation of state parliaments. That is because a valid act of the Commonwealth Parliament always overrides an act of a state parliament if there be a conflict between the two. The Commonwealth Parliament remains free to override its own *RDA* at whim. That is because a later, more specific act of parliament overrides an earlier, more general act if there be a conflict between the two. This has occurred particularly when the Commonwealth has come to legislate for native title in the wake of the *Mabo* and *Wik* decisions. In 1993 and again in 1998, the Commonwealth Parliament passed laws dealing with native title, and some provisions of those laws were arguably racially discriminatory and not consistent with the *RDA*.

The second concern has been that early in the development of the High Court jurisprudence of section 51(26) of the Constitution, people were lulled into thinking that the Commonwealth Parliament legislating for Aborigines under this race power could, or at least would, legislate only for their benefit and not to their detriment. And yet Sir Robert Menzies, our most constitutionally savvy prime minister, had always warned of the risk of detrimental laws being made. That is why he was not minded to support the referendum question, which then awaited proposal in 1967 by his successor Harold Holt. In 1998, when considering legislation aimed at precluding any further heritage investigations that might hold up the construction of the controversial Hindmarsh Island Bridge in South Australia, the High Court made it clear that the parliament could legislate adversely as well as benignly to local Aboriginal interests. There was no restriction on Parliament winding back a law that had conferred a benefit on Aborigines. Until then, many Aboriginal leaders presumed that the 1967 referendum conferred power on the Commonwealth Parliament to legislate only for the benefit of Aborigines and Torres Strait Islanders when legislation was race-specific to them.

It is one thing for a parliament to wind back or restrict a special benefit that it previously gave to Aborigines, and another for a parliament to legislate outright contrary to the interests and wishes of an Aboriginal group. Those agitating for greater constitutional change would like to see the *RDA,* or at least its key principles, binding and restricting the Commonwealth Parliament as well as the state parliaments. They would also like to guarantee as far as possible that the Commonwealth Parliament be able to legislate specifically for them as a racial group only when that would be beneficial for them, and not when it could be adverse to their interests or contrary to their wishes.

The Expert Panel set up in 2011 to advise the Gillard Government on how best to recognise Aborigines and Torres Strait Islanders in the Constitution recommended two ways of correcting these problems. First, it suggested that the Commonwealth's race power (section 51(26)) could be reworded and confined with a preambular statement acknowledging 'the need to secure the advancement of Aboriginal and Torres Strait Islander peoples'. Second, it suggested a broad constitutional prohibition of racial discrimination that would apply to the Commonwealth as well as the states and territories but would permit 'measures for the purpose of overcoming disadvantage' or 'ameliorating the effects of past discrimination'. It would also permit Commonwealth or state measures 'protecting the cultures, languages or heritage of any group'.[1]

Both suggestions are deeply flawed. There is no way the High Court will start second-guessing the Commonwealth Parliament on measures aimed at the advancement of Aboriginal communities or individuals. The court would be hard-pressed to develop the complex jurisprudence of anti-discrimination law without the detail of the *RDA* and the *International Convention on the Elimination of All Forms of Racial Discrimination* (*ICERD*), which have been judicially scrutinised now for 40 years in Australia. There would be some years of uncertainty as the High Court worked out a way of determining the limits of its second-guessing a parliament on what is discriminatory behaviour as stipulated in the Constitution, and what was the parliament's purpose in passing a discriminatory law.

One person's commitment to advance a disadvantaged group is another person's evidence of paternalism or commitment to subsume individual rights to the public good. The proposed new constitutional provision would be a one-line entry: 'Thou shalt not discriminate.' The 24-page *RDA*, with the accompanying 13-page *ICERD*, contains far more detail than that. The key provisions of the *RDA* do not even use the word 'discriminate'. Under the *RDA*, there is no general right to equality or right not to be discriminated against. If a person of one race enjoys any of the rights enumerated in the *ICERD* 'to a more limited extent than persons of another race', then the Commonwealth law kicks in to ensure that the person of that first race enjoys those rights to the same extent as others. Those rights may include the right of drinkers to own property (their beverages of choice) on an Aboriginal community as well as the right of other community residents 'to security of person and protection by the State against violence or bodily harm, whether inflicted by government officials or by any individual, group or institution'. Is a legislative limit on the first right appropriate in order to enhance the enjoyment of the second right? Or is any limit on the first right discriminatory? It is novel territory in Australia to transform these into constitutional questions.

Even if lawyers could agree on the likely effect of these proposals for constitutional change, the outcomes will be shrouded in such uncertainty that there could be no realistic expectation that the Australian voters would, by a super-majority, hand resolution of these issues carte blanche from the parliaments to the courts. Ultimately, the High Court might decide that a simple constitutional ban on race discrimination, with exceptions for affirmative action and cultural protection, does no more and no less than constitutionalise the existing *RDA* and *ICERD*. Then again, individual justices might take a long time to reach that position. Others might find it an untenable position, given that a constitutional provision is not to be interpreted in light of international instruments such as the *ICERD*. It is to be interpreted as a free-standing constitutional text.

Unfortunately the Expert Panel failed to heed the advice of Bob Ellicott, who as attorney-general successfully steered the three 1977 referendum questions to success. He warned the panel in his submission, 'In my view, for a referendum proposal to have a substantial chance of acceptance, it should contain no element of possible substantial confusion on legal or other grounds or of the proposal possibly undermining existing rights particularly State rights.'[2] A brief look at the key High

Court cases in the last 30 years highlights the complexity and uncertainty that would be unleashed by the Expert Panel's proposals on racial discrimination.

In 1982, the High Court for the first time had to rule on the constitutional validity of the *RDA*. The Commonwealth's Aboriginal Land Fund Commission had wanted to purchase the Archer River Pastoral Holding in Cape York for the benefit of John Koowarta and his people, who were the traditional owners of the land. The commission had entered into a written agreement with the lessees of the lease. The Queensland Government refused to transfer the lease. The Queensland minister acted in accordance with Cabinet policy. Explaining his refusal to transfer the lease, the minister wrote, 'The Queensland Government does not view favourably proposals to acquire large areas of additional freehold or leasehold land for development by Aborigines or Aboriginal groups in isolation.' The Queensland Cabinet had considered the transfer of the Archer River Pastoral Holding and formally decided:

1. That Cabinet's policy regarding Aboriginal reserve lands ... remain unchanged.
2. That in accordance with such policy and as it is considered that sufficient land in Queensland is already reserved and available for use and benefit of Aborigines, no consent be given to the transfer of Archer River Pastoral Holding No. 4785 to the Aboriginal Land Fund Commission.

By the narrowest majority of four to three, the High Court upheld the validity of the *RDA*, not as an exercise of legislative power under section 51(26) but as a valid exercise of legislative power under the external affairs power (section 51(29)). The court held that the parliament had power to make laws with respect to any matter when those laws faithfully reflected the provisions of an international treaty to which Australia was a party. The Commonwealth had signed *ICERD* on 13 October

1966 and ratified it on 30 September 1975. So now the Commonwealth Parliament had the power to enact a law that faithfully replicated the key provisions of the convention. In one of his last decisions before becoming governor-general, Sir Ninian Stephen deftly summed up the outcome of the case:

> The Minister was quite right in the view he took of the consequence were he to grant his approval. His withholding of approval, once explained by reference to the settled policy of his Government, amounted to a refusal to permit that to occur and accordingly constituted a refusal to permit persons, then possibly unknown to him but who in fact included Mr. Koowarta, to occupy land by reason of their race.[3]

The *RDA* could not be classified as a law made under section 51(26) because as Chief Justice Gibbs put it, 'A law which applies equally to the people of all races is not a special law for the people of any one race.'[4] Though there was no need to determine the limits of section 51(26) in this case, Sir Ninian Stephen did make an observation that triggered the first awareness that the race power might not always be exercised for the benefit of Aborigines: 'I regard the reference to special laws as confining what may be enacted under this paragraph to laws which are of their nature special to the people of a particular race. It must be because of their special needs or because of the special threat or problem which they present that the necessity for the law arises.'[5] Justice Lionel Murphy thought that the race power granting the Commonwealth Parliament the power to make laws for the people of any race could be exercised only for the benefit of the race specified in any Commonwealth legislation: 'In paragraph (26) "for" means "for the benefit of". It does not mean "with respect to", so as to enable laws intended to affect adversely the people of any race.'[6]

A year later, the High Court needed to consider again the race power (section 51(26)) in the *Tasmanian Dam* case.[7] The Commonwealth

Parliament had enacted the *World Heritage Properties Conservation Act 1983* to restrain the Tasmanian Government and their Hydro-Electric Commission from proceeding with a dam that would have threatened Aboriginal sites and heritage. Once again the Commonwealth relied upon the race power as well as the external affairs power. This time the court saw the race power as having some work to do in providing a constitutional basis for the Commonwealth legislation. A majority (justices Mason, Murphy, Brennan and Deane) upheld the Commonwealth law. Justice Mason made it clear that any law made under the race power could be either restrictive or benign for people of the race. He picked up on the idea floated by Sir Ninian Stephen in *Koowarta* and said, 'Its terms are wide enough to enable the Parliament (a) to regulate and control the people of any race in the event that they constitute a threat or problem to the general community; and (b) to protect the people of a race in the event that there is a need to protect them.' Justice Murphy maintained the same view as he did in *Koowarta*. He said, 'A broad reading of this power is that it authorises any law for the benefit, physical and mental, of the people of the race for whom Parliament deems it necessary to pass special laws.'[8] Justice Brennan said:

> No doubt paragraph (26) in its original form was thought to authorize the making of laws discriminating adversely against particular racial groups. The approval of the proposed law for the amendment of par. (26) by deleting the words 'other than the aboriginal race' was an affirmation of the will of the Australian people that the odious policies of oppression and neglect of Aboriginal citizens were to be at an end, and that the primary object of the power is beneficial. The passing of the *Racial Discrimination Act* manifested the Parliament's intention that the power will hereafter be used only for the purpose of discriminatorily conferring benefits upon the people of a race for whom it is deemed necessary to make special laws.[9]

This was stirring rhetoric that gave heart to many Aboriginal advocates. But it should be noted that Brennan did not say that the sole object of the power was beneficial, only that its primary object was beneficial. In a similar vein, Justice Deane said:

> As Professor Sawer comments, the architects of the Constitution paid no attention at all to the position of the Aboriginal people of Australia. Their express exclusion from the provisions of s.51(26) could not be attacked as adversely discriminatory since that grant of power was primarily seen as a power to permit adverse discrimination against the people of a particular race rather than as a power to pass a law for the benefit or protection of such people. As it became increasingly clear that Australia, as a nation, must be diminished until acceptable laws be enacted to mitigate the effects of past barbarism, the exclusion of the people of the Aboriginal race from the provisions of s.51(26) came to be seen as a fetter upon the legislative competence of the Commonwealth Parliament to pass necessary special laws for their benefit. The referendum of 27th May, 1967, deleting the reference in s.51(26) and deleting s.127 altogether, was carried by an overwhelming majority of the voters in every State of the Commonwealth. The power conferred by s.51(26) remains a general power to pass laws discriminating against or benefiting the people of any race. Since 1967, that power has included a power to make laws benefiting the people of the Aboriginal race.[10]

After the High Court's 1992 *Mabo* decision, the Commonwealth and state governments all needed to consider their response to native title so that they could return certainty to all other titles while also respecting native title and designing procedures to allow native titleholders to negotiate with others having an interest in their lands, especially miners. Prime Minister Paul Keating invested great energy in the design of the Commonwealth's *Native Title Act 1993* (*NTA*). Prior to the election that year, he conducted broad-ranging consultations. After winning the election, which he described as 'the sweetest victory of all', he set about formulating legislation that could pass the Senate, where the balance of power was held by the Greens and the Tasmanian senator Brian Harradine. In Western Australia, Richard Court's government decided that it would try and get around the proposed federal scheme by passing its own law, which replaced common law native title with a statutory entitlement to ongoing land use. Richard Court's claim was that there would then be no surviving common law native title in Western Australia on which any Commonwealth scheme would be able to operate.

The High Court was called upon to determine the validity of both schemes in *Western Australia* v *The Commonwealth*.[11] It struck down the Western Australian law and upheld the Commonwealth *NTA*. The Court found that the race power provided the constitutional basis for the Keating legislation. The whole bench, except Justice Dawson, who was the only judge in *Mabo* not to find that common law native title survived the assertion of British sovereignty, wrote a joint judgment in which they considered the reach of the race power. In doing so, they took into account what their predecessor Sir Ninian Stephen had said about the special needs or special threat of a racial group providing the particular necessity as the occasion for a special law within the race power. They said:

> If ... the requirement that a law enacted under s.51(26) be special were held to evoke a judicial evaluation of the needs of the people of a race or of the threats or problems that confronted them in order to determine whether the law was, or could be deemed to be, 'necessary', the Court would be required to form a political value judgment. Yet it is clear that that judgment is for the Parliament, not for the Court.[12]

The judges did leave in abeyance the question of whether the court might ever need to examine Parliament's judgment of necessity 'against the possibility of a manifest abuse of the races power'. There was no suggestion of such abuse in this case. The court was in no doubt that the *NTA* was a 'special' law, 'in that it confers uniquely on the Aboriginal and Torres Strait Islander holders of native title (the "people of any race") a benefit protective of their native title'.[13] That was the only task the court needed to perform. 'Whether it was "necessary" to enact that law was a matter for the Parliament to decide and, in the light of *Mabo (No 2)*, there are no grounds on which this Court could review the Parliament's decision, assuming it had power to do so.'[14]

Aboriginal advocates were worried that the court was indicating its unwillingness to buy into political value judgments about Parliament's decision to legislate in a manner not approved by affected Aborigines. The court would only consider upsetting Parliament's assessment of a law's necessity if there were evidence of manifest abuse of power. But even then the court might decide not to intervene.

Even more troubling for Aboriginal advocates was the court's matter-of-fact assessment that the *NTA*, being a later, more specific Commonwealth law, would prevail over the *RDA* if there were to be any conflict between the two. During the negotiation of the *NTA*, there had been detailed discussions about how to deal with native title, which may have existed on land that had been used for other purposes after the passage of the *RDA* in 1975. The High Court's basic approach in *Mabo* was that common law native title would have existed on most, if not all, lands on the Australian continent prior to 1788. After the assertion of British sovereignty, native title was progressively extinguished whenever the crown granted title such as freehold or an exclusive lease over land to any other person or when the crown used the land for a purpose inconsistent with the continuation of native title, for example the building of a post office or the dedication of a road. Prior to the *RDA*, native title was very fragile. It could be extinguished at whim by the crown, without consultation and without compensation. But after 1975, native title was at least protected from further state action because the *RDA* required that native titleholders enjoy their rights to property at least to the same extent as other property holders. So if other property holders, whether freeholders or leaseholders, were entitled to consultation and compensation before compulsory acquisition of their interests for a legitimate public purpose, and not just for transfer to another person, native titleholders would enjoy the same protection.

What then was the situation for native titleholders whose interests in land had been extinguished between 1975 and 1993 if their titles had been extinguished not for some public purpose but in the course of granting title to another person or corporation? And what was the situation for those property owners and miners who had been granted interests in land that the Crown had not dealt with before 1975? It was possible that their interests were invalid. At the very least, they might be liable for paying compensation to native titleholders who had lost their interests in their traditional country. The *NTA* contained a series of provisions dealing with these 'past acts' on native title land, ensuring validity and security for those who had obtained titles from the crown. The preamble of the *NTA* stated, 'The needs of the broader Australian community require certainty and the enforceability of acts potentially made invalid because of the existence of native title. It is important to provide for the validation of those acts.'

The Aboriginal advocates convinced the Keating Government to insert section 7(1) of the *NTA*, which provided: 'Nothing in this Act affects the operation of the *Racial Discrimination Act 1975*.' This was basically a face-saver for the government and the Aboriginal advocates during the negotiation of the legislation. The court was quite curt: 'It is difficult to identify the legal purpose which this provision is intended to serve. It does not affect the validation of past acts: section 7(2) expressly so declares.'[15] Section 7(2) provided: 'Subsection (1) does not affect the validation of past acts by or in accordance with this Act.'

The Keating Government rightly took pride in the fact that the *NTA* overall provided additional benefits to Aboriginal native titleholders than those they had obtained from the High Court in the *Mabo* judgment. The preamble of the *NTA* stated that the law was intended for the purposes of the *RDA* 'to be a special measure for the advancement and protection of Aboriginal peoples and Torres Strait Islanders, and is intended to further advance the process of reconciliation among all Australians'. But there was no getting away from the fact that some specific provisions in the *NTA* were designed to strip back the common law rights of the native titleholders for the benefit of other persons, such as miners who had been granted titles over native title land after the *RDA* came into force in 1975. Those specific provisions had to override the *RDA* so that the miners were guaranteed certainty of title without native titleholders being able to go back to court and argue that the mining interest was invalid because it had been granted in a racially discriminatory way. The native titleholders would have been able to argue that an equivalent mining interest would not have been granted over someone else's freehold title, so that it would be discriminatory to validate the mining interest granted over native title land even if compensation were payable.

During the 1993 negotiations with the Keating Government, the *RDA* was the great Aboriginal bargaining chip. It is what gave them a place at the table. For the first time in history, they actually sat at the Cabinet table and negotiated with government. The Aboriginal leaders could have walked away any time, saying that they were not interested in any native title legislation. They could have been satisfied just with ongoing protection of their native title by the *RDA*. Any government proposing legislation in response to the High Court *Mabo* decision, stripping back the protection of the *RDA* without consent or adequate consultation with Aboriginal groups, would have been seen to be unprincipled. The High Court later explained the negotiated outcome:

> The relationship of the *Native Title Act* with the *Racial Discrimination Act* has two aspects: first, the *Native Title Act* validates or permits the validation of past acts that were not of full force and effect because of the

operation of the *Racial Discrimination Act*; second, the *Native Title Act* affords protection to the holders of native title who heretofore have been protected by ... the *Racial Discrimination Act*, the regime established by the *Native Title Act* being more specific and more complex than the regime established by the *Racial Discrimination Act*.[16]

Other than the treatment of past acts, the High Court did not see anything in the *NTA* discriminating adversely against Aboriginal native titleholders. Even if there were inconsistencies between the two acts, the court said that 'both Acts emanate from the same legislature and must be construed so as to avoid absurdity and to give to each of the provisions a scope for operation'. If there were a direct conflict, the way to go was clear: 'The general provisions of the *Racial Discrimination Act* must yield to the specific provisions of the *Native Title Act* in order to allow those provisions a scope for operation.'[17]

When the Howard Government came to amend the *NTA* in the wake of the *Wik* decision and in conformity with its election promise of bucketloads of extinguishment, it too had to deal with a hostile Senate. This time the balance of power was in the hands of just one man, Senator Brian Harradine. Responding to Aboriginal requests, Harradine sought an improvement of the provisions, setting down the relationship between the *RDA* and the *NTA*. The most that government would agree to was the new section 7:

(1) This Act is intended to be read and construed subject to the provisions of the *Racial Discrimination Act 1975*.

(2) Subsection (1) means only that:
   (a) the provisions of the *Racial Discrimination Act 1975* apply to the performance of functions and the exercise of powers conferred by or authorised by this Act; and
   (b) to construe this Act, and thereby to determine its operation, ambiguous terms should be construed consistently with the

> *Racial Discrimination Act 1975* if that construction would remove
> the ambiguity.
>
> (3) Subsections (1) and (2) do not affect the validation of past acts or
> intermediate period acts in accordance with this Act.

Once again, there was no way that the government would permit the operation of the *RDA* to jeopardise the certainty given to past acts by the operation of the *NTA*.

If it so wished, the Commonwealth Parliament could specify that a particular function or power to be exercised under a later Commonwealth law, including an amendment of the *NTA*, was to be performed contrary to the *RDA*. In 1993 and 1998, the parliament was happy to ensure compliance with the *RDA* as much as possible while delivering certainty in relation to past acts and then in relation to the later created 'intermediate period acts', which occurred between 1 January 1994 and 23 December 1996.

The issue came to a head in the 1998 Senate debate on the Howard amendments. The Greens and the Democrats on the crossbenches wanted an amendment to ensure that the *RDA* prevailed over the *NTA* in all circumstances. This became known as 'the clause buster', in the sense that if the *RDA* were to prevail over every single clause of the *NTA* then there would be clauses of the *NTA* that no longer meant or achieved what they stated. For example, a clause of the *NTA* might purport to validate a mining title granted over native title land after 1975. But by applying the *RDA* to the clause, the mining title would be no more valid than if the government had purported to grant it over someone's freehold land without consultation or consent. The Democrats proposed this amendment:

> (1) To avoid doubt, it is expressly declared to be the intention of the Parliament that the provisions of the *Racial Discrimination Act 1975* shall prevail over any provisions of this *Native Title Amendment Bill 1997*.

> (2) Nothing in the *Native Title Amendment Act 1997* shall be taken to authorise any conduct, whether legislative, executive or judicial, that is inconsistent with the provisions or operation of the *Racial Discrimination Act 1975*.[18]

The government rejected this proposal out of hand. Senator Nick Minchin, the special minister of state, had the carriage of the legislation in the Senate on behalf of the government. He told the Senate:

> We are not prepared, as we have said many times, to open up an unholy uncertainty in the whole operation of the *Native Title Act* by subjecting it to the *Racial Discrimination Act* because, as you well know, the thousands of leases and licences et cetera that are and will be issued under the *Native Title Act* would each and severally be subject to potential challenge as being inconsistent.[19]

Just as significantly, the Labor Opposition could not see its way clear to support the Democrat amendment. Senator Nick Bolkus, who led the opposition during the debate, told the Senate that the Labor Party did not support the amendment because of its 'so-called clause-busting capacity'.[20] Senator Minchin acknowledged that the Labor Party 'was keen to ensure that this section was not the so-called clause buster, and we accept that you do not want this clause to have this effect'.[21] Senator Bob Brown, the leader of the Greens, was greatly upset by Senator Harradine's government-backed amendment, pointing out, 'Racially discriminatory provisions in this legislation will not be affected by this amendment. That is why the Greens tried to have what were called clause busting provisions.'[22] In government and in opposition, no major political party has had the least interest in legislating clause-busting provisions, making the *RDA* trumps in all circumstances. A constitutional guarantee of non-discrimination is a clause buster of nuclear proportions! It's just not on.

The Howard Government when elected in 1996 not only wanted to wind back some of the native title gains provided by Paul Keating's original *NTA*, they also thought the Hawke and Keating Labor governments had been too deferential to Aboriginal claims and perceptions on a number of policy fronts. They had been long dissatisfied with the protracted inquiries conducted into Aboriginal claims about sacred sites in the vicinity of the proposed Hindmarsh Island Bridge in South Australia.

The Commonwealth Parliament passed the *Hindmarsh Island Bridge Act 1997*, which had the effect of removing the area from any further investigation under the *Aboriginal and Torres Strait Islander Heritage Protection Act 1984*. This was a Commonwealth law that did not purport to do anything for the benefit of Aborigines. It just took away the special protection that had been provided for Aboriginal sacred sites. The general protective regime was left in place for all sacred sites. It just could not be invoked in the vicinity of the proposed Hindmarsh Island Bridge. The lawyers for Doreen Kartinyeri and the other Ngarrindjeri women claiming the existence of sacred sites at the proposed bridge site submitted to the court that the circumstances surrounding the passage of the 1967 referendum 'favoured, if they did not require, a construction of section 51(26) in its amended form which would support only those special laws which were for the "benefit" of the indigenous races'.[23]

Chief Justice Brennan and Justice McHugh thought the matter was fairly straightforward: 'the Parliament exercised its power under section 51(26) to enact the *Heritage Protection Act* and it has had at all times the same power to amend or repeal that Act. As the *Bridge Act* has no effect or operation other than reducing the ambit of the *Heritage Protection Act*, section 51(26) supports it.'[24] They thought it unnecessary and misleading to inquire into the nature of the power conferred by section 51(26) for the purposes of determining the validity of the *Bridge Act*: 'The *Bridge Act* can have no character different from, and must have the same validity as, the *Heritage Protection Act*.'[25] Ultimately, Justice

Gaudron reached the same conclusion but not before stating that 'it would be irrational and, thus, a manifest abuse of the races power if Parliament were to enact a law requiring or providing for the different treatment of the people of a particular race if it could not reasonably form the view that there was some difference requiring their different treatment'.[26]

Justices Gummow and Hayne went into more detail and put paid once and for all to the argument that a valid law would need to be for the benefit of Aborigines. They surveyed the history of the 1967 referendum campaign and the act of the Commonwealth Parliament preceding the popular vote:

> The circumstances surrounding the enactment of the 1967 Act, assuming regard may properly be had to them, may indicate an aspiration of the legislature and the electors to provide federal legislative powers to advance the situation of persons of the Aboriginal race. But it does not follow that this was implemented by a change to the constitutional text which was hedged by limitations unexpressed therein.[27]

Their honours observed that there was not a 'No' case put to the electors and that the 'Yes' case was largely confined to federalism issues, making it clear that the Commonwealth would now have power to act in relation to Aborigines wherever they lived, that the states would not lose their powers, and that the Commonwealth intended to co-operate with the states. 'It did not speak of other limitations upon the nature of the special laws beyond confirming that they might apply to the people of the Aboriginal race "wherever they may live" rather than be limited to the Territories.'[28] The judges thought that the omission of any mention of 'benefit' was 'consistent with a wish of the Parliament to avoid later definitional argument in the legislature and the courts as to the scope of its legislative power. That is the effect of what was achieved.'[29] Justice Kirby was a lone voice delivering a spirited dissent, analysing the political background to the 1967 referendum and concluding that the *Bridge Act* was 'detrimental to, and adversely discriminatory against, people of the Aboriginal race of Australia by reference to their race. As such it falls outside the class of laws which the race power in the Australian Constitution permits.'[30]

In light of these High Court decisions, the Expert Panel convened by Prime Minister Gillard thought there was 'little reason to doubt that the far-reaching judicial deference to the legislative judgment of Parliament concerning the merit of proposed laws, including their supposed beneficial effect in favour of Aboriginal and Torres Strait Islander peoples, is very likely to be followed for the foreseeable future'.[31] On this, the panel was undoubtedly correct.

Aborigines and Torres Strait Islanders can expect that any law made specifically about them by the Commonwealth Parliament will be upheld by the High Court as a valid exercise of power under the existing section 51(26), provided only that the law relates to some valid ground of discrimination between Aborigines or Torres Strait Islanders and others. Questions of benefit or detriment are academic once the parliament has passed the law. They are political rather than legal questions. If a new Commonwealth law is in conflict with the *RDA*, the new law will prevail because it is more recent and more specific. The Expert Panel thought this problem worthy of constitutional correction.

The panel asserted, 'By operation of the *Racial Discrimination Act* and section 109 of the Constitution, the States and Territories are already effectively subject to a constitutional prohibition on legislative or executive action which discriminates on the ground of race.'[32] But this is just not so. The states are effectively subject to a prohibition imposed by the Commonwealth Parliament. There may be circumstances when the Commonwealth Parliament thinks that the lifting of the prohibition is in the public interest, as both the parliaments dominated by the Keating and Howard governments did in passing native title legislation. Each time, the Commonwealth Parliament effectively suspended the *RDA*, allowing state parliaments and state governments to validate past acts, including the grant of state land titles between 1975 and 1993, without any cost or inconvenience to other landholders who took title from the crown in good faith unaware that native title existed or could have existed. Panel member Professor Megan Davis asserts that the *RDA* 'has quasi-constitutional status and binds the states and territories'.[33] This assertion overstates the binding nature of the *RDA* on the states and territories. The *RDA* binds the states and territories except when the Commonwealth Parliament decides to loosen the bond, as it has twice and for good reason when legislating for a comprehensive national native title regime in 1993 and 1998. Unlike the *RDA*, a constitutional ban on discrimination could never be lifted no matter what the public interest agreed by the major political parties. Those who favour a constitutional ban on racial discrimination ought to be supportive of the clause busters previously proposed by the Greens and Democrats against the sustained opposition of the Liberal, Labor and National parties, regardless of who is occupying the treasury benches.

Later state laws are not able to override the *RDA*. The states cannot discriminate against Aborigines or single them out for 'special' treatment unless the discrimination or special treatment can be classed as a special measure taken for the sole purpose of securing adequate advancement of Aborigines. Any state measure must be necessary to ensure equal enjoyment or exercise of human rights. There is much more scope for the High Court to scrutinise such laws made by state parliaments than Commonwealth laws made under the race power. But even here, Aboriginal advocates have been disappointed in the court's failure to overturn the assessments made explicitly or implicitly by parliaments. Often the cases have involved state schemes for limiting access to alcohol on Aboriginal communities.

In June 2013, the High Court of Australia delivered the final judgment on the long-running dispute about restrictive alcohol laws applied to Palm Island, just off the Queensland coast near Townsville and home to one of Australia's largest Aboriginal communities. In *Maloney* v *The Queen*, the High Court upheld the validity of a Queensland scheme that restricted alcohol sales and possession in the community. Joan Maloney was prosecuted for being in possession of two bottles of spirits because only mid-strength beer was authorised under the liquor plan, which had been put in place by the licensing authority after consultations with community groups, including the locally elected council. Each resident could have up to 11.25 litres of beer with less than 4 per cent alcohol content. Maloney accepted the need for an alcohol-management plan but she did not agree to the specific details of what had been put in place. There was division in the community about the appropriate way forward. Both the Queensland and Commonwealth governments submitted to the High Court that the laws were not racially discriminatory because they were targeted at communities with a demonstrated need for restrictive laws for the maintenance of peace and security in those communities, regardless of race. Governments argued that race was irrelevant. The High Court received evidence that the 'harm levels in the communities subject to regulatory amendment range from 7.5 times to 13.6 times Queensland's expected number of hospital admissions for assault; and from 11.2 times to 24.6 times the expected number of reported offences against the person'.[34]

The High Court, as the Queensland Court of Appeal had previously done, surveyed the detailed history of attempts by the Queensland Government to come to terms with the high levels of alcohol abuse and violence on Aboriginal communities. In December 1998 the state's minister for women's policy had established an Aboriginal and Torres Strait Islander Women's Task Force on Violence, which provided a detailed report on women's concerns in these communities. In 2001, Justice Tony Fitzgerald, at the request of the Queensland Government, undertook the Cape York Justice Study in relation to Indigenous communities on the Cape. Both these studies 'concluded that harmful levels of alcohol consumption in remote Indigenous communities were the chief precursor to violence, crime, injury and ill-health in these populations'.³⁵ Tony Fitzgerald had reported:

> While extremely high alcohol consumption levels continue there is little realistic possibility that the many other areas requiring change can be addressed. In these communities where massive alcohol consumption has virtually become the norm rather than aberrant behaviour, the policy focus should be on facilitating long-term generational and cultural change, rather than just on modifying the practices of individual drinkers. Such change cannot be viewed in isolation, but needs to be addressed as part of wider community development. Band-aid solutions to the alcohol problem in Cape York can no longer be justified. The consequences of excessive alcohol consumption over several generations have been so destructive and all pervasive that the capacity of Cape York Aboriginal families and communities to deal with them has been severely compromised.³⁶

All but one of the High Court judges rejected the government claims that the law was racially non-discriminatory. They preferred to classify the Queensland law as racially discriminatory on its face but classifiable as a special measure 'taken for the sole purpose of securing adequate advancement' of a disadvantaged racial group. This gave rise to claims in the national media by some Aboriginal residents of Palm Island and their elected representatives that they had not been adequately consulted about what was necessary for their 'advancement'. The National Congress of Australia's First Peoples had been given leave to appear in the case and had submitted that the scheme was discriminatory. Jody Broun, co-chair of the congress, claimed on the eve of the High Court hearing that the case would 'provide the opportunity for a watershed moment in Australian history' and would go to the heart of the conversation on constitutional reform requiring Aboriginal recognition and the scrapping of all race-based provisions. She asked, 'Is there any place in a modern Australia for race-based laws which do not treat everyone equally under the law?'[37] There are two great lines in the judgment of one of the newest High Court justices, Justice Stephen Gageler. He said, 'Geography was used as a proxy for race,' and 'Racial targeting is not negated by some persons of other races being caught in the net.'[38] But then he joined the majority claiming that such discriminatory laws were special measures.

All judges found a need to look back to one of the first racial discrimination cases dealing with state laws, *Gerhardy* v *Brown*, in which Justice Brennan, when inquiring whether a measure is a special measure being 'for the sole purpose of securing adequate advancement of the beneficiaries in order that they may enjoy and exercise equally with others human rights and fundamental freedoms', said, 'The wishes of the beneficiaries for the measure are of great importance (perhaps essential) in determining whether a measure is taken for the purpose of securing their advancement.'[39] In recent years, various international human rights bodies have been insisting that special measures be put in place only with the consent of the affected group. In the *Maloney* decision, Chief Justice Robert French said that you could not insist that consultation be a definitional element of a 'special measure'. He went on to say:

> Nor can such a requirement be imported into a text which will not bear it by the subsequent opinions of expert bodies, however distinguished. That being said, it should be accepted, as a matter of common sense, that prior consultation with an affected community and its substantial acceptance of a proposed special measure is likely to be essential to the practical implementation of that measure. That is particularly so where, as in this case, the measure said to be a 'special measure' involves the imposition on the affected community of a restriction on some aspect of the freedoms otherwise enjoyed by its members. It can also be accepted, as the appellant submitted, that in the absence of genuine consultation with those to be affected by a special measure, it may be open to a court to conclude that the measure is not reasonably capable of being appropriate and adapted for the sole purpose it purports to serve.[40]

The chief justice was convinced that there had been adequate consultation over the years. Not surprisingly, there was a division of opinion in the Palm Island community about appropriate measures for dealing with grog abuse and senseless violence. The Explanatory Notes to the 2002 *Communities Liquor Licences Act* recorded that the Fitzgerald Inquiry had found, 'Alcohol abuse and associated violence are so prevalent and damaging that they threaten the communities' existence and obstruct their development.'[41] Before recommending the making of a regulation declaring a community area to be a restricted area, the minister had to be satisfied that the declaration was necessary to achieve the objective. She was required to have consulted with the community justice group for the community area about the declaration or must have considered any recommendation made by that group.

All six sitting High Court justices wrote separate opinions in this case, highlighting that there is not yet a settled jurisprudence in the court for resolving these vexed issues. All members of the court were agreed that there was no need for a unanimous acceptance of a liquor scheme by the affected community for it to pass muster as a special measure. Justice Kenneth Hayne postulated two questions for determining if the Queensland regulation and scheme constituted a special measure:

> First, is there a racial group members of which are not enjoying or exercising human rights or fundamental freedoms to the same extent as persons of another race? Second, do the impugned provisions have a sole purpose which is conducive to the equal enjoyment and exercise of rights and freedoms by the relevant racial group and could the same goals be achieved to the same extent by some alternative means?[42]

The grog management plan for Palm Island was designed to minimise the adverse effects of alcohol-fuelled violence. Such minimisation is essential if members of the Palm Island community are to be assured equal enjoyment and exercise of their rights and freedoms with other citizens. Justice Susan Crennan noted that no party to the litigation had suggested:

> ... that the legislative purpose of protecting a community, and all individuals within that community, against alcohol-related violence and public disorder was an illegitimate or tendentious legislative purpose, or that it failed to qualify as a purpose capable of securing 'the adequate development and protection' or the 'adequate advancement' of the community, and its individuals, in relation to security of the person and freedom from violence.[43]

Justice Kenneth Hayne noted, 'Those who live in fear of violence cannot exercise their rights. They are not free. And when the violence is spread through a community, the members of that community cannot exercise their rights and freedoms.'[44]

The High Court judge with most experience in cases challenging community alcohol management plans is Justice Patrick Keane, who spent years on the Queensland Court of Appeal. He was not yet a member of the High Court when the *Maloney* appeal was heard. In one of the earlier Queensland cases, Keane waxed eloquent as to why judges should be wary about treading where parliaments have already sweated much in trying to set the appropriate balance. He wrote:

> It is difficult to accept that the opportunity to buy alcohol from a licensed local government authority can rationally be placed on the same level of importance in any frame of reference with the right of women and children to live free of alcohol-fuelled violence. But even if one assumes that the appellants are able to point to a fundamental freedom or human right with an equal claim to protection with the fundamental human right of women and children to be protected against personal violence, the striking of the balance between these competing human rights is ... a matter for the legislature.[45]

Keane is adamant that the *RDA* and international human rights instruments, such as *ICERD*, do not take away from a state parliament 'the power and responsibility to strike the balance of priority between human rights and freedoms where those rights are in competition with each other'.[46] None of these instruments sets down a hierarchy of rights that instructs the decision-maker to give priority to any particular right over another when these rights come into conflict. It is difficult to counter Keane's claim that such a specified hierarchy would be expected if the final word were being left to unelected judges. Keane staked his claim for the supremacy of parliament: 'Absent some statement of priority in the instruments which establish the rights and freedoms protected by section 10 of the *RDA*, a decision-maker forced to choose between right and right is left to make an intuitive value judgment between incommensurable values. This kind of judgment is readily seen to be the province of the legislature rather than the judiciary.'[47]

Those who advocate a broadening of judicial scrutiny of these sorts of provisions would do well to consider Justice Keane's passionate plea for the unheard victims of alcohol abuse on Aboriginal communities:

> The women and children whose right to personal freedom from violence apparently motivated the enactment of the amending Act were not represented as parties in this Court. This Court's attention was focused, inevitably, upon the parties before it and their arguments in support of their rights and interests. It is, I think, salutary to reflect upon the possibility that had the women and children of Aurukun and Kowanyama the means and opportunity to make their voices heard in litigation, their argument might have been that, prior to the enactment of the amending Act, the law which then permitted the appellants to act as licensed suppliers of alcohol infringed s 10 of the *RDA* in that, the then law, by permitting local authorities to act as licensed suppliers of alcohol, their rights under Article 5(b) of *CERD* were enjoyed by them to a lesser degree than by other residents of Queensland. The legislature

is not subject to the constraints which are inherent in the judicial process. The legislature is able to vindicate the interests of the women and children of Aurukun and Kowanyama who were not represented in this Court. The Court should recognise that its ability responsibly to set aside the balance struck by the legislature between competing human rights is limited by the very nature of the judicial process. The Courts' ability to set aside the political judgment of the legislature is necessarily confined to cases where the balance struck by the legislature is demonstrably unreasonable in the sense that no reasonable legislature could have struck that balance.[48]

No doubt there are many lawyers, and perhaps even many citizens, who disagree with Keane's preference for parliament to make these policy choices. But there will be many more citizens who agree that this is a matter for parliaments and not for the courts.

There is no way that the Australian public will vote for a referendum proposal that transfers the responsibility for these decisions from the parliaments to the courts, particularly at this time when there is no clarity from the judiciary about how they would exercise this newfound power. When presently asked to determine whether a law is a special measure under the *RDA*, the High Court has always shown great deference to the assessment of Parliament. A constitutional change would provide a new basis for urging the court to abandon that deference. It would call into question the assessment made by Justice Brennan in 1985:

> But the character of a special measure depends in part on a political assessment that advancement of a racial group is needed to ensure that the group attains effective, genuine equality and that the measure is likely to secure the advancement needed. When the character of a measure depends on such a political assessment, a municipal court must accept the assessment made by the political branch of government which takes the measure. It is the function of a political branch to make the assessment. It is not the

function of a municipal court to decide, and there are no legal criteria available to decide, whether the political assessment is correct. The court can go no further than determining whether the political branch acted reasonably in making its assessment.[49]

Were the Constitution amended to prohibit racial discrimination except when a measure was passed for the purpose of overcoming disadvantage or ameliorating the effects of past discrimination, the court would be constitutionally obliged to make the political assessment that was previously made by the parliament. On past form, most judges would be uncomfortable performing this task.

There is another problem with inserting a general constitutional ban on discrimination. Most of the cases that are not special measures cases tend to deal with section 10 of the *RDA*, which operates as a top-up provision, ensuring that members of a racial group presently enjoying one of the specified rights in Article 5 of *ICERD* to a lesser extent than do other persons will be guaranteed equal enjoyment of that right. Article 5 of *ICERD* contains a diffuse catalogue of rights. For the purposes of the alcohol cases, the courts have had to consider the following rights from that catalogue:

- The right to equal treatment before the tribunals and all other organs administering justice;
- The right to security of person and protection by the State against violence or bodily harm;
- Political rights, in particular the rights to participate in elections, to take part in the Government, and to have equal access to public service;
- The right to own property alone as well as in association with others;
- The right of access to any place or service intended for use by the general public, such as transport, hotels, restaurants, cafés, theatres and parks.

As Justice Keane often points out, there is no hierarchy of these rights stipulated in the international covenant. When it comes to an individual claiming the right to own property in the form of alcohol, how is that right to be weighed against the right of non-drinking adults and children to security of person and protection against violence or bodily harm? Presumably some of the assessment procedure for trading off one right against another is relevant when it comes to determining whether a parliament or government has discriminated against a person or group on the grounds of race. In *Maloney*, Justice Hayne warned, 'Reference to "discrimination" is apt to bring with it conceptual baggage which has been developed in other contexts but which finds no reflection in the text of section 10.' Section 10 deals with the enjoyment of rights and 'questions about the *enjoyment* of rights do not necessarily require consideration of the concepts that are often associated with "discrimination"'.[50]

Were a referendum inserting a general prohibition of racial discrimination in the Constitution to be carried, the High Court over the next 10 or 20 years might well develop a jurisprudence for such a prohibition very similar to that which has been developed with the more detailed *RDA*, which invokes the catalogue of specified rights listed in *ICERD*. But then again it might not. It is this sort of uncertainty that kills off referenda proposals and for good reason.

Were the Expert Panel's constitutional prohibition of racial discrimination to be carried, no doubt the National Congress of Australia's First Peoples would hope that it would mean no more alcohol-management plans or federal intervention strategies, except those that are sought by local communities and ensure treatment similar to that received by all other local communities. Some governments and Aboriginal advocates for marginalised adults and children would hope that it would permit parliamentary experiments with initiatives aimed at improving the lives and service delivery for those who suffer most from alcohol abuse. As we have seen in recent years, not all hopes can be realised. If the Expert Panel's referendum proposal were carried, no legal expert could accurately predict which stream of hope would be more likely to prevail. The outcome would depend more on the unelected judges of the High Court than on the elected members of territory, state and Commonwealth parliaments. There is no way that a majority of people in four of the six states will support such uncertainty, for such questionable long-term gain. No doubt the assurance will be offered that the ultimate High Court outcomes will be similar to what we have now. In which case, why run the risk of jeopardising the whole referendum next time around?

At the 2014 Garma Festival in Arnhem Land, there was a spirited disagreement between Aboriginal leaders Nova Peris and Noel Pearson about income management and the issuing of a 'basics card', which restricts the class of groceries that can be purchased by social welfare recipients living on remote Aboriginal communities. Peris was shocked to enter a shopping centre in Alice Springs to find two different queues: one for those with the basics card, and one for other shoppers. Those in the basics card queue were all Aboriginal. They had to stop and wait, and have their groceries checked. In the other queue, 'people happily went through and used their ATM cards to purchase whatever they wanted'. Pearson retorted:

> There's another kind of queue I've seen. It's the queue in front of the ATM machine in front of the bowls club where the poker machines are. What do we do about that queue? And the question about intervention, what do we do when the kids aren't getting a feed, they're being neglected? Should we intervene and support that family, to make sure there's food in the fridge and they're able to tackle their addictions, by making sure the rent is paid and the food is in the fridge or do we stand back and say, no, we won't intervene and we'll let the child protection authorities intervene later and take the kids away? Which one do we want: to support the family so that the child can stay with Mum and Dad or stand back and let the child be taken away by the child protection authorities? In Cairns you

drive around the streets, the buses have got advertisements asking for more foster parents, asking people from the public to volunteer as foster parents to take Aboriginal children in. So, you know, it's easy to say we shouldn't intervene and so on but by us not intervening, that's why our children are 3% of the population but 60% of the kids in child protection not living with their mothers and fathers.[51]

There is little to be gained from a referendum that, if successful, would grant the High Court more say about which queue is preferable. That is primarily a matter for elected parliaments being attentive to local Aboriginal communities and their leaders, with the High Court continuing to ensure compliance with the *Racial Discrimination Act*.

CHAPTER 8

THE ROAD TO RECOGNITION FOR INDIGENOUS AUSTRALIANS
Moving beyond the 2012 Expert Panel report

In November 2010, Prime Minister Julia Gillard, when establishing the Expert Panel to consult the community and advise her government on how best to provide constitutional recognition of Indigenous Australians, said, 'The First Peoples of our nation have a unique and special place in our nation. We have a once-in-50-year opportunity for our country.'[1] The Expert Panel included four members of parliament, the co-chairs of the National Congress of Australia's First Peoples, the Aboriginal and Torres Strait Islander Social Justice Commissioner from the Australian Human Rights Commission, and 15 other members, of whom seven were Indigenous Australians. There was good representation of the nation's respected Aboriginal leadership, including Patrick Dodson, Marcia Langton and Noel Pearson. There was good legal and political experience in members like Fred Chaney, Henry Burmester, Mark Leibler and Megan Davis.

The government did a fine job in putting together a broadly representative and competent panel. The panel was very thorough in their community consultations, social research, polling and canvassing of options. The panel even used the services of Mark Textor, who claims to be 'Australia's most successful pollster and campaign strategist', and who often works for the Liberal Party. The Expert Panel recommended four changes to the Constitution:

Item 1

Repeal section 25 and section 51(26) of the Constitution.

Item 2

Insert after section 51:

Section 51A   Recognition of Aboriginal and Torres Strait Islander peoples

Recognising that the continent and its islands now known as Australia were first occupied by Aboriginal and Torres Strait Islander peoples;

Acknowledging the continuing relationship of Aboriginal and Torres Strait Islander peoples with their traditional lands and waters;

Respecting the continuing cultures, languages and heritage of Aboriginal and Torres Strait Islander peoples;

Acknowledging the need to secure the advancement of Aboriginal and Torres Strait Islander Peoples;

the Parliament shall, subject to this Constitution, have power to make laws for the peace, order and good government of the Commonwealth with respect to Aboriginal and Torres Strait Islander peoples.

Item 3

Insert after section 116:

Section 116A   Prohibition of racial discrimination

(1) The Commonwealth, a State or a Territory shall not discriminate on the grounds of race, colour or ethnic or national origin.

(2) Subsection (1) does not preclude the making of laws or measures for the purpose of overcoming disadvantage, ameliorating the effects of past discrimination, or protecting the cultures, languages or heritage of any group.

Item 4

Insert as section 127A:

Section 127A Recognition of languages

(1) The national language of the Commonwealth of Australia is English.

(2) The Aboriginal and Torres Strait Islander languages are the original Australian languages, a part of our national heritage.

In response to the Expert Panel's report, the parliament set up a Joint Select Committee on Constitutional Recognition of Aboriginal and Torres Strait Islander Peoples. On 13 February 2013, the parliament marked the fifth anniversary of the National Apology adopted by the parliament on the motion of Prime Minister Kevin Rudd and supported by the leader of the opposition Brendan Nelson. Their successors, Julia Gillard and Tony Abbott, spoke well when passing the largely symbolic *Aboriginal and Torres Strait Islander Peoples Recognition Act 2013* through the House of Representatives. Prime Minister Julia Gillard said she was 'conscious that on this special anniversary we acknowledge the courage that enabled Kevin Rudd to offer the apology and the generosity of spirit that enabled Indigenous Australians to accept it'.[2] She spoke of the Constitution as 'a foundation document [which] is more than just a set of rules and procedures. It can articulate a nation's sense of itself. But our nation cannot articulate such a sense of self when there are still great unanswered questions in our midst. How do we share this land and on what terms? How adequate are our national laws and symbols to express our history and our hopes for the future?' She said, 'No gesture speaks more deeply to the healing of our nation's fabric than amending our nation's founding charter.'[3]

With a real show of bipartisanship, Tony Abbott complimented Prime Minister Gillard on her 'fine speech' and without any fanfare proceeded to put to rest John Howard's previous critique of the 'black armband view' of history. He told Parliament:

Australia is a blessed country. Our climate, our land, our people, our institutions rightly make us the envy of the earth, except for one thing – we have never fully made peace with the First Australians. This is the stain on our soul that Prime Minister Keating so movingly evoked at Redfern 21 years ago. We have to acknowledge that pre-1788 this land was as Aboriginal then as it is Australian now. Until we have acknowledged that we will be an incomplete nation and a torn people. We only have to look across the Tasman to see how it could have been done so much better. Thanks to the Treaty of Waitangi in New Zealand two peoples became one nation. So our challenge is to do now in these times what should have been done 200 or 100 years ago to acknowledge Aboriginal people in our country's foundation document. In short, we need to atone for the omissions and for the hardness of heart of our forebears to enable us all to embrace the future as a united people.[4]

We should not underestimate the significance of John Howard's successor giving credit to Paul Keating for his 1992 Redfern speech, before then invoking the Treaty of Waitangi and calling for atonement. Abbott was indicating that he wanted to put to rest some of the divisions of the past in this vexed policy space. He was anxious to put some daylight between his perspective on Australian history and that enunciated by John Howard so strongly early in his prime ministership, when Howard had told Parliament:

I profoundly reject ... the black armband view of Australian history. I believe the balance sheet of Australian history is a very generous and benign one. I believe that, like any other nation, we have black marks upon our history but amongst the nations of the world we have a remarkably positive history. I think there is a yearning in the Australian community right across the political divide for its leader to enunciate more pride and sense of achievement in what has gone before us. I think we have been too apologetic about our history in the past ... I believe it is tremendously important that we understand, particularly as we approach the centenary of the Federation of Australia, that the Australia achievement has been a heroic one, a courageous one and a humanitarian one.[5]

Abbott was the first Liberal leader to praise Keating's Redfern speech. He was the first Liberal leader to distance himself deliberately from Howard's all too trenchant and one-dimensional rejection of that view of Australian history which acknowledged the lack of heroism, the lack of courage and the lack of humanitarianism that had marked so much of the relations between Aborigines and the new settlers.

A new generation of Aboriginal and Torres Strait Islander leaders were gathered in the public gallery for the speeches by Gillard and Abbott. Together with those novices were many of the leaders from earlier campaigns over the Northern Territory land rights legislation, *Mabo*, *Wik*, native title and reconciliation. They then proceeded to the National Press Club, which was packed to the rafters with supporters. The speakers at the press club were two of the up-and-coming Aboriginal and Torres Strait Islander leaders, Tanya Hosch and Jason Glanville. Each of them spoke proudly of their diverse heritage. One of the benefits of the National Apology has been that Australians with a mixed heritage are now proud to proclaim it and share its benefits with the community at large. Tanya Hosch told the Press Club:

> I was blessed to be raised in a family that is a model for the kind of nation I want Australia to be. A family where race isn't a divide, but an enricher. A family that is proud of the many strands of its heritage, and particularly of our Indigenous heritage. A family that integrates the best of all of our traditions and cultures, and which has nurtured me to play a part in bringing about this big moment in the life of our nation.[6]

Jason Glanville told the story of his great-grandmother leaving the mission with her two-year-old child and coming to the New South Wales country town of Cootamundra and building a home. He said:

In the Cootamundra Town Hall, where once my great-grandmother was barred from being able to vote, a stained glass window now hangs. It's a picture story. In it, she is telling bedtime stories to her grandchildren in the language of their ancestors. The town that once excluded this amazing Aboriginal woman has now immortalised her remarkable story. At long last, it has recognised her. And regards her story as a source of pride. It's time our Constitution did too.[7]

I was privileged to sit at a table with many erstwhile campaigners like Lowitja O'Donoghue, Patricia Turner and Jackie Huggins. But, alas, Karen Middleton was the only serving journalist from the Press Gallery to join the Press Gallery Committee in asking questions.

Later in the week, I was dining with some of the gallery and I quizzed them about their absence. They told me there was not the same interest in Indigenous affairs nowadays. There is plenty of work to be done if a referendum is to get up in the foreseeable future. In the wake of the National Apology, there is a new generation of Indigenous Australians able to show us the way. Tony Abbott summed up the task and hinted at the obstacles ahead when he told Parliament, 'I believe that we are equal to this task of completing our Constitution rather than changing it.'[8] Hopefully there will be unanimity about what constitutes completion and there will be patience and respect shown as we discuss what constitutes change to be put off for another time.

By mid-March 2013, both houses of parliament had unanimously passed the *Aboriginal and Torres Strait Islander Peoples Recognition Act 2013*, which provided the following recognition and acknowledgment:

> The Parliament, on behalf of the people of Australia, recognises that the continent and the islands now known as Australia were first occupied by Aboriginal and Torres Strait Islander peoples.
>
> The Parliament, on behalf of the people of Australia, acknowledges the

continuing relationship of Aboriginal and Torres Strait Islander peoples with their traditional lands and waters.

The Parliament, on behalf of the people of Australia, acknowledges and respects the continuing cultures, languages and heritage of Aboriginal and Torres Strait Islander peoples.[9]

Significantly these three acknowledgments follow the wording proposed by the Expert Panel in the first three clauses of Item 2, their proposed preamble for section 51A. The parliament made no attempt to replicate the fourth and problematic acknowledgment proposed by the panel, namely 'the need to secure the advancement of Aboriginal and Torres Strait Islander peoples'.

Since 1967, the Australian Constitution has made no reference to Aborigines and Torres Strait Islanders. Prior to 1967, people 'of the aboriginal race' were exempt from the Commonwealth Parliament's power to make laws with respect to the people of any race 'for whom it is deemed necessary to make special laws'. Most Australians agree that it is time for the Constitution to make positive reference to Indigenous Australians, thereby affirming their status as equal citizens free from all vestiges of racial discrimination and recognising their status as Indigenous Australians. This can be done only by a super-majority of the Australian population at referendum with a majority of voters in four of the six states voting in favour. This will happen only if any proposal is supported and strongly backed by the major political parties. We are now a sufficiently mature, inclusive democracy to know this cannot happen unless a broad range of respected Indigenous leaders has first approved the proposal. The report of the Expert Panel, including key Aboriginal leaders and academics and members of the major political parties, has been a useful starting point. But it is not the final word.

The panel was right to recommend that any referendum proposals be first discussed with all political parties, the independent members of the Commonwealth Parliament, and also 'State and Territory governments and oppositions', and that any referendum proceed only 'when it is likely to be supported by all major political parties, and a majority of state governments'.[10] The atmosphere in our last national parliament was so toxic that these conditions could not possibly have been met before the 2013 election, as the panel had hoped. It is even doubtful that they could be met before the 2016 election.

Uncontroversially, the panel recommended that the outdated and now racist section 25 of the Constitution be repealed. As previously noted, section 25 provides:

> For the purposes of the last section, if by the law of any State all persons of any race are disqualified from voting at elections for the more numerous House of the Parliament of the State, then, in reckoning the number of the people of the State or of the Commonwealth, persons of that race resident in that State shall not be counted.

The previous section, 24, deals with the House of Representatives being composed of members chosen directly by the people of the Commonwealth. Gone are the days when the Commonwealth would contemplate people of a particular race being excluded from the franchise for the House of Representatives. That much is easy. All fair-minded Australians agree that section 25 should go. This has been common ground since at least 1988, when the Constitutional Commission recommended the repeal of the section. It is a racially discriminatory provision, and there is no way that any state parliament would disqualify people of a particular race from voting in the future. To give them their due, they did not in the past either.

The Expert Panel presented the government with a number of measures going beyond the simple 1988 suggestion of the Constitutional Commission that section 25 be repealed and section 51(26) be replaced with a power to make laws 'with respect to Aborigines and Torres Strait Islanders'. The panel suggested the splendid words of acknowledgment now replicated in the *Aboriginal and Torres Strait Islander Peoples Recognition Act 2013*. The panel proposed that these words form the preamble for a new section 51A. I wonder whether they would not be better placed at the beginning of the Constitution, as an 'Acknowledgment' of the place of Indigenous Australians in the nation's history, life and future.

At the moment the Constitution does not contain any preamble. The Constitution is attached to the UK Parliament's *Commonwealth of Australia Constitution Act 1900*, which has its own preamble in a form often used in acts of the Imperial Parliament. If Australia were ever to become a republic, presumably we will replace this act, which contains what by then will be a very outdated preamble and covering clauses that will have outlived their purpose. It would be time to cut the apron strings, placing the Australian Constitution on its own feet. But that is not part of the present enterprise.

The Constitution, like an act of parliament, could have its own preamble. This has been a constant refrain in the national conversation ever since the 1998 Constitutional Convention. At the 1999 referendum, John Howard proposed his favoured preamble drawn up in consultation with the poet Les Murray.[11] It did not win favour with the public. Since then, people have looked at the possibility of a preamble making the appropriate acknowledgment of Indigenous perspectives and aspirations. A preamble generally has no legal effect but it may be referred to by judges if it were to assist in resolving an ambiguity in the text in the body of the legal instrument that follows. A preamble would usually state the reasons for wanting to enact a law or Constitution. That is why we need to be wary about a preamble that deals only with Aboriginal matters. There were many other reasons for enacting the Constitution 114 years ago. If we were now to draw up a preamble that stated a comprehensive vision of the society desired in the twenty-first century, then we would need to consider including all manner of things, including for example a commitment to gender equality. When people speak about an Aboriginal preamble, they are really talking about the need for the Constitution to begin with an acknowledgment of the key facts about the Aboriginal past, present and future. Thus my suggestion: an Acknowledgment, rather than a preamble.

When considering section 51(26), the Expert Panel recommended a provision stipulating that the Commonwealth Parliament have power to make laws 'with respect to Aboriginal and Torres Strait Islander peoples'. Aware that such a law-making power theoretically could be exercised in a manner adverse to Aboriginal and Torres Strait Islander peoples, the panel suggested a special preamble for the newly proposed Section 51A, 'acknowledging the need to secure the advancement of Aboriginal and Torres Strait Islander peoples'. I am one of those contemporary Australians who flinches at the word 'advancement'. It is a very 1970s word. From where and to what would the parliament be wanting to 'advance' Aborigines? Especially in Queensland, there are Aborigines and Torres Strait Islanders who still have vivid, negative memories of Sir Joh Bjelke-Petersen's Department of Aboriginal and Islander Advancement.

A broad preambular statement before any new head of power will be an invitation to disaffected citizens to litigate policy questions in the High Court. For example, groups opposed to Commonwealth legislation introduced by governments of both political persuasions in the last ten years enacting the ongoing 'federal intervention' on Aboriginal communities in the Northern Territory will turn to the High Court, expecting a ruling on whether the legislation is classifiable as being for the 'advancement' of Indigenous Australians. What criteria could a court possibly develop to answer such a question?

Those worried that the Commonwealth Parliament might use any 'race power' to act against the interests of Aborigines might want to consider whether the legislative power should relate to objects rather than people. The Commonwealth Parliament could be given the power to make laws with respect to the cultures, languages, heritage and relationships with lands and waters of Aboriginal and Torres Strait Islander peoples. This approach would be consistent with what Noel Pearson was suggesting in his 2013 Whitlam Lecture:

> The Race Power should also be removed and replaced with a new power allowing governments to pass necessary laws specific to Indigenous affairs, such as Native Title and Indigenous heritage laws. But the new Indigenous affairs power should not be used for matters of public welfare or government socioeconomic assistance. These matters should be addressed not on the basis of Indigeneity, but on the basis of individual and community need. This distinction should be made clear in the drafting.[12]

Another of the Expert Panel's suggestions is the previously noted inclusion of a one-line prohibition of racial discrimination: 'The Commonwealth, a State or a Territory shall not discriminate on the grounds of race, colour or ethnic or national origin', followed by a double-pronged special measures exemption for laws or measures having 'the purpose of overcoming disadvantage, ameliorating the effects of past discrimination, or protecting the cultures, languages or heritage of any group'. As previously noted, I had happily proposed a similar clause in 1996. But in the wake of the *Wik* decision and the subsequent 1998 Senate debate, I changed my mind.

The panel was wanting to address the Aboriginal concerns about the perceived failure by the High Court to rein in the parliament from legislating in a discriminatory or adverse fashion. In the previous chapter, I analysed the key High Court decisions and indicated what a quantum leap it would be to make this constitutional change. Understandably, many other members of the community will look to lawyers not to answer whether racial discrimination is a good or bad thing, nor to work out what special measures should be permitted, but rather to determine whether the insertion of such a clause in a Constitution that does not have a comprehensive bill of rights is workable and desirable, and to assess how such a stark constitutional provision would sit with the complex plethora of existing laws prohibiting such discrimination.

As previously noted, the general non-discrimination clause proposed is a variant on the equality right proposed by the 1988 Constitutional Commission, which tentatively put forward a comprehensive constitutional bill of rights. That commission first proposed a modest improvement and expansion of the few rights presently articulated in our Constitution and then the addition of a new Chapter VIA of our Constitution entitled 'Rights and Freedoms'. They treated these two matters separately,

> ... not because the rights and freedoms presently protected by the Constitution are necessarily more important than rights and freedoms which are not so protected, but rather because we estimate that proposals to alter the Constitution to strengthen and extend existing guarantees are less likely to be misunderstood than proposals to incorporate in the Constitution guarantees of an entirely new kind.[13]

In the end, not even the former set of rights won acceptance at the 1988 referendum; and of course, no major political party was interested in proposing the latter.

The 1988 Constitutional Commission was very upfront in acknowledging:

> ... that adoption of the proposed new Chapter on Rights and Freedoms would produce a radical change in the effective allocation of power as between Parliaments and the Courts. It would, for practical purposes, give to the courts the last word in deciding a wide range of issues which are sometimes very difficult and which many people regard as issues which cannot always be satisfactorily resolved by methods of adjudication.[14]

They proposed an equality right with some similarity to the non-discrimination clause proposed by the Expert Panel. But it was part of a general chapter of proposed amendments on rights and freedoms. A comparison of the two proposals is useful.

Each proposal provided everyone with a right to freedom from discrimination on the ground of race, colour or ethnic or national origin. The 1988 proposal also included within the right the freedom from discrimination on the ground of sex, marital status, or political, religious or ethical belief. The Constitutional Commission also proposed that the 1988 constitutional entrenchment of this right be accompanied by a reworking of section 116, which presently provides restrictions only on the Commonwealth making any law establishing any religion, imposing religious tests or observances, or prohibiting the free exercise of religion. The commission recommended that the restriction on Commonwealth intrusion into religion be applied to the executive and the judiciary and not just to parliament in its law-making function. The new broad-reaching restriction would be applied to the states and territories as well.

The 1988 proposal included a clause that provided: 'The Rights and Freedoms guaranteed by this Chapter may be subject only to such reasonable limits prescribed by law as can be demonstrably justified in a free and democratic society.'[15] It also included a clause, 'The rights and freedoms guaranteed by this Chapter do not abrogate or restrict any other right or freedom that a person may have.'[16] You need to be careful when inserting just one constitutional right in a Constitution without words of limitation for balancing all other rights. As argued in the previous chapter, when you are trying to build on the jurisprudence of the 40-year-old *RDA*, you cannot just write a one-line blank cheque for the judiciary.

We need to abandon this suggestion from the Expert Panel if we are to get to the next base for Indigenous recognition in the Constitution. I make this claim aware that the Joint Select Committee on Constitutional Recognition of Aboriginal and Torres Strait Islander

Peoples in its July 2014 interim report stated unanimously that for any referendum to be successful there would be a need for a constitutional guarantee that prevents the Commonwealth from discriminating against Aborigines and Torres Strait Islanders when making laws.[17] At the 2014 Garma Festival in Arnhem Land, Bill Shorten, Labor's leader of the opposition, threw down the gauntlet:

> Many Indigenous people have made it clear to me that they believe banning racism in our Constitution is vital. The Expert Panel on Constitutional recognition proposed a new section 116A for this very purpose. We are some way from finalising any referendum proposal. But imagine, striking out old laws tainted by imperialism and prejudice – and replacing them with a safeguard against racial discrimination. What an uplifting moment for all Australians – not just our Aboriginal and Torres Strait Islander brothers and sisters.[18]

This sounds like the promise of a constitutional clause-buster that would preclude both state and Commonwealth parliaments from ever being able to legislate provisions such as the native title amendments in 1993 and 1998, provisions aimed at providing certainty and benefits for a range of citizens, not just native titleholders. Once this proposal is closely studied by our politicians, it might win support from the Democrats and the Greens but it could not win support from the major parties if they continue to follow the cogent legal advice they each received in 1993 and 1998, trying to work out how to balance the principle of non-discrimination against the need to provide certainty of land title for all landholders in the wake of *Mabo* and *Wik*. A simple test of the resolve of our parliamentarians' commitment to constitutional entrenchment of non-discrimination (without a bill of rights) would be to ask them immediately to amend the *Native Title Act* providing, as the Greens and Democrats unsuccessfully proposed in 1998, that the *RDA* prevails over all provisions of the *Native Title Act*.

In their October 2014 progress report, the members of the joint select committee stepped back from insisting on a constitutional guarantee against adverse discrimination. It is still their preferred option but as an alternative they have suggested the vague option of 'enacting an Act of Recognition'.[19] The committee has come to appreciate that there are real problems with a freestanding constitutional ban on racial discrimination.

The Expert Panel's fourth item for consideration of constitutional amendment is the insertion of a new section 127A, recognising that English is the national language and that Aboriginal and Torres Strait Islander languages are the original Australian languages and part of our national heritage. The joint select committee has already recommended against this proposal, saying that the objective 'would be better achieved by other means'.[20]

The Expert Panel has given us some great talking points. But there is a lot more work to be done before we settle on a constitutional formula for decent and workable constitutional recognition of Indigenous Australians. The conservative side of politics has always been more successful than Labor in proposing constitutional change in Australia. That is not because Liberals or Nationals are more committed than Labor to constitutional change. The Australian Constitution is a very democratic instrument; our politicians cannot amend it without the approval of the people. The people are very unlikely to approve an amendment proposed by politicians unless both sides of the parliamentary chamber support the change. Even then, the people may suspect that the politicians are in cahoots, acting against the interests of the people.

In the field of Aboriginal affairs, a referendum proposed by an Abbott Government will be more likely to win support from the parliamentary opposition than one that would have been proposed by the Gillard or Rudd Labor governments. This has nothing to do with the personalities of the leaders; it has everything to do with the Coalition being the more difficult side of politics to bring on board with constitutional change when it is in opposition. Now is the time to move on constitutional change. The actual fiftieth anniversary of the 1967 referendum falls on a Saturday some time after the next federal election – 27 May 2017. There have been too many false starts on both sides. It is now time for both sides of the parliamentary chamber to commit themselves to a referendum after the next election, no matter which side wins government. The referendum should be held on Saturday 27 May 2017.

Prior to his winning the 2013 election, Tony Abbott spoke at the Sydney Institute and repeated some of the themes from his very welcome parliamentary speech backing the *Aboriginal and Torres Strait Islander Peoples Recognition Act 2013*. Each time, he has broken from the John Howard mould and demonstrated a bipartisan spirit by referring to Paul Keating's 1992 Redfern speech. He told the Sydney Institute, 'There may come a time, perhaps some decades hence, when we can be relaxed and comfortable about the circumstances of Indigenous Australians – but it's not now. Our failure to come to grips with this remains, in Paul Keating's resonant phrase, a stain on our nation's soul.'[21]

Having demonstrated his willingness to move beyond the anti–black armband view of history, each time he has been quick to indicate that he is not opening the Pandora's box of wide-ranging constitutional reform. The cautious sting was in the tail of his parliamentary speech: 'I believe that we are equal to this task of completing our Constitution rather than changing it.'[22] In March 2013, he underlined that caution when he told the Sydney Institute:

> An acknowledgment of Aboriginal people as the first Australians would complete our Constitution rather than change it. Aboriginal people need to know that they will never be regarded as just an historical footnote to modern Australia. Done well, such an amendment could be a unifying and liberating moment, even surpassing the 1967 change or the apology, so it's worth making the effort.
>
> Within 12 months of taking office, an incoming Coalition government would put forward a draft amendment and establish a bipartisan process

to assess its chances of success. The difficulty of crafting an amendment that satisfies Aboriginal people while reassuring the wider community that we are not creating two classes of citizen should not be under-estimated.

Australians of all political persuasions have differing views about what constitutes completion, and whether it requires any change. We need to get used to the idea that there is a divergence of Aboriginal opinion about the desirable content of the Constitution, and about how best to proceed to seek constitutional change. The 2013 election of Adam Giles, the first Aboriginal chief minister of the Northern Territory, presented the nation with an Indigenous leader who unashamedly speaks as a Liberal in the John Howard mould about Indigenous affairs. He says, 'Our future in the Northern Territory is about jobs, jobs, jobs, not welfare, welfare, welfare.'[23] He jokes that his Aboriginal father would be 'turning in his grave' to know his son was now a conservative. When working for the Howard Government, reviewing Indigenous policies, he realised that 'welfare and socialism are what's killing Aboriginal people'. Within the Indigenous communities as well as among Australians generally, there is a range of views as to what constitutes completion without substantive change of the Constitution. And there are those who think completion without real change is not worth the paper it is written on.

In his 2013 parliamentary speech, Tony Abbott pointed across the Tasman at the Treaty of Waitangi, whereby 'two peoples became one nation'.[24] Things are not that simple and complete in New Zealand. The conservative government there had to cut a deal with the Maori Party in 2008, setting up a Constitutional Advisory Panel that looked at a range of issues, including 'the role of the Treaty of Waitangi within New Zealand's constitutional arrangements'. The panel had to counter allegations that it had a secret agenda 'about making the treaty an overriding piece of law which cancels all other law out'.[25] The panel reported to the government in December 2013 and their report does not disclose any strong yearning to complete their Constitution in the near future.

In their recommendations on the Treaty of Waitangi, the panel 'invites and supports the people of Aotearoa New Zealand to continue the conversation about the place of the Treaty in our constitution'.[26] The panel had to acknowledge the tension and diversity of viewpoints in New Zealand about the Treaty, ranging from the need to base any written Constitution on the Treaty to the need to wind back the operation of the Treaty. The panel noted that 'some fear the potential undermining or negation of Treaty rights, others fear their implementation'.[27] This was their conclusion:

> The Panel acknowledges that many New Zealanders remain sceptical that the Treaty can be a constructive element of our constitution and so may be reluctant to participate in a conversation about its future. Based on the Conversation, however, the Panel believes it is not viable to wind back the clock. The Treaty is already a fundamental element of our constitutional arrangements. It would be unfair, unjust and unrealistic to go back on the commitments made to iwi and hapū by successive governments. Nor do the arguments of equality put forward by some proponents of this view sufficiently acknowledge the diversity of this country's people.
>
> The Treaty is not inherently divisive – its purpose was to establish a relationship between two peoples in one nation. Any divisions arise from a failure to meet those obligations, not from meeting them. The question is not just whether the Treaty is part of the constitution, but how it is best reflected and what we want to achieve by reflecting it.
>
> The Crown cannot turn back on the commitments made in the Treaty and subsequently without the risk of social and political tensions. Any decisions made in such a crisis situation are unlikely to be enduring.[28]

On Australia Day 2014, Tony Abbott returned to the parallel between completing the Australian Constitution and the Treaty of Waitangi. Without being critical of our Australian forebears who were products of their time, he said, 'I think that we can complete their great work in the next few years by finally doing what the New Zealanders were able to do back in the 1860s with the Treaty of Waitangi.'²⁹ In New Zealand, there is no sense of completion with the Treaty; its implementation and incorporation into the constitutional fabric of the country will long remain an ongoing contested issue. I well recall Sir David Lange, the expansive ex–prime minister of New Zealand, once laughing at us Australians during an after-dinner speech in 1989. He told us that we are always seeking the final settlement of indigenous grievances. He said the best you could ever do was seek durable agreements that lasted a generation or two. That sounds more like ongoing change than completion. There is a lot of hard work to be done to complete or change the Australian Constitution, but something should be achievable by May 2017.

The Australian Parliament's Joint Select Committee on Constitutional Recognition of Aboriginal and Torres Strait Islander Peoples convened one roundtable discussion before the 2013 election. On 30 April 2013, three Senate members of the committee were in attendance – Trish Crossin for Labor, George Brandis for the Coalition, and Rachel Siewert for the Greens. Given the political volatility in the lead-up to that election, the committee was not able to advance consideration of the issue. Following the election of the Abbott Government, the parliament agreed on 2 December 2013 that a joint committee with a similar mandate be appointed to inquire into and report on steps that can be taken to progress towards a successful referendum on Indigenous constitutional recognition. As previously noted, the eight-member committee is chaired by government member Ken Wyatt, an Aboriginal man from Western Australia. The deputy chair of the committee is opposition senator Nova Peris, an Aboriginal woman from the Northern Territory who, as a delegate at the 1998 Constitutional Convention, said that she 'would like to see a model for a republic that gives an indigenous woman – perhaps my daughter – the chance of becoming our head of state'.³⁰ The committee is considering the recommendations of the Expert Panel, but is not bound or constrained by those recommendations. The committee will present its final report by 30 June 2015.

At the April 2013 roundtable, Mick Gooda, the Aboriginal and Torres Strait Islander Social Justice Commissioner who had been a member of the Expert Panel, said, 'You can take some hints from the panel's foreword, that we understood that there would be a political process following the submission of our report and what we put in might not come out the same way as it was originally presented.'[31] Lisa Strelein from the Australian Institute of Aboriginal and Torres Strait Islander Studies said, 'What we should be looking for is the best option that will succeed, not the option that is most popular.'[32] Gary Highland, who had been executive officer for the Expert Panel, conceded the need for any constitutional change to be 'technically sound' but that many of the Indigenous Australians who appeared before the panel were not so much interested in legal technicality. They knew what they wanted: 'We want recognition, we do not want racism and we did not want to end up worse off as a part of this process.'[33] Tim Gartrell, the campaign director for Recognise, the people's movement set up by Reconciliation Australia to recognise Aboriginal and Torres Strait Islander peoples in our Constitution, spoke of 'the tension between trying to make the most of this historic opportunity and keeping it simple'.[34]

Senator George Brandis, who is now attorney-general, readily conceded that section 25 of the Constitution 'is obsolete really'.[35] So it is gone. Mick Gooda pointed out that the appearance of the word 'race' in the Constitution of a liberal democracy of the twenty-first century was an anomaly. Senator Brandis then posed an interesting question: 'If you want to get rid of race from the Constitution entirely then presumably that also means not having any references to a specific race, including Aboriginal and Torres Strait Islander peoples, does it not?'[36] After some discussion, Mick Gooda told the committee:

> Senator Brandis sort of hit the nail on the head for me and, without divulging what happened at the expert panel, it was always a concern to me that we were removing race and we were putting race back in for one particular group. This is what worries me. The research tells us that, if one group is seen to benefit more than anyone else in Australia, we will lose the referendum. For me, that would be the easiest thing to run a no case against – the whole lot – because we are recommending that it goes in the package.[37]

Peter Dawson, appearing for the Indigenous Youth Engagement Council, expressed reservations about the word 'advancement'. Some of their members were wary about Indigenous Australians always being seen to be disadvantaged, with a frozen socio-economic position in time.[38] In their submission, the Youth Council warned that 'advancement' could be inconsistent with the principle of self-determination. The chair of the committee, Labor senator Trish Crossin from the Northern Territory, agreed that 'advancement' 'seems a bit demeaning' and 'a bit of a put-down really'.[39]

Senator Brandis thought that the proposed section 51A with a new head of power preceded by an internal preamble in the Constitution was 'a bit of a lawyer's nightmare', although it might be seen as 'a smart political compromise'. He was adamant that the inclusion of 'advancement' in any preambular introduction of a new parliamentary power would not limit the parliament in its consideration of a proposed law and that, after all, 'what "advancement" means is always going to be subjective'.[40] He added, 'Any measure that a government takes in relation to Aboriginal and Torres Strait Islander peoples is going to represent as being for their good. Then people will argue about whether, in fact, it is for their good. And that is a policy argument.' Brandis gave an example of a conservative government wanting to cut welfare payments to Aborigines for their own good so that they might become more self-reliant. In policy terms, he suggested that this could be put as a measure for Indigenous advancement:

> Let us say you had a government that took a very, let us say, Thatcherite view of the welfare system, and the ministers in that government decided 'We're going to cut back a whole lot of welfare payments that are specifically designed to assist Aboriginal and Torres Strait Islander peoples' and their political opponents said, 'You can't do that. This is not for the advancement of Aboriginal people' and they replied, 'Yes it is, because we think the real vice in Aboriginal Australia is welfare dependency and we think this tough love will end up improving the lot of future generations of Aboriginal people.' That is a policy argument. The problem here is you are conflating a policy argument with an argument about constitutional limitations.[41]

Parliament would be hardly likely to make a law with a significant majority of members thinking or stating that they were legislating with the purpose of disadvantaging Indigenous Australians. Brandis took the example of the federal intervention on remote Aboriginal communities in the Northern Territory – a policy initiative that has been strongly debated in recent years but which enjoyed the support of Coalition and Labor governments with only minor variations to the tough laws imposed on these communities. Brandis said:

> But the parliament might have an opinion that a law was beneficial for Aboriginal people and some members of the Aboriginal community might have the view that it was against their interests. We had that very debate over the Northern Territory intervention, when the parliament was of the view that these laws were beneficial to Aboriginal people in the Northern Territory, and there were plenty of Aboriginal people in the Northern Territory who had the same view and there were plenty of people who had the opposite view.[42]

Brandis was right when he claimed, 'So just to say something is for the advancement of the Aboriginal people does not get you over the proposition that different people will have different legitimately held views about what is advancement and what is not.'[43] The realpolitik of any reform was admitted by Brandis when he warned the Aboriginal representatives at the roundtable, 'Our advice from research which tested work that Recognition Australia [sic] have done is that one thing that would kill this referendum is if its opponents are able to say that this is divisive or it provides special rights for one group of people that are not enjoyed by others. The further you go down that line, the more you give those who want to make that argument a hook.'[44]

Things did not get any easier when it came to a consideration of the proposed prohibition of racial discrimination. While providing a constitutional ban on discrimination by the Commonwealth, the states or a territory on the grounds of race, colour or ethnic or national origin, it would not preclude the making of laws or measures 'for the purpose of overcoming disadvantage, ameliorating the effects of past discrimination, or protecting the cultures, languages or heritage of any group'. Trish Crossin got it in one when she said, 'Again, I am looking at Mr and Mrs Joe Suburb, and they are going to say: "What the hell does that mean? I don't know, so I am going to vote no."' And later she said, 'This wording, though, is wording that I think ordinary Joe Blow is not going to relate to. They will say, "No, I don't get this. No."'[45] As a retiring Labor senator from the Northern Territory with a proven track record of support for Indigenous rights, Trish Crossin is close to being the canary down the mine when assessing the political utility of these sorts of suggestions. George Brandis could see exactly the same problem arising as with the 'advancement' debate:

> I would just point out to you that the qualifying words in subsection (2) of proposed section 116A really open up the same argument we were having before about advancement because, to use once again the intervention in the Northern Territory as the example here, those who thought that was a good thing would say, 'If it discriminates, then it's a measure for the

purpose of overcoming disadvantage', and people who had a different view would say, 'No, it's not. It's pure discrimination and this is a bad law.' That is going to be a policy argument.[46]

If anything, Brandis understated the likely impact of the proposed section 116A. Every Commonwealth or state law or practice dealing specifically with Indigenous persons or issues would be reviewable by a court being asked to rule whether the targeted law or measure was made for the purpose of overcoming disadvantage, ameliorating the effects of past discrimination or protecting Aboriginal culture, language or heritage. Without a constitutional bill of rights, Australians are not in the habit of routinely referring such questions to the unelected judiciary. Our preference to date has been to have elected politicians make such policy decisions and then to set up an interchange between the politicians and the judges, with the politicians ultimately having the last word. By constitutionalising these issues, we give the judges the last word.

Consider the case of a state government deciding that it will not give any further preferential treatment to outstation communities wanting health and education services delivered in circumstances – distance, remoteness and small population – in which, but for the community being Aboriginal, there would have been no prospect of such service delivery. The politicians or bureaucrats would say that such measures were not discriminatory or that if they were, they were implemented for the purpose of overcoming the disadvantage, especially to children remaining in remote, under-resourced areas with limited opportunity for education, training and 'advancement'. The government's critics would say that the measures were discriminatory and that rather than overcoming disadvantage, they would risk further contributing to disadvantage. The critics' case would be arguable, and the final decision would rest with the High Court of Australia.

The added problem and unintended consequence is highlighted by the High Court native title cases and the subsequent native title acts passed by the Commonwealth Parliament, first at the initiative of the Keating Government and then of the Howard Government. The High Court in *Mabo* found that native title existed and survived the assertion of sovereignty by the crown. It could be extinguished by the crown granting title to another person or by the crown using the land in a manner inconsistent with the continuation of native title. The High Court found that native title was very fragile until 1975 because it was so readily extinguished. With the protection of the *RDA*, native title was thereafter more secure from extinguishment by the states. But the Commonwealth Parliament was still free to deal with native title as it saw fit. During the negotiation of the native title acts, it was acknowledged that there may have been some inadvertently discriminatory dealings with some native title holdings by the new Commonwealth laws. But these discriminatory dealings were said to be offset by other provisions of the legislation. In 1993, the Keating Government was able to point to agreement to those offsets with the key Indigenous groups. None of this would have been possible if section 116A was part of the Constitution. It would have acted as a clause buster, pre-empting any trade-offs.

Indigenous supporters might think that would be all for the best. It may be, subject to two caveats. In *Mabo*, the High Court by six to one found that native title survived in some instances, enjoying the protection of the *RDA*. If the comprehensive constitutional protection were in place, it is less likely that the High Court, at least by the same majority, would have found native title to exist and survive. And it is highly improbable that the High Court, which decided by just four to three in *Wik* that native title could co-exist on a pastoral lease, would have reached the same conclusion given that it would have been impossible for even the Commonwealth Parliament to design a law that accommodated both sets of rights, unless of course the new law were to interfere with the pastoralists' rights as much as with any existing native title rights. The second caveat is that the additional complexity in native title law, should common law native title be proven to exist, would send a clarion call to the electorate not to risk this once again by carrying such a constitutional amendment. Let there be no doubt. A constitutional ban on discrimination would place in doubt the future validity of many mining and pastoral titles on native title land, which were previously validated with certainty by the Keating legislation in 1993 or the Howard legislation in 1998.

The Expert Panel's proposed section 116A obtained little support from either Crossin or Brandis. Brandis thought it 'fundamentally contradictory to have a Constitution that recognises Indigenous Australians and allows for special laws to be made in their favour, if we want to approach this from a point of view of a nation free from all forms of discrimination'. He thought there was a need to be upfront about the logical inconsistency of the task confronting the committee – a task that is 'philosophically, morally and historically supportable because of the unique place of Aboriginal and Torres Strait Islander peoples in this continent'.[47] Les Malezer, co-chair of the National Congress of Australia's First Peoples, insisted that the general prohibition on discrimination and the exemption for special measures was standard in legislation such as the *RDA* and in international instruments. Brandis was unimpressed: 'it is one thing to have a provision like that in a law that is amendable by the parliament; it is a much graver thing to have it in the Constitution, which is unlikely ever to be amended to remove it.' When considering the pragmatic politics of the matter, he was *ad idem* with Trish Crossin that such a measure would be unlikely to garner community support, as it would be 'vulnerable to opposition from those who say, "this is about giving Aboriginal people special rights that other people don't have."'[48]

By the end of the roundtable, Brandis was suggesting a way forward. Parliament has already unanimously supported the first three statements of acknowledgment and recognition as proposed in the Expert Panel's section 51A. But it has steered away from the fourth acknowledgment concerning 'advancement'. So the fourth statement should be dropped while the first three are incorporated in any referendum package. He would separate the words of acknowledgment from the clause, granting the Commonwealth power to make laws with respect to the wellbeing of Aborigines and Torres Strait Islanders. He would propose a constitutional ban on racial discrimination but make it subject to the Commonwealth Parliament's power to make laws with respect to the wellbeing of Aborigines and Torres Strait Islanders. This was his summation:

> [Y]ou do not want to entirely remove the capacity for special measures, so you introduce section 116A(1) with the qualifying words 'subject to section 51A'. That seems to me to be a logically neat package. You can tell Aboriginal people that the goal of recognition and the goal of empowerment and the capacity of the parliament to make laws for their benefit have all been achieved by this package, as well as the removal of racially discriminatory provisions from the Constitution, section 25 and section 51(26), and a general prohibition against racial discrimination in section 116A, while preserving the capacity to make special laws for their wellbeing. I think the argument you are then going to have is not going to be with the Aboriginal people; it is going to be with the general community and particularly the conservative community. The removal of subsection (2) of 116A, in my opinion, would make that argument easier for the proponents to make.[49]

Though a key member of the Expert Panel that recommended a constitutional prohibition of racial discrimination, Noel Pearson has since moved completely away from the idea of section 116A, preferring to expunge all notions of race from the Constitution. In *A Rightful Place*, his *Quarterly Essay* published in September 2014, Pearson abandons the call for a constitutional anti-discrimination provision, being prepared to rely on the *RDA* to protect against the 'illegitimate concept' of racial discrimination.[50] Instead of a constitutional prohibition on racial discrimination, he suggests 'incorporation of a requirement that indigenous peoples get a fair say in laws and policies made about us'. He proposes a new representative body for Indigenous Australians, which could ensure that they 'have a voice in their own affairs'.[51] While there is no prospect that such a body would be included in the Constitution at this time, a successful referendum could provide the impetus for the Commonwealth Parliament to institute committee processes and other safeguards requiring parliament and the executive to be more attentive to Indigenous voices when legislating and determining national policy targeted at Indigenous Australians.[52]

The fourth item put forward by the Expert Panel was the recognition of languages. George Brandis thought his side of politics would quite like a constitutional affirmation that English is the national language. Greens senator Rachel Siewart admitted that, although a member of the Expert Panel, she never liked this proposal: 'I have had people almost yelling at me about not wanting' a constitutional statement that English is the national language.[53] Brandis was sanguine about an affirmation that Aboriginal and Torres Strait Islander languages 'are the original Australian languages', but strongly contested the assertion that they are 'a part of our national heritage'.[54] It needed to be understood that such an affirmation gave no protection to these languages, nor would it add to what was already included in the preambular statement of respect for these languages. Trish Crossin doubted the need for the clause at all, and Brandis warned that it ran a real risk of causing offence to the 30 per cent of the population who were non-Indigenous and from non-English-speaking backgrounds.[55] Out in the backblocks, he foresaw scare campaigns being run by opponents claiming that the referendum, if passed, would require people to learn an Aboriginal language. I see little utility in a languages clause being inserted in the Constitution, especially if Aboriginal languages are already included in the Acknowledgment.

The Abbott team went to the September 2013 election with a policy commitment to establishing 'a special committee to progress Constitutional Recognition to be chaired by the Attorney-General, with deputy chairman to include the Minister for Indigenous Affairs and Mr Ken Wyatt AM, the first Indigenous member of the House of Representatives. Senior Indigenous leaders would also sit on the committee.' Clearly George Brandis will play a key role in determining the Abbott Cabinet's position on what provisions ultimately get put to a referendum.

On 17 December 2013, Tony Abbott spoke at a function at Mark Leibler's law firm in Melbourne with Noel Pearson in attendance. He spoke of the need for symbols in effecting national reconciliation and expressed the hope that the promised referendum would surpass the 1967 referendum and the 2008 apology in providing a unifying moment for the nation. He said, 'The best thing we could do for Aboriginal Australia right now is push on as quickly as we can with constitutional recognition. We have it in our hearts to do this.'[56] When speaking about the content of any proposed referendum, Noel Pearson observed on Australia Day 2014 that 'a new policy paradigm has become dominant, based on culture and economic development'. What is truly new since 1967 is that 'cultural identity and modern development is understood as complementary rather than anathema'.[57] Michael Dodson spoke of two objectives: 'recognise in Australia's Constitution a simple but important fact – that someone was here first'; and 'remove the discrimination that still lingers in sections of our Constitution'.[58] This can be done with an appropriate Acknowledgment, a repeal of section 25, and a rewording of section 51(26). Anything further will be piecemeal, creating additional uncertainty and complexity, transferring power from parliament to the High Court when we have not made the decision to vest the High Court with the constitutional authority to arbitrate all human rights.

Now is the time for consideration of future constitutional options. The panel appointed under the *Aboriginal and Torres Strait Islander Peoples Recognition Act 2013* to review the work of the Expert Panel and the proposals being developed by Reconciliation Australia reported to Parliament in September 2014. The panel was required to identify which proposals 'would be most likely to obtain the support of the Australian people'. The panel reported, 'Research shows that there is strong support for changes that recognise the place and history of Indigenous Australians and the removal of references to race. Australians want to address inequality in our Constitution but are wary of "special treatment" for one group of people on the basis of race.'[59] This panel and the joint parliamentary committee should be able to provide the Abbott Government with options more workable and more likely to be passed than the broad range of options proposed by the Expert Panel. What is essential is that Aborigines and Torres Strait Islanders not be left thinking that this process is simply a watering down of proposals that were appropriate.

If a cross-section of key Aboriginal leaders were to reject the revised Expert Panel proposals, there would be no point in our proceeding with putting them to a referendum. If some proposals from the Expert Panel are, as I have argued, unworkable or too uncertain in outcome, they should be abandoned. My modest suggestion is that the workable proposals put forward by the panel provide the building blocks for a successful referendum campaign.

The Expert Panel correctly set four hurdles for any referendum proposal to jump: it must contribute to a more unified and reconciled nation; it must benefit and accord with the wishes of our Indigenous peoples; it must be capable of being supported by an overwhelming majority of Australians from across the political and social spectrums; and it must be technically and legally sound.[60] Unfortunately, the Expert Panel overreached itself with its non-discrimination proposal, falling at the last two hurdles. New contorted arrangements agreed to by both sides of politics have been put in place to salvage the good aspects of the work done by the panel. There is now more work being done by another appointed panel and by a parliamentary committee. With goodwill on all sides, we will get there by 2017, with some declaring completion, and others predicting change.

In addition to the repeal of section 25, I would suggest two additional changes to the Constitution for consideration by the newly appointed panel and parliamentary committee: the addition of an Acknowledgment and the amendment of section 51(26). The first additional change draws on the words proposed by the Expert Panel in the first three paragraphs of the introduction to their proposed section 51A. The key words of the proposed Acknowledgment have already found unanimous endorsement in the Commonwealth Parliament's *Aboriginal and Torres Strait Islander Peoples Recognition Act 2013*, with the parliament speaking 'on behalf of the people of Australia'.[61] We should add this Acknowledgment at the commencement of the Constitution immediately prior to 'Chapter I: The Parliament':

> **Acknowledgment**
> We, the people of Australia, recognise that the continent and the islands of Australia were first occupied by Aboriginal and Torres Strait Islander peoples.
> We acknowledge the continuing relationship of Aboriginal and Torres Strait Islander peoples with their traditional lands and waters.
> We acknowledge and respect the continuing cultures, languages and heritage of Aboriginal and Torres Strait Islander peoples.

We should amend section 51(26) so that the Commonwealth Parliament shall, subject to the Constitution, have power to make laws for the peace, order and good government of the Commonwealth with respect to:

> the cultures, languages and heritage of the Aboriginal and Torres Strait Islander peoples and their continuing relationship with their traditional lands and waters.

This way, as a nation we might have more hope of taking what Patrick Dodson and Mark Leibler have described as the next logical next step to achieving 'full inclusion of Aboriginal and Torres Strait Islander peoples in the Constitution by recognising their continuing cultures, languages and heritage as an important part of our nation and by removing the outdated notion of race'.[62]

If these amendments are carried overwhelmingly by referendum on 27 May 2017, we should once again provide the inspiration and political imperative for our politicians to attend to the proper place for Aboriginal and Torres Strait Islander citizens in the Commonwealth of Australia, completing the task we commenced 50 years ago. Hasluck, Stanner, Dexter and Coombs would be well pleased, despite their disagreements, and all of us would owe each of them some debt.

EPILOGUE

NO SMALL CHANGE

Guaranteeing choices from
the Dreaming and the Market

When Harold Holt decided to leave Sir Robert Menzies' constitutional scepticism behind and ride the wave of popular support for constitutional change recognising the place of Aborigines in the Constitution, he carried with him a Cabinet that presumed that any constitutional change would still mean business as usual. They were of the 'completion without change' school. Paul Hasluck, the most experienced Cabinet minister in Aboriginal affairs, was left outside the tent after the referendum. Holt realised that the overwhelming support for the referendum required that he do something with a new broom. The appointment of the three-member Council for Aboriginal Affairs provided the intellectual catalyst and the prod in the side of the bureaucracy for change well beyond the bounds envisaged by the Holt Cabinet and most of the voters.

Later, prime ministers Gorton and McMahon had to wrestle with the changes without controlling the process or the outcomes. This culminated in McMahon misreading the public mood about land rights when he issued his Australia Day statement in 1972, attempting to address Aboriginal land needs and claims without going the extra step to land rights. In his caution to grant only leases or a form of title less than inalienable freehold, McMahon had drawn on the expertise of men of high degree like Richard Blackburn, Bob Ellicott, WEH Stanner,

Barrie Dexter and Nugget Coombs, but he failed to follow through their recommendations. Not even they could predict where the public mood would go. The Labor Opposition rode the crest of the wave of change in the public mood and was able to add land rights to its election policies in 1972, providing a further point of differentiation from an ageing Coalition Government.

Without the strong 1967 referendum result, Stanner, Dexter and Coombs would not have had the political capital to instigate the changes from assimilation to self-determination and from *terra nullius* to land rights. The changes came in part because the old paradigms had fractured. Showdowns such as Yirrkala and Wave Hill convinced the Australian public that local Aboriginal communities were entitled to more 'say' in what was happening on their traditional lands. The public who readily acknowledged this entitlement to more 'say' could see the case for recognising some rights of these communities to their traditional lands, especially when no other persons had yet been granted rights over those lands. The Yirrkala land rights case demonstrated that there was more than one forum where Aborigines could agitate their claims. The issue was charged with law, morality and politics. The government might exercise some control over the politics, but it had no control over the development of the common law by the courts and little control over the public discourse about the immorality of the ongoing dispossession of Aborigines who had not previously been excluded from their traditional lands. When law and public morality are out of synch, there is room in the political process for change.

We the Australian people are again considering how to amend the Constitution for the benefit of Indigenous Australians. We are at a stage in history when we acknowledge as a nation the right of Aborigines and Torres Strait Islanders to their traditional lands where other Australians have not been granted titles to those lands. We also acknowledge that there are still ongoing effects of dispossession and that it is our national responsibility through our Commonwealth Parliament to address those ongoing effects. In the past we justified the failure to recognise land rights with the assurance that such recognition might arrest rather than facilitate assimilation, which was a well-intentioned policy, designed for the good of Aborigines. Now we acknowledge that property rights are not contingent on benign social outcomes. And assimilation cannot occur effectively except by choice.

Once land rights have been acknowledged and granted as best they can be, given the history that has intervened, we come back to the question about how best to maximise realistic life choices for Aborigines and their communities. They need to be at the table, being heard and represented in our courts and parliaments, in our public debates and in the internal deliberations of interdepartmental committees of government. Governments and Aborigines need to work together to weigh the conflicting goods, knowing that not every public service can be provided on a remote outstation and that the performance of spiritual responsibilities for land is less likely to occur when traditional owners and their descendants are living in a town or city. Sir William Deane, when a High Court judge, set the challenge:

> One cannot but be conscious of the diversity of the views that have been expressed about the identification, extent and resolution of the problems involved in the mitigation of the effects which almost two centuries of alien settlement have had on the lives and culture of the Australian Aboriginals. Even among men and women of goodwill there is no obvious consensus about ultimate objectives. At most, there is a degree of consensus about some abstract generalised propositions: that, within limits the Aboriginals are entitled to justice in respect of their homelands; that, within limits, those Aboriginals who wish to be assimilated within the ordinary community should be assisted in their pursuit of that wish; that, within limits, those Aboriginals who desire separately to pursue and develop their traditional culture and lifestyle upon their ancestral homelands should be encouraged, assisted and protected in that pursuit and

development. It is in the identification and resolution of the problems involved in determining 'the limits' that consensus breaks down and that the greatest difficulties lie. The cause of the Aboriginal peoples will not be advanced if those difficulties are ignored. To the contrary, the difficulties will only be exacerbated.[1]

As governor-general, Deane delivered the inaugural Vincent Lingiari Lecture and distinguished 'complete assimilation and integration' from the 'general acceptance of the Aboriginal right of choice'. The dispute was no longer about the right of Aborigines to 'effective choice' but about the level of government support warranted for giving effect to the choices made. He rightly claimed, 'It is now accepted by persons of goodwill that those Aborigines who desire separately to pursue and develop their traditional culture and lifestyle within our multi-cultural nation should be encouraged, assisted and protected in that pursuit and development, and that those who wish to be assimilated within the ordinary community should be assisted in that wish.'[2] Assimilation is no longer a bad word; neither is self-determination. Neither term captures the complexity of what needs to be negotiated, informing the choices of Indigenous persons and of governments.

After the forthcoming referendum process, Aborigines and Torres Strait Islanders will be freshly engaged with governments as they determine how best to live as people of the Dreaming and of the Market, being open as Noel Pearson would say to positive experiences from Cape York to New York. They will wrestle with how best to ensure the balance between security and utility of land; to deliver essential services to remote communities while providing opportunities for children in those communities to receive good education, health and opportunity; to protect community members from alcohol abuse while acting in a racially non-discriminatory way towards heavy drinkers; and to close the gap while respecting the choice of those individuals and communities who want to pursue the lifestyle of their ancestors. In his 1958 presidential address to the Australian and New Zealand Association for the Advancement of Science, Stanner spoke of 'Continuity and Change among the Aborigines', theorising about the 'quite marked disinterest the Aborigines have shown and still show in so many kinds of European activity'. That disinterest has lessened in most Aborigines and Torres Strait Islanders. But there is a healthy scepticism and a hope that the old ways of the ancestors might still have value for those whose pace of life has changed. Stanner invited his non-Indigenous readers to consider a few of the contrasts:

> We are deeply interested in futurity. We try to foresee, forestall and control it by every means from astrology and saving to investment and insurance: the Aborigines are scarcely concerned with it at all; it is not a problem for them. Their 'future' differentiates itself only as a kind of extended present, whose principle is to be continuously at one with the past. This is the essence of the set of doctrines I have called The Dreaming. Our society is organised by specialised functions which cut across groups; theirs on a basis of segmentary groups … Theirs is a self-regulating society knowing nothing of our vast apparatus of state instrumentalities for authority, leadership and justice. Ours is a market civilisation, theirs not. Indeed there is a sense in which The Dreaming and The Market are mutually exclusive. What is The Market? In its most general sense it is a variable locus in space and time at which values – the values of anything – are redetermined as human needs make themselves felt from time to time. The Dreaming is a set of doctrines about values – the values of everything – which were determined once and for all in the past. The things of the Market – money, prices, exchange values, saving, the maintenance and building of capital – which so sharply characterise our civilisation, are precisely those which the Aborigines are least able to grasp and handle. They remain incomprehensible for a long time. And they are among the foremost means of social disintegration and personal demoralisation.[3]

Stanner concluded:

> If we tried to invent two styles of life, as unlike each other as could be, while still following the rules which are necessary if people are to live together at all, one might well end up with something like the Aboriginal and the European traditions.[4]

Most Indigenous Australians maintain a foot in each of these worlds. Some, like Liam Marrantya to whom this book is dedicated, end up without a foothold in either. For the majority in the third century since the assertion of British sovereignty, the Market is now more determinative of their identity than the Dreaming, with the result that there is less strained straddling to be done. Perhaps it is my own religious impulse, but I think it is impossible for most human beings to straddle two such different worlds without a deep, nurtured and nurturing spirituality. Those of us who have never had to straddle two such diverse worlds are not those best placed to advise how to overcome the 'social disintegration and personal demoralisation', especially in a society as secular and materialist as Australia. Governments that place a deep faith in the Market and in community 'interventions' enforced by instrumentalities of the state may be well intentioned, but unless they consult and work collaboratively with local Aboriginal leaders, who carry the deep spiritual insights of the Dreaming, they will be sure to make big mistakes, waste precious resources and forfeit trust.

If the forthcoming referendum is overwhelmingly successful, as it should be and as it needs to be, the Abbott Government and their successors will have to call key Aboriginal and Torres Strait Islander leaders to the table to assess the way forward. This time the key people called to the table will not be exclusively, or even chiefly, those with the attributes of Stanner, Dexter and Coombs. The successors to Charles Perkins will take their rightful place. Even if their political masters think the referendum does nothing more than complete the Constitution, they will know from what occurred between 1967 and 1972 that an overwhelming expression of the will of the people for just dealing provides a springboard for realigning law, morality and politics. The public, the parliament, the courts, the tent embassy and the bureaucracy will each have their role. There will be no substitute for those with the wisdom, compassion and connections to create the spaces for reform, as did Stanner, Dexter and Coombs. What will matter is not so much the legal reach of the constitutional reform but the breadth and depth of the public sentiment in support.

With an increasing and secure land base, Indigenous Australians will need to reflect on how best to provide realistic life choices for their young people, including the provision of government services equitably delivered and the enjoyment of culture and heritage. These will be particularly acute questions in regional and remote areas, especially where the spiritual commitment to land has waned in the face of readily available alcohol and other life options in towns and cities. Some will want to recast the balance between security of land title for future generations and utility of land title for present communities and individuals anxious to use land for economic development.

This time the likes of Stanner, Dexter and Coombs will be found in Indigenous ranks as well as elsewhere. Tapping into the nation's sense of moral entitlements and the range of realistic life choices which appeal to contemporary Aborigines, they will be boosted by the affirmation of the will of the Australian people that the odious policies of oppression and neglect be put at an end once and for all, and that all affordable steps be taken to mitigate the effects of past barbarism.[5] There will be High Court judgments and assessments by international tribunals that provide unexpected encouragement and new directions despite the inertia of those elected politicians who will have hoped that a referendum would put it all behind us.

When proposing the first-ever motion in the new Parliament House acknowledging Aborigines and Torres Strait Islanders, Prime Minister Bob Hawke quoted Dr Coombs:

It's a politician's job to recognise when the will is there to do something; but they also have a responsibility to create that will. It's never divisive to correct injustice. The fact of injustice is divisive and will continue to be until we correct it and learn to live with it. People who benefit from injustice will oppose this, but you don't stop working for justice simply because people around you don't like it.[6]

It's time to amend the Constitution modestly but with the expectation that due acknowledgment of Indigenous Australians will effect the big changes needed so that they might enjoy their realistic choices of belonging to the Dreaming and the Market that constitute modern Australia.

APPENDIX 1

PREVIOUS SUGGESTIONS FOR CONSTITUTIONAL CHANGE AND FOR PARLIAMENTARY ACKNOWLEDGMENT OF ABORIGINAL AND TORRES STRAIT ISLANDER PEOPLES

1974 Bonner Motion

That the Senate accepts the fact that the indigenous people of Australia, now known as Aborigines and Torres Strait Islanders, were in possession of this entire nation prior to the 1788 First Fleet landing at Botany Bay, urges the Australian Government to admit prior ownership by the said indigenous people, and introduce legislation to compensate the people now known as Aborigines and Torres Strait Islanders for dispossession of their land.

1988 House of Representatives Motion on Opening of New Parliament House

That this House –
(1) acknowledges that:
    (a) Australia was occupied by Aborigines and Torres Strait Islanders who had settled for thousands of years before British settlement at Sydney Cove on 26 January 1788;
    (b) Aborigines and Torres Strait Islanders suffered dispossession

and dispersal upon acquisition of their traditional lands by the British Crown; and
(c) Aborigines and Torres Strait Islanders were denied full citizenship rights of the Commonwealth of Australia prior to the 1967 Referendum;

(2) affirms:
(a) the importance of Aboriginal and Torres Strait Islander culture and heritage; and
(b) the entitlement of Aborigines and Torres Strait Islanders to self-management and self-determination subject to the Constitution and the laws of the Commonwealth of Australia; and

(3) considers it desirable that the Commonwealth further promote reconciliation with Aboriginal and Torres Strait Islander citizens providing recognition of their special place in the Commonwealth of Australia.

Amendment moved by John Howard

Paragraph (2) (b), after 'the entitlement of Aborigines and Torres Strait Islanders to self-management and self-determination' insert ', in common with all other Australians,'.

1988 Constitutional Commission

We recommend against altering or repealing the preamble to the *Commonwealth of Australia Constitution Act 1900*, and against inserting any new preamble to the Constitution.

We recommend that section 25 of the Constitution should be repealed.

We recommend that section 51 of the Constitution be altered by
i. omitting paragraph (26); and

ii. inserting the following paragraph so that the Federal parliament has power to make laws with respect to:
(26) Aborigines and Torres Strait Islanders

We recommend that the Constitution be altered by inserting Chapter VIA – Rights and Freedoms as set out below:

including:
Equality Rights
124G
(1) Everyone has the right to freedom from discrimination on the ground of race, colour, ethnic or national origin, sex, marital status, or political, religious, or ethical belief.
(2) Subsection (1) is not infringed by measures taken to overcome disadvantages arising from race, colour, ethnic or national origin, sex, marital status, or political, religious or ethical belief.

1989 Aboriginal and Torres Strait Islander Commission Act

Section 3 *Objects*
The objects of this Act are, in recognition of the past dispossession and dispersal of the Aboriginal and Torres Strait Islander peoples and their present disadvantaged position in Australian society:
(a) to ensure maximum participation of Aboriginal persons and Torres Strait Islanders in the formulation and implementation of government policies that affect them;
(b) to promote the development of self-management and self-sufficiency among Aboriginal persons and Torres Strait Islanders;
(c) to further the economic, social and cultural development of Aboriginal persons and Torres Strait Islanders; and

(d) to ensure co-ordination in the formulation and implementation of policies affecting Aboriginal persons and Torres Strait Islanders by the Commonwealth, State, Territory and local governments, without detracting from the responsibilities of State, Territory and local governments to provide services to their Aboriginal and Torres Strait Islander residents.

1991 Council for Aboriginal Reconciliation Act

Preamble

Because:
(a) Australia was occupied by Aborigines and Torres Strait Islanders who had settled for thousands of years, before British settlement at Sydney Cove on 26 January 1788; and
(b) many Aborigines and Torres Strait Islanders suffered dispossession and dispersal from their traditional lands by the British Crown; and
(c) to date, there has been no formal process of reconciliation between Aborigines and Torres Strait Islanders and other Australians; and
(d) by the year 2001, the centenary of Federation, it is most desirable that there be such a reconciliation; and
(e) as a part of the reconciliation process, the Commonwealth will seek an ongoing national commitment from governments at all levels to co-operate and to co-ordinate with the Aboriginal and Torres Strait Islander Commission as appropriate to address progressively Aboriginal disadvantage and aspirations in relation to land, housing, law and justice, cultural heritage, education, employment, health, infrastructure, economic development and any other relevant matters in the decade leading to the centenary of Federation, 2001:

1993 Native Title Act

Preamble

This preamble sets out considerations taken into account by the Parliament of Australia in enacting the law that follows.

The people whose descendants are now known as Aboriginal peoples and Torres Strait Islanders were the inhabitants of Australia before European settlement. They have been progressively dispossessed of their lands. This dispossession occurred largely without compensation, and successive governments have failed to reach a lasting and equitable agreement with Aboriginal peoples and Torres Strait Islanders concerning the use of their lands.

As a consequence, Aboriginal peoples and Torres Strait Islanders have become, as a group, the most disadvantaged in Australian society.

The people of Australia voted overwhelmingly to amend the Constitution so that the Parliament of Australia would be able to make special laws for peoples of the aboriginal race.

The Australian Government has acted to protect the rights of all of its citizens, and in particular its indigenous peoples, by recognising international standards for the protection of universal human rights and fundamental freedoms through:

(a) the ratification of the International Convention on the Elimination of All Forms of Racial Discrimination and other standard-setting instruments such as the International Covenants on Economic, Social and Cultural Rights and on Civil and Political Rights; and
(b) the acceptance of the Universal Declaration of Human Rights; and
(c) the enactment of legislation such as the *Racial Discrimination Act 1975* and the *Australian Human Rights Commission Act 1986*.

The High Court has:
(a) rejected the doctrine that Australia was *terra nullius* (land belonging to no-one) at the time of European settlement; and
(b) held that the common law of Australia recognises a form of native title that reflects the entitlement of the indigenous inhabitants of Australia, in accordance with their laws and customs, to their traditional lands; and
(c) held that native title is extinguished by valid government acts that are inconsistent with the continued existence of native title rights and interests, such as the grant of freehold or leasehold estates.

The people of Australia intend:
(a) to rectify the consequences of past injustices by the special measures contained in this Act, announced at the time of introduction of this Act into the Parliament, or agreed on by the Parliament from time to time, for securing the adequate advancement and protection of Aboriginal peoples and Torres Strait Islanders; and
(b) to ensure that Aboriginal peoples and Torres Strait Islanders receive the full recognition and status within the Australian nation to which history, their prior rights and interests, and their rich and diverse culture, fully entitle them to aspire.

The needs of the broader Australian community require certainty and the enforceability of acts potentially made invalid because of the existence of native title. It is important to provide for the validation of those acts.

Justice requires that, if acts that extinguish native title are to be validated or to be allowed, compensation on just terms, and with a special right to negotiate its form, must be provided to the holders of the native title. However, where appropriate, the native title should not be extinguished but revive after a validated act ceases to have effect.

It is particularly important to ensure that native titleholders are now able to enjoy fully their rights and interests. Their rights and interests under the common law of Australia need to be significantly supplemented. In future, acts that affect native title should only be able to be validly done if, typically, they can also be done to freehold land and if, whenever appropriate, every reasonable effort has been made to secure the agreement of the native titleholders through a special right to negotiate. It is also important that the broader Australian community be provided with certainty that such acts may be validly done.

A special procedure needs to be available for the just and proper ascertainment of native title rights and interests which will ensure that, if possible, this is done by conciliation and, if not, in a manner that has due regard to their unique character. Governments should, where appropriate, facilitate negotiation on a regional basis between the parties concerned in relation to:

(a) claims to land, or aspirations in relation to land, by Aboriginal peoples and Torres Strait Islanders; and
(b) proposals for the use of such land for economic purposes.

It is important that appropriate bodies be recognised and funded to represent Aboriginal peoples and Torres Strait Islanders and to assist them to pursue their claims to native title or compensation.

It is also important to recognise that many Aboriginal peoples and Torres Strait Islanders, because they have been dispossessed of their traditional lands, will be unable to assert native title rights and interests and that a special fund needs to be established to assist them to acquire land.

The Parliament of Australia intends that the following law will take effect according to its terms and be a special law for the descendants of the original inhabitants of Australia.

The law, together with initiatives announced at the time of its introduction and others agreed on by the Parliament from time to time, is intended, for the purposes of paragraph 4 of Article 1 of the International Convention on the Elimination of All Forms of Racial Discrimination and the *Racial Discrimination Act 1975*, to be a special measure for the advancement and protection of Aboriginal peoples and Torres Strait Islanders, and is intended to further advance the process of reconciliation among all Australians.

The Parliament of Australia therefore enacts:

1998 Constitutional Convention

That the Constitution include a Preamble, noting that the existing Preamble before the Covering Clauses of the Imperial Act which enacted the Australian Constitution (and which is not itself part of our Constitution) would remain intact.

The Preamble to the Constitution should contain the following elements:

- Introductory language in the form 'We the people of Australia';
- Reference to 'Almighty God';
- Reference to the origins of the Constitution, and acknowledgment that the Commonwealth has evolved into an independent, democratic and sovereign nation under the Crown;
- Recognition of our federal system of representative democracy and responsible government;
- Affirmation of the rule of law;
- Acknowledgment of the original occupancy and custodianship of Australia by Aboriginal peoples and Torres Strait Islanders;
- Recognition of Australia's cultural diversity;
- Affirmation of respect for our unique land and the environment;
- Concluding language to the effect that '[We the people of Australia] asserting our sovereignty, commit ourselves to this Constitution'; and
- A provision allowing ongoing consideration of constitutional change.

John Howard's 1999 Exposure Draft of Proposed New Preamble to the Australian Constitution

With hope in God, the Commonwealth of Australia is constituted by the equal sovereignty of all its citizens.

The Australian nation is woven together of people from many ancestries and arrivals. Our vast island continent has helped to shape the destiny of our Commonwealth and the spirit of its people.

Since time immemorial our land has been inhabited by Aborigines and Torres Strait Islanders, who are honoured for their ancient and continuing cultures.

In every generation immigrants have brought great enrichment to our nation's life.

Australians are free to be proud of their country and heritage, free to realise themselves as individuals, and free to pursue their hopes and ideals. We value excellence as well as fairness, independence as dearly as mateship.

Australia's democratic and federal system of government exists under law to preserve and protect all Australians in an equal dignity which may never be infringed by prejudice or fashion or ideology nor invoked against achievement.

In this spirit we, the Australian people, commit ourselves to this Constitution.

2012 Report of the Expert Panel on Constitutional Recognition of Indigenous Australians

Item 1
Repeal section 25 and section 51(26) of the Constitution.

Item 2
Insert after section 51:

Section 51A Recognition of Aboriginal and Torres Strait Islander peoples

Recognising that the continent and its islands now known as Australia were first occupied by Aboriginal and Torres Strait Islander peoples;

Acknowledging the continuing relationship of Aboriginal and Torres Strait Islander peoples with their traditional lands and waters;

Respecting the continuing cultures, languages and heritage of Aboriginal and Torres Strait Islander peoples;

Acknowledging the need to secure the advancement of Aboriginal and Torres Strait Islander Peoples;

the Parliament shall, subject to this Constitution, have power to make laws for the peace, order and good government of the Commonwealth with respect to Aboriginal and Torres Strait Islander peoples.

Item 3
Insert after section 116:

Section 116A Prohibition of racial discrimination

(1) The Commonwealth, a State or a Territory shall not discriminate on the grounds of race, colour or ethnic or national origin.

(2) Subsection (1) does not preclude the making of laws or measures for the purpose of overcoming disadvantage, ameliorating the effects of past discrimination, or protecting the cultures, languages or heritage of any group.

Item 4
Insert as section 127A:

Section 127A Recognition of languages

(1) The national language of the Commonwealth of Australia is English.

(2) The Aboriginal and Torres Strait Islander languages are the original Australian languages, a part of our national heritage.

2014 Interim Report, Joint Select Committee on Constitutional Recognition of Aboriginal and Torres Strait Islander Peoples

A successful referendum on Indigenous constitutional recognition will need to meet three primary objectives. To be successful at a referendum, the committee considers that a successful proposal must:
- recognise Aboriginal and Torres Strait Islander peoples as the first peoples of Australia;
- preserve the Commonwealth's power to make laws with respect to Aboriginal and Torres Strait Islander peoples; and
- in making laws under such a power, prevent the Commonwealth from discriminating against Aboriginal and Torres Strait Islander peoples.

2014 Progress Report, Joint Select Committee on Constitutional Recognition of Aboriginal and Torres Strait Islander Peoples

The committee recommends that the Parliament consider three structural options for constitutional recognition of Aboriginal and Torres Strait Islander peoples that follow, noting the committee's view that any proposal must preserve both existing Commonwealth laws relying on section 51(26) and the Commonwealth's power to make laws with respect to Aboriginal and Torres Strait Islander peoples.

OPTION 1 – New section 51A with a broad prohibition of racial discrimination incorporating the Expert Panel's section 116A amendment

51A   Recognition of Aboriginal and Torres Strait Islander Peoples
Recognising that the continent and its islands now known as Australia

were first occupied by Aboriginal and Torres Strait Islander peoples;
Acknowledging the continuing relationship of Aboriginal and Torres Strait Islander peoples with their traditional lands and waters;
Respecting the continuing cultures, languages and heritage of Aboriginal and Torres Strait Islander peoples;
The Parliament shall, subject to this Constitution, have power to make laws for the peace, order and good government of the Commonwealth with respect to Aboriginal and Torres Strait Islander peoples.

116A   Prohibition of racial discrimination
(1) The Commonwealth, a State or a Territory shall not discriminate on the grounds of race, colour or ethnic or national origin.
(2) Subsection (1) does not preclude the making of laws or measures for the purpose of overcoming disadvantage, ameliorating the effects of past discrimination, or protecting the cultures, languages or heritage of any group.

OPTION 2 – New section 51A with a limited prohibition of discrimination by the Commonwealth against Aboriginal and Torres Strait Islander peoples

51A   Recognition of Aboriginal and Torres Strait Islander peoples
Recognising that the continent and its islands now known as Australia were first occupied by Aboriginal and Torres Strait Islander peoples;
Acknowledging the continuing relationship of Aboriginal and Torres Strait Islander peoples with their traditional lands and waters;
Respecting the continuing cultures, languages and heritage of Aboriginal and Torres Strait Islander peoples;
(1) The Parliament shall, subject to this Constitution, have power to make laws for the peace, order and good government of the Commonwealth with respect to Aboriginal and Torres Strait Islander peoples, but not so as to discriminate adversely against them.

(2) Subsection (1) does not preclude the making of laws or measures for the purpose of overcoming disadvantage, ameliorating the effects of past discrimination, or protecting the cultures, languages or heritage of Aboriginal and Torres Strait Islander peoples.

OPTION 3 – Redraft section 51(26) to allow the Commonwealth Parliament to make laws with respect to Aboriginal and Torres Strait Islander peoples with the option of enacting an Act of Recognition

51   Legislative Powers of the Parliament
The Parliament shall, subject to this Constitution, have power to make laws for the peace, order, and good government of the Commonwealth with respect to:
(26)   Aboriginal and Torres Strait Islander peoples.

APPENDIX 2

RECOMMENDED CHANGES TO THE CONSTITUTION

1. Insert after the words: 'This Constitution is divided as follows:', the word: 'Acknowledgment'.
2. Immediately prior to the heading 'Chapter 1' include these words:

Acknowledgment
We, the people of Australia, recognise that the continent and the islands of Australia were first occupied by Aboriginal and Torres Strait Islander peoples.

We acknowledge the continuing relationship of Aboriginal and Torres Strait Islander peoples with their traditional lands and waters.

We acknowledge and respect the continuing cultures, languages and heritage of Aboriginal and Torres Strait Islander peoples.

3. Repeal section 25 of the Constitution.
4. Repeal section 51(26) and insert in lieu the following sub-paragraph:

the cultures, languages and heritage of the Aboriginal and Torres Strait Islander peoples and their continuing relationship with their traditional lands and waters:

ENDNOTES

PREFACE *A Personal Journey*
1 Quoted by Justice Murphy in *Neal* v *The Queen* (1982) 149 CLR 305 at p. 316.
2 *ibid.*, p. 317.
3 *ibid.*, p. 326.
4 Peter Sutton, *The Politics of Suffering*, Melbourne University Publishing, 2011 edition, p. 1.
5 Noel Pearson, 'A Fair Place in Our Own Country: Indigenous Australians, Land Rights and the Australian Economy', Castan Public Lecture, Castan Centre for Human Rights Law, Monash University, June 2004.
6 Justice Brennan in *Neal* v *The Queen* (1982) 149 CLR 305 at p. 326.
7 French CJ, Hayne, Crennan, Kiefel, Bell, Gageler and Keane JJ in *Bugmy* v *The Queen* [2013] HCA 37 (2 October 2013).
8 Letter by Sir Joh Bjelke-Petersen to Bishop William Murray, 8 February 1979.
9 Marcia Langton, *The Quiet Revolution: Indigenous People and the Resources Boom*, Boyer Lectures 2012, ABC Books, 2013, p. 149.

INTRODUCTION *The Case for Modest Constitutional Change*
1 *The Sydney Morning Herald*, 1 January 2014.
2 *The Australian*, 19 July 2014.
3 *ibid.*, 25 July 2014.
4 *Final Report of the Aboriginal and Torres Strait Islander Act of Recognition Review Panel*, September 2014, p. 7.

5   Report of the Expert Panel, *Recognising Aboriginal and Torres Strait Islander Peoples in the Constitution*, 2012, p. v.
6   Joint Select Committee on Constitutional Recognition of Aboriginal and Torres Strait Islander Peoples, *Interim Report*, July 2014, p. 29.
7   ibid., p. 18.
8   In my 1996 Roma Mitchell Oration, 'Thirty Years On, Do We Need a Bill of Rights?', I suggested an addition of Chapter VIA to the Constitution to deal with rights and freedom. My proposed section 124A was:
    - Everyone has the right to freedom from discrimination on the ground of race, colour, ethnic or national origin.
    - This right is not infringed by measures taken to overcome disadvantages arising from race, colour, ethnic or national origin.
    - Neither is it infringed by measures recognising the entitlement to self-determination of Aborigines and Torres Strait Islanders or protecting their sacred sites, native title, land rights, customary law, or cultural traditions.

    Despite the 1993 Senate debate on the *Native Title Bill* and the 1995 High Court decision in the *Native Title Act* case, I was in 1996 still open to the possibility of a constitutional ban on racial discrimination. But then came the High Court's *Wik* decision at the end of 1996 and the 1998 Senate debate on the amendments proposed in the wake of that decision. In the 1995 *Native Title* case decision, the High Court had clarified that, contrary to the view of some Labor members, Paul Keating's 1993 native title legislation was not strictly subject to the *Racial Discrimination Act* (RDA). The unexpected *Wik* decision held that native title could co-exist with the rights of a pastoralist on a pastoral lease. How then could the rights of the pastoralist prevail over the rights of the native title holders if there was a conflict of rights, given that the RDA would operate to ensure that native title rights were not less secure than the pastoralist's rights? The Labor Party in opposition could not see its way clear to joining with the Democrats and the Greens, ensuring that the *Native Title Act* was made strictly subject to the RDA. Both the Coalition Government and the Labor Opposition were convinced that it was essential that the law provide certainty for pastoralists' rights and for all other land titles granted after 1975, regardless of the RDA. In my opinion, they were right.

CHAPTER 1 *Approaching the Forthcoming Referendum*

1   Quoted in Report of the Expert Panel, *Recognising Aboriginal and Torres Strait Islander Peoples in the Constitution*, 2012, p. 15.

2   Paul Hasluck, *Black Australians: A Survey of Native Policy in Western Australia, 1829–1897*, Melbourne University Press, 1942, p. 205.
3   *ibid.*, second edition, 1970, 'Preface' dated 30 September 1969, pp. 4–5.
4   Paul Hasluck, Statement to Native Welfare Conference, Canberra, 26 January 1961, and Statement in the House of Representatives, 20 April 1961.
5   Commonwealth Parliamentary Debates, House of Representatives, p. 89, 14 August 1963.
6   Commonwealth Parliamentary Debates, House of Representatives, p. 3952, 10 December 1965.
7   In the matter of the *Conciliation and Arbitration Act 1904–1965* and the Cattle Station Industry (Northern Territory) Award 1951, Commonwealth and Conciliation Arbitration Commission, 1965, 651 at p. 668.
8   *ibid.*, p. 669.
9   *ibid.*
10 James Gobbo, *Something to Declare: A Memoir*, Miegunyah Press, 2010, p. 106.
11 *ibid.*, p. 107.
12 Quoted in Bill Bunbury, *It's Not the Money, It's the Land*, Fremantle Arts Centre Press, 2002, p. 104.
13 Bain Attwood and Andrew Markus, *The 1967 Referendum*, Aboriginal Studies Press, second edition, 2007, p. 110, citing Snedden's submission to Cabinet, 22 February 1965.
14 Commonwealth Parliamentary Debates, House of Representatives, pp. 2638–39, 11 November 1965.
15 Cited by Robert French, 'The Race Power: A Constitutional Chimera' in *Australian Constitutional Landmarks*, HP Lee and George Winterton (eds), Cambridge University Press, 2003, 180 at p. 208.
16 Paul Hasluck, *Shades of Darkness: Aboriginal Affairs 1925–1965*, Melbourne University Press, 1988, p. 124.
17 Cabinet minute quoted in Attwood and Markus, *op. cit.*, p. 42.
18 Argument in favour of the proposed *Constitution Alteration (Aboriginals) Act 1967*, National Archives of Australia, at http://vrroom.naa.gov.au/print/?ID=24248
19 Cabinet Minute, Decision 507, 15 August 1967.
20 *ibid.*
21 Cabinet Minute, Decision 712, 31 October 1967.
22 Barrie Dexter, 'Pandora's Box', unpublished manuscript, 2011, chapter 1, p. 3.
23 *ibid.*, p. 5.
24 Letter by Sam Lipski to Tony Eggleton, 10 October 1967.
25 Dexter, *op. cit.*, p. 10.

26 Hasluck, *Shades of Darkness, op. cit.*, p. 123.
27 *ibid.*
28 Dexter, *op. cit.*, chapter 2, p. 3.
29 Letter by AP Elkin to HC Coombs, 2 November 1967.
30 WEH Stanner, Address to Belconnen Churches, 1 July 1969, p. 10, WEH Stanner Collection, Australian Institute of Aboriginal and Torres Strait Islander Studies (AIATSIS), Series I, Box 15, Item 293.
31 Cited by Dexter, *op. cit.*, chapter 2, p. 3.
32 Dexter, *op. cit.*, chapter 2, pp. 5–6.
33 Prime Minister's Department, Notes of Discussion between Coombs, Stanner and Moy, 7 December 1967.
34 WEH Stanner, *White Man Got No Dreaming*, Australian National University Press, 1979, p. 225.
35 Hasluck, *Shades of Darkness, op. cit.*, p.143.
36 Noel Pearson, 'The Reward for Public Life Is Public Progress', 2013 Whitlam Oration, University of Western Sydney, 13 November 2013, p.16, available at http://www.whitlam.org/__data/assets/pdf_file/0008/535553/2013_WHITLAM_ORATION1.pdf.
37 Hasluck, *Shades of Darkness, op. cit.*, p. 145.
38 See my remarks at the launch of the Miriam Rose Foundation, Darwin, 22 October 2013, at http://www.eurekastreet.com.au/article.aspx?aeid=38418.
39 Commonwealth Parliamentary Debates, House of Representatives, p. 140, 23 August 1988.
40 Letter by WEH Stanner to Frank Brennan, 4 October 1981.
41 Diane Barwick, Jeremy Beckett and Marie Reay, *Metaphors of Interpretation: Essays in Honour of WEH Stanner*, Australian National University Press, 1985, p. 44.

CHAPTER 2 *The Collapse of Terra Nullius and Forced Assimilation*
1 Paul Hasluck, Opening Statement, Meeting of Ministers and Government Officers, Canberra, 26 January 1961.
2 Letter by Charles Perkins to Paul Hasluck, undated. Hasluck replied on 27 January 1961.
3 Letter by Charles Perkins to Paul Hasluck, 1 February 1961.
4 Recorded interview with Peter Howson and Ray Evans, Oral History Section, National Library of Australia, TRC5444, 27 April 2005.
5 Kim E Beazley, *Father of the House: The Memoirs of Kim E. Beazley*, Fremantle Press, 2009, p. 157.

6   Letter by Reverend CF Gribble to JD Jago, Convenor, Commission on Aboriginal Affairs, Methodist Social Service Department, Melbourne, 26 March 1963.
7   Prime Minister's Press Release, 17 February 1963.
8   *The Spectator*, Victorian and Tasmanian Methodist Conference, 6 March 1963.
9   Commonwealth Parliamentary Debates, House of Representatives, p. 1796, 23 May 1963.
10 Recorded interview with Howson and Evans, *op. cit.*
11 Commonwealth Parliamentary Debates, House of Representatives, p. 932, 12 September 1963.
12 *ibid.*
13 Cited at *ibid.*, p. 933.
14 *ibid.*
15 *ibid.*, p. 927.
16 *ibid.*, p. 928.
17 *ibid.*, p. 935.
18 House of Representatives, Parliament of the Commonwealth of Australia, *Report from the Select Committee on Grievances of Yirrkala Aborigines, Arnhem Land Reserve*, Part II – Minutes of Evidence, 1963, p. 29.
19 Letter by CF Gribble to EA Wells, 25 September 1963.
20 House of Representatives, *Report from the Select Committee on Grievances of Yirrkala Aborigines, Arnhem Land Reserve, op. cit.*, pp. 37–38.
21 *ibid.*, p. 38.
22 *ibid.*, pp. 40–41.
23 *ibid.*, p. 10, para. 43.
24 *ibid.*, p. 10, para. 46.
25 *ibid.*, p. 11, para. 61.
26 *ibid.*, p. 8, para. 20.
27 *ibid.*, p. 12, para. 69.
28 *ibid.*, p. 13.
29 Letter by CF Gribble to AE Wells, 11 November 1963.
30 Cited by Edgar Wells, *Reward and Punishment in Arnhem Land 1962–1963*, Aboriginal Studies Press, 1982, p. 116.
31 Ministerial Statement by CE Barnes on 'Northern Territory – Gove Bauxite Deposits' to House of Representatives, Commonwealth Parliamentary Debates, House of Representatives, p. 924, 15 September 1965.
32 House of Representatives, *Report from the Select Committee on Grievances of Yirrkala Aborigines, Arnhem Land Reserve, op. cit.*, para. 66.
33 Commonwealth Parliamentary Debates, House of Representatives, p. 9, 12 March 1968.

34 Barrie Dexter, 'Pandora's Box', *op. cit.*, chapter 3, p. 15.
35 HC Coombs, Address to Federal Council for the Advancement of Aborigines and Torres Strait Islanders, Canberra, 12 April 1968, National Library of Australia, Papers of HC Coombs, Box 44, Item 372.
36 Dexter, *op. cit.*, chapter 6, p. 10.
37 Letter by Barrie Dexter to HC Coombs, 10 May 1968. Dexter formed the view that the minister was attempting to develop different lines of policy 'by going behind our backs and dealing directly with his ministerial colleagues. This has merely served to confuse his colleagues and their departments and has no doubt caused officers in the latter two to be sure that my office is of no significance in the development of policy.'
38 Cabinet Minute, Decision 252, 22 May 1968.
39 Cabinet Minute, Decision 314, 2 July 1968.
40 Cabinet Minute, Decision 391 (M), 25 July 1968.
41 Address by the Prime Minister the Rt Hon. John Gorton at the Conference of Commonwealth and State Ministers Responsible for Aboriginal Affairs at Parliament House, Canberra, 12 July 1968.
42 WEH Stanner, Address to External Affairs Department, 16 July 1969, p. 7, WEH Stanner Collection, AIATSIS, Series I, Box 15, Item 295.
43 WEH Stanner, *After the Dreaming*, Lecture 4: 'Confrontation' in *White Man Got No Dreaming*, Australian National University Press, 1979, p. 230. For example, this paragraph was quoted by Justice Brennan in *R* v *Toohey; Ex parte Meneling Station Pty Ltd* (1982) 158 CLR 327.
44 *ibid.*, pp. 235–36.
45 Letter by FX Purcell to WEH Stanner, 23 December 1968.
46 Transcript, ABC Guest of Honour, 5 January 1969, National Archives of Australia, Series A2354, 1967/5 Part 2, Item Barcode 3193016, pp. 536–38.
47 Letter by WEH Stanner to Julius Stone, 13 January 1969, WEH Stanner Collection, AIATSIS, Series I, Box 15, Item 276.
48 Stanner, *After the Dreaming, op. cit.*, p. 5, 'Introduction'.
49 WEH Stanner, Note to CAA, 25 September 1969.
50 Letter by HC Coombs to Fred Chaney, 3 March 1970.
51 Paul Hasluck, *Light That Time Has Made*, National Library of Australia, 1995, p. 52.

CHAPTER 3 *The Promise of the 1967 Referendum*
1 Jeremy Long, 'The Pintubi Patrols: Welfare Work with Desert Aborigines', *Australian Territories*, vol. 4, no. 5, 1964, 43 at p. 48.

2   Jeremy Long, 'The Pintubi Patrols: Welfare Work with Desert Aborigines – The Later Phases', *Australian Territories*, vol. 4, no. 6, 1964, 24 at p. 25.
3   *ibid.*, pp. 32–33.
4   Ronald Berndt, 'The Gove Dispute: The Question of Australian Aboriginal Land and the Preservation of Sacred Sites', *Anthropological Forum*, vol. 1, no. 2, 1964, pp. 258–95.
5   Jeremy Long, Notes on Professor Berndt's Paper 'The Gove Dispute', addressed to The Director, Welfare Branch, 63/2650, 18 February 1965.
6   WEH Stanner, 'The Yirrkala Writ and the Department of Interior's Paper', Council for Aboriginal Affairs, 21 January 1969, WEH Stanner Collection, AIATSIS, Series I, Box 15, Item 278.
7   Peter Nixon, Press Statement, 25 January 1969.
8   Memo from WEH Stanner to FX Purcell, 29 January 1969, pp. 5–6, WEH Stanner Collection, AIATSIS, Series I, Box 15, Item 277.
9   Letter by WEH Stanner to FX Purcell, 14 February 1969, WEH Stanner Collection, AIATSIS, Box 15, Item 280.
10 WEH Stanner, 'The Yirrkala Case', paper for private seminar, Australian National University, 28 February 1969, WEH Stanner Collection, AIATSIS, Series I, Box 15, Item 279.
11 WEH Stanner, paper for CAA commenting on Draft Submission by the Department of the Interior on the Yirrkala Case, 11 March 1969, WEH Stanner Collection, AIATSIS, Series I, Box 15, Item 286.
12 WEH Stanner, transcript of longhand notes taken in the Supreme Court of the Northern Territory, 1 April 1969, p. 1, WEH Stanner Collection, AIATSIS, Series 15, Item 5.
13 *ibid.*, p. 13.
14 Letter by WEH Stanner to WC Wentworth, 1 April 1969, WEH Stanner Collection, AIATSIS, Series I, Box 15, Item 287.
15 Memo from HC Coombs to Minister-in-Charge of Aboriginal Affairs, 15 April 1969.
16 Letter by HC Coombs to EJ Hook, 28 April 1969.
17 Memo from First Assistant Crown Solicitor to Secretary, Attorney-General's Department, 2 May 1969.
18 Letter by EJ Hook to HC Coombs, 13 May 1969.
19 Letter by Peter Nixon to WC Wentworth, 5 May 1969.
20 Memo from RS Swift, Deputy Secretary, to Assistant Secretary, Department of the Interior, 26 May 1969.
21 Jeremy Long, 'Interests in Land in the Gove Peninsula', undated and unpublished.

22 Memo by EE Payne to Acting Secretary, Department of the Interior, 12 June 1969.
23 Bill Harris QC and Malcolm McLelland, Joint Memorandum of Advice, *Commonwealth of Australia* v *Mathaman*, 21 March 1970, written confirmation of advice first given orally on 5 June 1969 after meeting of counsel on 4 June 1969.
24 WEH Stanner, Address to Belconnen Churches Group, 1 July 1969, WEH Stanner Collection, AIATSIS, Series I, Box 15, Item 293.
25 Letter by WEH Stanner to FX Purcell, 11 July 1969.
26 Letter by WEH Stanner to Les Hiatt, 20 August 1969, WEH Stanner Collection, AIATSIS, Series I, Box 16, Item 301.
27 Quoted at (1971) 17 *Federal Law Reports* 141 at p. 160.
28 WEH Stanner, 'Yirrkala Notes', 18–25 November 1969, WEH Stanner Collection, AIATSIS, Series I, Box 16, Item 302.
29 *ibid.*
30 Council for Aboriginal Affairs, 'Discussions with Methodist Overseas Mission, CAA and Nabalco', National Archives of Australia, Item 502802.
31 Letter by RB Hutchison to Purcell and Purcell, Solicitors, 31 December 1969.
32 Interview of Robert Ellicott QC with Frank Brennan, 17 July 2012.
33 Transcript, *Milirrpum* v *Nabalco*, 25 May 1970, p. 33.
34 Robert Ellicott QC, Memorandum to the Attorney-General, 11 June 1970.
35 Memorandum from RS Swift, Department of the Interior, to Assistant Secretary NT (G&SA), 'Yirrkala Program', 18 June 1970.
36 Commonwealth Parliamentary Debates, House of Representatives, p. 967, 3 September 1970.
37 *ibid.*, p. 968.
38 *ibid.*, p. 969.
39 *ibid.*, p. 970.
40 *ibid.*, p. 971.
41 Interview of Robert Ellicott QC with Frank Brennan, 29 May 2012.
42 *ibid.*, 17 July 2012.
43 Transcript, *Milirrpum* v *Nabalco*, 7 September 1970, p. 916.
44 *ibid.*
45 *ibid.*, p. 923.
46 *ibid.*, p. 973.
47 *Milirrpum* v *Nabalco Pty Ltd* (1971) 17 FLR 14, p. 178.
48 *ibid.*, p. 187.
49 AE Woodward, 'Three Wigs and Five Hats', Eric Johnston Lecture, Northern Territory Library Service, Darwin, 1989, p. 6.

50 Draft letter by WEH Stanner to AE Woodward, 12 October 1970, WEH Stanner Collection, AIATSIS, Series I, Box 16, Item 317. Stanner added a note at the head of the letter on 23 December 1973: 'I kept this unsent letter to record my views in 1970.' As such, it is an invaluable resource for knowing the thoughts of Stanner during the course of the *Milirrpum* litigation, just a month after his testing cross-examination by Ellicott.
51 Commonwealth Parliamentary Debates, Senate, p. 1636, 29 October 1970.
52 Transcript, *Milirrpum* v *Nabalco*, 10 November 1970, p. 2344.
53 *ibid.*, p. 1370.
54 *ibid.*, 16 November 1970, pp. 2514–15.
55 *ibid.*, p. 2515.
56 WEH Stanner, Address to Aboriginal Graduation Dinner, 12 February 1971, WEH Stanner Collection, AIATSIS, Series I, Box 17, Item 324.
57 WEH Stanner, Address to University Congregation, Australian National University, 1 April 1971, WEH Stanner Collection, AIATSIS, Series I, Box 17, Item 325.
58 William McMahon, 'Aboriginal Affairs Policy', Conference of Commonwealth and State Ministers Responsible for Aboriginal Affairs, Cairns, 23 April 1971, p.1.
59 *Milirrpum* v *Nabalco Pty Ltd* (1971) 17 FLR 141, p. 262.
60 *ibid.*, p. 272.
61 *ibid.*
62 *ibid.*, p. 267.
63 *ibid.*, p. 198.
64 Edward Woodward, 'Three Wigs and Five Hats', *op. cit.*, p. 6.
65 Edward Woodward, *One Brief Interval*, Miegunyah Press, 2005, p. 99.
66 *ibid.*, p. 106.
67 Transcript, *Milirrpum* v *Nabalco*, 24 November 1970, pp. 2871–72.
68 *Australian Law Journal*, vol. 45, 1971, p. 773.
69 *Australian Law Journal*, vol. 46, 1972, p. 45.
70 *ibid.*, p. 206.
71 *Australian Law Journal*, vol. 47, 1973, p. 152.
72 Memorandum from RJ Ellicott to the Attorney-General, 28 April 1971, pp. 3–4.
73 Commonwealth Parliamentary Debates, House of Representatives, p. 2217, 29 April 1971.
74 Cabinet Minute, Submission No. 76, 29 April 1971.
75 Cabinet Minute, Decision No. 150, 4 May 1971.
76 Letter by Robert Ellicott to Frank Brennan, 12 February 2014.

CHAPTER 4 *After the 1971 Gove Land Rights Case*

1. Letter by Yirrkala elders to Prime Minister McMahon, 6 May 1971.
2. Sir John Bunting, Note of Meeting between Yirrkala delegation and Prime Minister, Canberra, 6 May 1971.
3. WEH Stanner, Statement on Land Policy for the Council for Aboriginal Affairs, 22 May 1971, WEH Stanner Collection, AIATSIS, Series I, Box 17, Item 327.
4. Barrie Dexter, 'Pandora's Box', unpublished manuscript, chapter 19, p. 1.
5. Letter by HC Coombs to Peter Howson, 28 May 1971.
6. Peter Howson, *The Life of Politics: The Howson Diaries*, Viking Press, 1984, p. 734, 10 June 1971.
7. *ibid.*, p. 755, 3 August 1971.
8. *ibid.*, pp. 755–76, 4 August 1971.
9. *ibid.*, p. 758, 11 August 1971.
10. Letter by Charles Perkins to Prime Minister McMahon, 18 June 1971.
11. Memorandum from HC Coombs, 'Notes on Conversation with the Minister on 21 June 1971 in Canberra', distributed to the Council for Aboriginal Affairs, 23 June 1971.
12. Letter by Charles Perkins to Prime Minister McMahon, 20 August 1971.
13. Letter by Prime Minister McMahon to Charles Perkins, 25 October 1971.
14. Memorandum from Charles Perkins to Council for Aboriginal Affairs, 12 July 1971, p. 20.
15. *ibid.*, p. 23.
16. Memorandum from Barrie Dexter to HC Coombs, 27 July 1971.
17. Barrie Dexter, Note for File, Meeting with the Minister on 23 August 1971, 7 October 1971.
18. WEH Stanner, 'Some Notes on "Assimilation"', 1 September 1971.
19. Howson, *The Life of Politics, op. cit.*, p. 770, 16 September 1971.
20. Howson, *The Life of Politics, op. cit.*, p. 775, 1 October 1971.
21. WEH Stanner, Address to Third Monday Group, 22 September 1971, WEH Stanner Collection, AIATSIS, Series I, Box 17, Item 334.
22. Council for Aboriginal Affairs, Submission to Cabinet, 7 July 1971.
23. Dexter, 'Pandora's Box', *op. cit.*, chapter 24, p. 4.
24. Briefing by Barrie Dexter to Peter Howson, 12 October 1971.
25. Howson, *The Life of Politics, op. cit.*, p. 778, 13 October 1971.
26. *ibid.*, p. 779, 13 October 1971.
27. *ibid.*, p. 781, 18 October 1971.
28. Record of Conversation between HC Coombs and Prime Minister McMahon, 19 October 1971.
29. Dexter, 'Pandora's Box', *op. cit.*, chapter 24, pp. 19–20.

30 Howson, *The Life of Politics, op. cit.*, p. 781, 19 October 1971.
31 *ibid.*, p. 783, 21 October 1971.
32 *ibid.*, p. 784, 25 October 1971.
33 *ibid.*, p. 789, 7 November 1971.
34 *ibid.*, p. 792, 19 November 1971.
35 Letter by Sir Richard Blackburn to Ian Viner, 25 June 1976.
36 Robert Ellicott, 'Recognition of Aboriginal Land Claims on Reserves in the Northern Territory', 16 November 1971, p. 16.
37 HC Coombs, *Kulinma*, Australian National University Press, 1978, p. 171.
38 Howson, *The Life of Politics, op. cit.*, pp. 794–95, 25 November 1971.
39 Peter Howson, Submission to Cabinet Committee on Aboriginal Affairs, Submission No. 457, 2 December 1971, p. 4.
40 *ibid.*, p. 5.
41 *ibid.*, p. 6.
42 *ibid.*, p. 7.
43 *ibid.*, p. 8.
44 *ibid.*, p. 9.
45 Cabinet Minute, Decision 613(AA), 6 December 1971.
46 Howson, *The Life of Politics, op. cit.*, p. 799, 6 December 1971.
47 WEH Stanner, Observations at Anthropology Seminar on 'HW Scheffler: "Kariera-like Systems"', 9 December 1971, WEH Stanner Collection, AIATSIS, Series I, Box 17, Item 336.
48 Howson, *The Life of Politics, op. cit.*, p. 806, 21 December 1971.
49 *ibid.*, 22 December 1971.
50 Memorandum from Charles Perkins to Council for Aboriginal Affairs, 17 December 1971.
51 Memorandum from WEH Stanner to Barrie Dexter, 11 January 1972.
52 *ibid*.
53 Howson, *The Life of Politics, op. cit.*, p. 813, 6 January 1972.
54 Dexter, 'Pandora's Box', *op. cit.*, chapter 24, p. 40.
55 Statement by HC Coombs, 26 January 1972.
56 *The Age*, 26 January 1972.
57 *The Canberra Times*, 27 January 1972.
58 *The Australian*, 27 January 1972.
59 Quoted by Scott Robinson, 'The Aboriginal Embassy' in *The Aboriginal Tent Embassy: Sovereignty, Black Power, Land Rights and the State*, Gary Foley, Andrew Schaap and Edwina Howell (eds), Routledge, 2014, p. 5.
60 Howson, *The Life of Politics, op. cit.*, p. 819, 7 February 1972.
61 *The Canberra Times*, 27 January 1972.

CHAPTER 5 *Australia Day 1972*

1   *The Canberra Times*, 8 February 1972.
2   Peter Howson, *The Life of Politics: The Howson Diaries*, Viking Press, 1984, p. 820, 9 February 1972.
3   *ibid.*, p. 822, 14 February 1972.
4   Gary Foley, 'Reflection on the First Thirty Days' in *The Aboriginal Tent Embassy: Sovereignty, Black Power, Land Rights and the State*, Gary Foley, Andrew Schaap and Edwina Howell (eds), Routledge, 2014, p. 39.
5   Commonwealth Parliamentary Debates, House of Representatives, p. 122, 23 February 1972.
6   Peter Nixon, *The Peter Nixon Story*, Connor Court Publishing, 2012, pp. 69–70.
7   Commonwealth Parliamentary Debates, House of Representatives, pp. 122–23, 23 February 1972.
8   *ibid.*
9   *ibid.*, p. 123.
10 *ibid.*, p. 124.
11 *ibid.*
12 *ibid.*, p. 125.
13 *ibid.*, p. 128.
14 *ibid.*, p. 129.
15 *ibid.*
16 *ibid.*, p. 130.
17 *ibid.*
18 *ibid.*, p. 140.
19 *ibid.*, p. 141.
20 *ibid.*, p. 146.
21 *ibid.*
22 Letter by WEH Stanner to Sister Marita, 2 March 1972, WEH Stanner Collection, AIATSIS, Series 5, Item 21.
23 Letter by Barrie Dexter to HC Coombs in London, first week of July 1971.
24 Committee of Aboriginal Affairs, Cabinet Minute, Decision no. 1303(AA), 24 August 1972.
25 WEH Stanner, 'Fictions, Nettles and Freedoms' in *White Man Got No Dreaming*, Australian National University Press, 1979, 299 at pp. 304, 316.
26 *ibid.*, p. 302.
27 *ibid.*, 317.
28 Council for Aboriginal Affairs, Minutes, 27–28 September 1972, pp. 10–11.
29 Letter by HC Coombs to Peter Howson, 14 September 1972.

30 WEH Stanner, 'After the Dreaming – Whither?', *White Man Got No Dreaming*, *op. cit.*, 299 at p. 338. The address was delivered on 28 October 1972.
31 Campaign launch for the Australian Labor Party, Election 1972, delivered by Gough Whitlam at Blacktown Civic Centre, 13 November 1972.
32 William McMahon, Campaign Speech, 14 November 1972, available at Museum of Australian Democracy website: http://electionspeeches.moadoph.gov.au/speeches/1972-william-mcmahon.
33 HC Coombs, *Kulinma*, Australian National University Press, 1978, p. 174.
34 The proposed Bureau of Advice and Aid for Aborigines was a CAA idea that never won government support. On 21 July 1975, the Whitlam Cabinet 'agreed not to take up at this stage the Minister's proposals for the drafting of legislation to establish a Bureau of Advice and Aid', Decision No. 3719 in response to Submission No. 1839.
35 Gordon Bryant, Cabinet Submission 302, 1973, p. 2, attached to Decision No. 622(WEL), Welfare Committee, Cabinet Minutes, 10 May 1973.
36 Letter by Jim Cavanagh to Prime Minister Whitlam, 24 December 1974.
37 Charles Perkins, *A Bastard like Me*, Ure Smith, Sydney, 1975, p. 173.
38 *ibid.*, p. 196.
39 Letter by Prime Minister Whitlam to Queensland Premier Bjelke-Petersen, 20 October 1974.
40 Gough Whitlam, Message for 40 Years Freedom Day Festival, Daguragu, 18 August 2006.
41 *Koowarta v Bjelke-Petersen* (1982) 153 CLR 168.
42 *Mabo (No 2) v Queensland* (1992) 175 CLR 1.
43 Gough Whitlam, *The Whitlam Government 1972–75*, Viking Press, 1985, p. 467.
44 Quoted by Whitlam, *ibid.*, p. 468.
45 HC Coombs, 'Aboriginal Australians: 1967–1976; a Decade of Progress', Murdoch Lecture, Perth, 1976, p. 1.
46 *ibid.*, p. 17.
47 Letter by Barrie Dexter to Ian Viner, 24 December 1976.
48 Letter by Ian Viner to Barrie Dexter, 11 February 1977.
49 ABC Television, *Q&A*, 4 August 2014.

CHAPTER 6 *The Need for Constitutional Change*
1 Commonwealth Parliamentary Debates, Senate, p. 71, 11 July 1974.
2 Commonwealth Parliamentary Debates, Senate, p. 1271, 19 September 1974.
3 *ibid.*, p. 1272.

4   *ibid.*, p. 1273.
5   Cabinet Minute, Decision No. 3226, 17 February 1975.
6   Commonwealth Parliamentary Debates, Senate, p. 367, 20 February 1975.
7   *ibid.*, p. 370.
8   Constitutional Commission, *Report of the Advisory Committee on Individual and Democratic Rights Under the Constitution*, 1987, p. 72.
9   Constitutional Commission, *Final Report of the Constitutional Commission*, vol. 1, 1988, p. 104.
10 *ibid.*, p. 109.
11 *ibid.*, p. 110.
12 *ibid.*
13 *ibid.*, p. 157.
14 *ibid.*, p. 156.
15 *ibid.*, p. 157.
16 Constitutional Commission, *Report of the Advisory Committee on Individual and Democratic Rights under the Constitution*, 1987, p. 73.
17 Constitutional Commission, *Final Report of the Constitutional Commission*, vol. 2, 1988, p. 715.
18 *ibid.*, p. 718.
19 Commonwealth Parliamentary Debates, House of Representatives, pp. 140 and 162, 23 August 1988.
20 *ibid.*, p. 146.
21 *Report of the Constitutional Convention*, Transcript of Proceedings, vol. 3, pp. 262–63, 4 February 1998.
22 *ibid.*
23 *ibid.*, p. 264.
24 *ibid.*, vol. 4, p. 519, 9 February 1998.
25 *ibid.*, p. 496.
26 *ibid.*, p. 497.
27 *ibid.*, p. 810, 11 February 1998.
28 *ibid.*, p. 497, 9 February 1998.
29 *ibid.*, p. 743, 11 February 1998.
30 Australian Labor Party, *National Platform and Constitution 2004*, pp. 109–10.
31 Australian Labor Party, *National Platform and Constitution 2007*, p. 207.
32 *National Human Rights Consultation Report*, 2009, Recommendation 18, p. xxxiv.
33 AE Woodward, Aboriginal Land Rights Commission, *Second Report*, 1974, p. 35.
34 *ibid.*, pp. 35–36.

35 *ibid.*, p. 36.
36 Memorandum from FG Brennan to the Minister of Aboriginal Affairs, 27 April 1976.
37 Aboriginal Land Rights Commission, Transcript, Alice Springs, pp. 49–50, 18 February 1974.
38 *ibid.*, p. 62.
39 *ibid.*, p. 63.
40 *ibid.*, p. 68.
41 *ibid.*, p. 119, 20 February 1974.
42 *ibid.*, p. 135, referring to section 4, *Aborigines Act 1934–1939 (South Australia)*.
43 Aboriginal Land Rights Commission, Transcript, Darwin, p. 176, 25 February 1974.
44 Woodward, Aboriginal Land Rights Commission, *op. cit.*, p. 14.
45 *ibid.*
46 AE Woodward, Submission to Inquiry into the Reeves Report on the Aboriginal Land Rights (Northern Territory) Act, Standing Committee on Aboriginal and Torres Strait Islander Affairs, p. 11.
47 *ibid.*, p. 17.
48 Transcript, Standing Committee on Aboriginal and Torres Strait Islander Affairs, 2 June 1999.
49 *The Weekend Australian*, 2–3 August 2014.
50 Woodward, Aboriginal Land Rights Commission, *op. cit.*, p. 35.
51 AE Woodward, *One Brief Interval*, The Miegunyah Press, 2005, p. 135.
52 *ibid.*, p. 141.
53 *Wik Peoples* v *The State of Queensland & Ors* (1996) 187 CLR, 1 at p. 87.
54 Woodward, Aboriginal Land Rights Commission, *op. cit.*, p. 36.
55 Woodward, *One Brief Interval, op. cit.*, p. 139.
56 AE Woodward, 'Land Rights and Land Use: A View from the Sidelines', 23rd Australian Legal Convention, 1985, p. 27.
57 *ibid.*
58 Department of Natural Resources and Mines, 'Providing Freehold Title in Aboriginal and Torres Strait Islander Communities', Queensland Government, 2012, p. 4.
59 Morling Review Panel, *Report*, 2013, pp. 9–10.
60 (1992) 175 CLR 1 at p. 175.
61 Commonwealth Parliamentary Debates, Senate, p. 5499, 21 December 1993.
62 (1998) 195 CLR 96.

63 *Fejo* v *The Northern Territory of Australia* D7/1998 [1998] HCATrans 247 (22 June 1998). Justice McHugh also said, 'What you have got to take into consideration, at least as far as I am concerned, is this, that *Mabo* was a development of the law, and in developing the law the Court takes into account what expectations may be defeated. ... If the Court took the view that an estate in fee simple extinguished native title, why should we now develop that to defeat the expectations on which *Mabo* itself was founded? I mean, the pastoral leases themselves, if that issue had come before – or had been involved in *Mabo* as part of the *Mabo* issue, again, I am not sure, just speaking for myself, whether I would have subscribed to the *Mabo* doctrine. But in the setting of the time, and given the reservations in *Mabo*, it seemed to me proper that the Court should take the step that it did, because it was going to affect basically unalienated Crown land. So the position was, in one sense, the same as it was in 1788.'
64 *Western Australia* v *Ward* (2002) 213 CLR 1 at pp. 240–41. This case deals with the claim by the Miriuwung and Gajerrong peoples to lands in the East Kimberley region of Western Australia, including part of the Ord River scheme.
65 (2002) 213 CLR 401 at p. 454.
66 (2002) 213 CLR 1 at pp. 398–99.
67 Noel Pearson, 'Where We've Come From and Where We're at with the Opportunity That Is Koiki Mabo's Legacy to Australia', Mabo Lecture, AIATSIS Native Title Conference 2003, 'Native Title on the Ground', Alice Springs, 3–5 June 2003.
68 *Mabo* v *Queensland (No 2)* (1992) 175 CLR 1 at p. 104.
69 National Native Title Tribunal, *Annual Report 2011–12*, p. 19.
70 *The Weekend Australian*, 2–3 August 2014.

CHAPTER 7 *Aboriginal Concerns about Discrimination and Adverse Treatment*
1 Report of the Expert Panel, *Recognising Aboriginal and Torres Strait Islander Peoples in the Constitution*, 2012, Recommendations, p. xviii.
2 Robert Ellicott, Submission to the Expert Panel on Recognising Aboriginal and Torres Strait Islander Peoples in the Constitution, 2012, Submission 3525.
3 *Koowarta* v *Bjelke-Petersen* (1982) 153 CLR 168 at p. 222.
4 ibid., p. 187.
5 ibid., p. 210.
6 ibid., p. 242.

7   *The Commonwealth* v *Tasmania* (1983) 158 CLR 1.
8   *ibid.*, p. 158.
9   *ibid.*, p. 242.
10 *ibid.*, pp. 272–73.
11 *Western Australia* v *The Commonwealth (Native Title Act Case)* (1995) 183 CLR 373.
12 *ibid.*, p. 460.
13 *ibid.*, p. 462.
14 *ibid.*
15 *ibid.*, p. 483.
16 *ibid.*, p. 460.
17 *ibid.*, p. 484.
18 Senator John Woodley, Commonwealth Parliamentary Debates, Senate, p. 5037, 6 July 1998.
19 Commonwealth Parliamentary Debates, Senate, p. 5040, 6 July 1998.
20 *ibid.*, p. 5037.
21 *ibid.*, p. 5039.
22 *ibid.*, p. 5041.
23 *Kartinyeri* v *The Commonwealth* (1998) 195 CLR 337 at p. 381.
24 *ibid.*, p. 357.
25 *ibid.*, p. 358.
26 *ibid.*, p. 367.
27 *ibid.*, p. 382.
28 *ibid.*, pp. 382–83.
29 *ibid.*, p. 383.
30 *ibid.*, p. 422.
31 Report of the Expert Panel, *Recognising Aboriginal and Torres Strait Islander Peoples in the Constitution*, 2012, p. 150.
32 *ibid.*, p. 158.
33 Megan Davis, correspondence on *A Rightful Place*, in *Quarterly Essay*, issue 56, November 2014, 73 at p. 78.
34 *Maloney* v *The Queen* (2013) 298 ALR 308 at p. 342 (statistics quoted by Justice Crennan).
35 *Aurukun Shire Council & Anor* v *CEO Office of Liquor Gaming and Racing in the Department of Treasury* (2012) 1 Qd R 1 at p. 23 (McMurdo P).
36 Tony Fitzgerald QC, *Cape York Justice Study*, Department of Premier and Cabinet, Brisbane, 2001, vol. 2, p. 76.
37 *The Australian*, 11 December 2012.
38 *Maloney* v *The Queen*, *op. cit.*, at p. 406.

39 *Gerhardy* v *Brown* (1985) 159 CLR 70 at p. 135.
40 *Maloney* v *The Queen, op. cit.*, at p. 317.
41 *ibid.*, p. 318.
42 *ibid.*, p. 337.
43 *ibid.*, pp. 345–46.
44 *ibid.*, pp. 337–38.
45 *Aurukun Shire Council & Anor* v *CEO Office of Liquor Gaming and Racing in the Department of Treasury, op. cit.*, at p. 70.
46 *ibid.*
47 *ibid.*, p. 71.
48 *ibid.*
49 *Gerhardy* v *Brown* (1985) 159 CLR 70 at p. 138.
50 *Maloney* v *The Queen, op. cit.*, p. 329. Also Justice Susan Keifel, rejecting a submission by the Australian Human Rights Commission, said that 'the elimination of racial discrimination, cannot itself be a right for the purposes of sections 10 and 8' of the *RDA*. She said at pp. 351–52: 'Section 10 cannot operate in the manner intended with respect to a broad right not to be discriminated against. In its operation, section 10 is not directly informed by the purpose of a law, but rather by the differential effect that a law has upon the enjoyment of a human right or fundamental freedom. If section 10 was to be understood to refer only to one right, which clearly it does not, and then to equate that right with the broader objective of the *RDA* and the Convention, it would be expected that a law made in contravention of the protection so provided would be invalid outright, rather than remaining valid but being modified by section 10. Section 10 cannot be taken as intended to refer to such a broadly framed right. Further, to identify a right in the way contended for is to deny the possibility that a law may nevertheless be a special measure under section 8 and therefore a law to which section 10 does not apply.'
51 ABC Television, *Q&A*, 4 August 2014.

CHAPTER 8 *The Road to Recognition for Indigenous Australians*

1 *The Australian Financial Review*, 8 November 2010.
2 Commonwealth Parliamentary Debates, House of Representatives, p. 1120, 13 February 2013.
3 *ibid.*, p. 1122.
4 *ibid.*, p. 1123.
5 Commonwealth Parliamentary Debates, House of Representatives, p. 6155, 30 October 1996.

6   Tanya Hosch, Address to National Press Club, Canberra, 13 February 2013, available at http://www.recognise.org.au/wp-content/uploads/shared/uploads/custom/489c2b031191954f50c4.pdf.
7   Jason Glanville, Address to National Press Club, 13 February 2013, available at http://www.recognise.org.au/wp-content/uploads/shared/uploads/custom/28647a4f87b2e426d170.pdf.
8   Commonwealth Parliamentary Debates, House of Representatives, p. 1123, 13 February 2013.
9   Preamble, *Aboriginal and Torres Strait Islander Peoples Recognition Act 2013*.
10 Report of the Expert Panel, *Recognising Aboriginal and Torres Strait Islander Peoples in the Constitution*, 2012, p. xix.
11 See Appendix 1.
12 Noel Pearson, 2013 Whitlam Oration, University of Western Sydney, 13 November 2013, available at http://www.whitlam.org/__data/assets/pdf_file/0008/535553/2013_WHITLAM_ORATION1.pdf.
13 Constitutional Commission, *Final Report*, vol. 1, 1988, p. 446.
14 ibid., p. 496.
15 Constitutional Commission, *Final Report*, vol. 2, 1988, p. 1019. Section 124C of Proposed Bill No. 17, *The Constitution Alteration (Rights and Freedoms) 1988*.
16 *ibid.*, section 124D.
17 Joint Select Committee on Constitutional Recognition of Aboriginal and Torres Strait Islander Peoples, *Interim Report*, July 2014, p. 29.
18 Bill Shorten, Keynote Address, Garma Festival, 3 August 2014.
19 Joint Select Committee on Constitutional Recognition of Aboriginal and Torres Strait Islander Peoples, *Progress Report*, October 2014, p. x.
20 *ibid.*, p. 3.
21 Tony Abbott, Address to Sydney Institute, 15 March 2013, cited in *The Sydney Papers Online*, Issue 20.
22 Commonwealth Parliamentary Debates, House of Representatives, p. 1123, 13 February 2013.
23 *The Australian*, 16 March 2013.
24 Commonwealth Parliamentary Debates, House of Representatives, p. 1123, 13 February 2013.
25 'Constitution Review Panel Denies "Hidden Agenda"', *The New Zealand Herald*, 26 February 2013.
26 Constitutional Advisory Panel, *New Zealand's Constitution: A Report on a Conversation*, November 2013, p. 16.
27 *ibid.*, p. 33.

28 *ibid.*, p. 35.
29 *The Australian*, 27 January 2014.
30 Constitutional Convention, *Report*, Transcript of Proceedings, vol. 4, p. 743, 11 February 1998.
31 Joint Select Committee on Constitutional Recognition of Aboriginal and Torres Strait Islander Peoples, Roundtable, *Hansard*, 30 April 2013, p. 2.
32 *ibid.*, p. 5.
33 *ibid.*, p. 8.
34 *ibid.*, p. 30.
35 *ibid.*, p. 9.
36 *ibid.*, p. 10.
37 *ibid.*, p. 12–13.
38 *ibid.*, p. 15.
39 *ibid.*, p. 16.
40 *ibid.*, p. 17.
41 *ibid.*, p. 20.
42 *ibid.*, p. 16.
43 *ibid.*, p. 17.
44 *ibid.*, p. 19.
45 *ibid.*, p. 22.
46 *ibid.*, p. 21.
47 *ibid.*, p. 23.
48 *ibid.*, p. 25.
49 *ibid.*, p. 26.
50 Noel Pearson, *A Rightful Place: Race, Recognition and a More Complete Commonwealth*, Quarterly Essay, issue 55, 2014, p. 53.
51 *ibid.*, p. 67.
52 It could be timely to revisit two recommendations of the 2009 National Human Rights Consultation. Recommendations 15 and 16 provided: 'The Committee recommends that a "statement of impact on Aboriginal and Torres Strait Islander peoples" be provided to the Federal Parliament when the intent is to legislate exclusively for those peoples, to suspend the *Racial Discrimination Act 1975* (Cth) or to institute a special measure. The statement should explain the object, purpose and proportionality of the legislation and detail the processes of consultation and the attempts made to obtain informed consent from those concerned. The Committee recommends that, in partnership with Indigenous communities, the Federal Government develop and implement a framework for self-determination, outlining consultation protocols, roles and responsibilities (so that the communities have meaningful

control over their affairs) and strategies for increasing Indigenous Australians' participation in the institutions of democratic government.'
53   Joint Select Committee on Constitutional Recognition of Aboriginal and Torres Strait Islander Peoples, *op. cit.*, p. 31.
54   *ibid.*, p. 29.
55   *ibid.*, p. 31.
56   *The Australian*, 17 December 2013.
57   *The Australian*, 27 January 2014.
58   *The Sydney Morning Herald*, 27 January 2014.
59   *Final Report of the Aboriginal and Torres Strait Islander Peoples Act of Recognition Review Panel*, September 2014, p. 5.
60   Report of the Expert Panel, *Recognising Aboriginal and Torres Strait Islander Peoples in the Constitution*, 2012, p. 4.
61   *Aboriginal and Torres Strait Islander Peoples Recognition Act 2013*, Section 3 (1)–(3).
62   Report of the Expert Panel, *Recognising Aboriginal and Torres Strait Islander Peoples in the Constitution*, 2012, p. v.

EPILOGUE *No Small Change*

1   *Gerhardy* v *Brown* (1985) 159 CLR 70 at p. 151.
2   Sir William Deane, 'Some Signposts from Daguragu', Inaugural Vincent Lingiari Lecture, Northern Territory University, Council for Aboriginal Reconciliation, 1996, pp. 21–22.
3   WEH Stanner, *White Man Got No Dreaming*, Australian National University Press, 1979, p. 58.
4   *ibid.*, p. 59.
5   cf Justices Brennan and Deane, *The Commonwealth* v *Tasmania* (1983) 158 CLR 1 at pp. 242, 272–73.
6   Commonwealth Parliamentary Debates, House of Representatives, p. 137, 23 August 1988.

INDEX

1967 Referendum 1, 7, 19–21, 26–7, 39, 58, 80, 153, 176, 181–2, 234
   amendment of s 51(26) 3, 16–20, 219, 225, 234
   current situation compared 35, 200
   effects of 80, 92, 124, 176, 178, 181–2, 201
   fiftieth anniversary 263
   overwhelming Yes vote 20–1, 58
   repeal of s 127 19, 20

Abbott Government 29, 33, 34, 193, 195, 262, 266, 275–7, 285
Abbott, Tony x, xi, 2, 4, 198, 250–3, 263–6, 276
Aboriginal Advancement Trust Account 64, 65, 133
Aboriginal and Torres Strait Islander Commission (ATSIC) 193, 195
Aboriginal and Torres Strait Islander Commission Act 1989 193, 290
Aboriginal and Torres Strait Islander peoples
   compensation for dispossession 183, 184, 211
   constitutional recognition *see* constitutional recognition
   definition of Aboriginal 25
   distinction between classes 9
   financial assistance for schooling 25
   industrial laws applying to 13–15
   laws impacting only on 1–2
   life of choice xviii, xx, 200, 283–7
   parliamentarians 5, 183
   power to legislate with respect to 3, 6, 219
   prior ownership of land, acknowledging 183, 192
   relationship with land 67–8, 79, 91, 104–7, 114
   remote communities xix, 77
   removal of children 9
   representative body, proposed 275
   special measures for 11, 239, 243–4
   voting rights 41
   wards of the state (NT) 10, 16, 40, 41
   welfare mentality 14, 184
Aboriginal and Torres Strait Islander Peoples Recognition Act 2013 250, 253, 256, 263, 276, 278
Aboriginal and Torres Strait Islander Social Justice Commissioner 248
Aboriginal languages 5, 6, 250, 262, 275, 278, 297
Aboriginal policy
   assimilation 9–14, 25, 28, 32, 47, 50, 53, 65, 66, 71, 126, 128–31

Interdepartmental Committee report 132–3, 140, 146, 147
land rights *see* land rights
mainstreaming 74–5, 158
Milirrpum decision, after 121–54
reconciliation 192–4
self-determination xvi, xxi, 28, 29, 32, 34, 72, 158, 165, 178, 192, 268
single Australian society 157, 192
stages of 108–10
Aboriginal reserves 47–9, 77–8
  abuse of women on xiv, xvi, 237, 240
  economic development 132, 141
  effect of living on xiv, xvii
  'federal intervention' laws 1–2, 257, 269
  Hasluck's view 47–9
  leases for economic purposes 103, 132, 136
  mining on *see* mining Aboriginal land
  Northern Territory 42–3, 77–8, 131, 151
  Queensland 124, 174
Aboriginal tent embassy 153, 156, 157, 164, 185
Aborigines Benefits Trust Fund 103
Advisory Committee on Individual and Democratic Rights under the Constitution (Rights Committee) 186–9
Alaskan Eskimo people xxi, 153
alcohol abuse xvii, 179, 237–8, 240, 283
alcohol restrictions 2, 171, 236–45
Anderson, John 4
Anderson, Michael 153
Archer River Pastoral Holding 222
assimilation 9–14, 25, 28, 32, 47, 50, 53, 65, 66, 71, 126, 128–31, 282

Ballard, John 121
Barnard, Lance 171
Barnes, CE 12, 53, 57
Barton, Edmund 8
Barwick, Diane 147
Barwick, Garfield 116
basics card 246
Beazley, Kim Snr 41, 44, 45, 50, 51

Berndt, Ronald 78–9, 93, 94
Bjelke-Petersen, Joh xii, xiii, xviii, xix, 27, 124, 153, 167, 173–4, 176, 178, 257
Blackburn, Richard 90, 98, 105, 107, 110, 112–18, 130, 137–40, 280
Blackshield, Tony 84
Bolkus, Nick 232
Bonner, Neville 183–5, 187, 194, 195, 217, 288
  Bonner Motion 1974 183–4, 187, 288
Bowen, Lionel 186
Bowen, Nigel 19
Boyer Lectures xx, 26, 67, 70–3, 83, 93
Brandis, George 266–71, 273, 275, 276
Brennan, Frank ix–xvi, xxi, 30–1, 253, 258, 277
Brennan, Gerard xiii, xv, xvii, 202–4, 209, 224, 225, 233, 239, 243
Broun, Jody 238
Brown, Bob 232
Bryant, Gordon 17, 44, 50, 154, 172
Buchanan, Cheryl xiii
Bugmy, William xvii
Bunting, John 121, 123
Burmester, Henry 248
Byers, Maurice 186

Callinan, Ian 215
Calwell, Arthur 44, 45
Campbell, Enid 186
Canada, land rights in 102, 160, 211
Carmody, Kev 15
Casey, Richard 59
Castan, Ron 186
Cavanagh, Jim 172–4, 177, 183–5
Central Land Council 203
Chaney, Fred 74, 248
Chaney, Fred Snr 74
Chaseling, Wilbur 43, 54–5, 105–7
Chipp, Don 157
Coe, Paul 156, 184
compensation 97, 103, 183, 184, 211
Constitution
  Aboriginal people not mentioned 254
  amendment *see* constitutional amendment

INDEX

'completion' of x, 2, 4, 32
intentions of drafters 8, 256
legislative powers 2–3
nature of 2, 186
recognition of Indigenous Australians *see* constitutional recognition
s 25 3–6, 189, 191, 198, 249, 255, 267, 274, 276, 296, 301
s 51(26) *see* race power (s 51(26))
s 127 repeal 19, 20, 185
UK Act, attached to 2, 186, 256
constitutional amendment 3, 185
1967 amendments 16–20, 185
1977 amendments 186, 221
consultation required 33–4
proposals for *see* constitutional amendment proposals
requirements for 3
review panel 4
s 51(26) 3, 16–20, 185, 219, 225, 234
s 127 repeal 19, 20, 185
constitutional amendment proposals 4–7, 288–300
Constitutional Commission 1988 189–91, 259–60, 288–90
Constitutional Convention 1998 194–8, 256, 266, 295
discrimination ban 6–7, 200, 245, 249, 260, 270–3, 275, 297, 298, 299
Expert Panel recommendations 249–50, 254–62, 267, 273, 296–7
expunging notions of race 275
Howard's proposed preamble 1999 256, 296
Joint Select Committee reports 298
s 25 repeal 4–6, 189, 191, 198, 249, 255, 267, 274, 276, 278, 296, 301
s 51(26) 4, 6, 190, 191, 198, 257–8, 276, 278, 300
s 51(26) repeal 296, 301
s 51A 249, 254, 256, 257, 268, 273, 274, 278, 297, 298
s 116A 249, 261, 270–4, 297, 298, 299
s 127A 250, 262, 297
constitutional bill of rights 6, 186, 191, 198–200, 259, 271

Constitutional Commission 1988 186, 188–91, 200, 255, 259–60, 289
Distribution of Powers Committee (Powers Committee) 186, 190
rights and freedoms chapter 259–60
Constitutional Convention 1998 194–8, 256, 266, 295
constitutional recognition 1, 2, 5, 76, 186, 196–8, 249–79
Aboriginal and Torres Strait Islander Peoples Recognition Act 2013 250, 253, 256, 263, 276, 278
Aboriginal languages 5, 6, 250, 262, 275, 278, 297
Acknowledgment, suggested 6, 256–7, 278, 301
'advancement', use of word 249, 254, 257, 268–70
Expert Panel on xi, 5, 74, 220, 221, 235, 245, 248–67, 273, 277–8
Joint Select Committee on 197, 250, 260, 262, 266
objectives of referendum 5–6, 32–3
preamble 187–9, 195–7, 254, 256–7, 296
proposed amendments *see* constitutional amendment proposals
Recognise movement xi, 4, 34, 267, 270
recommendations of Expert Panel 249–50, 254–62, 267, 273, 296–7
referendum, proposed 2, 4, 5–6, 32–3, 254, 263, 277
special committee 275–6
Coombs, HC ('Nugget') 22, 24–6, 36–8, 60, 62–4, 70–1, 74–5, 84, 87–93, 96, 101, 120, 121, 123, 127–30, 133–7, 142, 143, 146, 151, 152, 154, 158, 163–5, 167, 173, 175–7, 180–2, 214, 279, 281, 285, 286
Council for Aboriginal Affairs (CAA) 21–8, 36, 42, 59–67, 70–6, 80, 85, 87, 93, 100, 113, 122–34, 141–53, 160, 163–7, 169, 171–3, 177, 178, 280
Aboriginal membership 126, 127
divisions between Interior and 80, 123, 127–9, 146

meeting with ALP Parliamentary Committee on Aboriginal Affairs 166, 169
Council for Aboriginal Reconciliation 193, 194
Council for Aboriginal Reconciliation Act 1991 291
Council for Ministers of Aboriginal Affairs 123
Court, Richard 226
Cowen, Zelman xiii
Craven, Greg 195, 196
Crennan, Susan 241
criminal justice system xvi–xviii
Cross, Manfred 162, 172
Crossin, Trish 266, 268, 270, 273, 275

Daes, Erica-Irene 76
Daly River tribes 31, 38, 106
Davis, Megan 236, 248
Dawson, Daryl 213, 214, 226
Dawson, Peter 268
Dean, RL 51
Deane, William 181, 216, 224, 225, 282–3
Department of Aboriginal Affairs 73–4, 169, 171–4
Department of the Interior 59, 60, 64, 70, 74, 80, 85, 100, 123, 127–9, 134, 141, 145–6, 149, 171
Dexter, Barrie 22–5, 36–8, 60, 62, 70, 71, 81, 96, 101, 120, 122, 127, 130, 133, 135, 136, 148, 150, 151, 156, 163, 165, 171–3, 176–80, 214, 279, 281, 285, 286
discrimination *see also* racial discrimination
  constitutional ban on 6–7, 200, 245, 249, 260, 270–3, 275, 297, 298, 299
Djerrkura, Gatjil 195
Dodson, Michael 37, 276
Dodson, Patrick 1, 5, 37, 74, 192, 248, 278
Dunstan, Don 154, 190

Eggleton, Tony 22
Elkin, AP 10, 22, 24, 38

Ellemor, AF 55–6
Ellicott, Bob 97–100, 104–7, 118–20, 137, 140–2, 186, 221, 280
Elliott, Jack 203, 204
Engel, Frank 124
equal pay case (NT) 13–16, 211
equality under law xvii
Evans, Gareth 172
Expert Panel on Constitutional Recognition xi, 5, 74, 220, 221, 235, 245, 248–67, 277–8
  recommendations 249–50, 254–62, 267, 273, 296–7

Federal Council for Aboriginal Advancement (FCAA) 16–18, 44
Federal Council for the Advancement of Aborigines and Torres Strait Islanders (FCAATSI) 26, 61, 164, 166, 172
'federal intervention' 1–2, 257, 269
Fitzgerald Inquiry 237–8, 240
Fitzgerald, Tony 237–8
Fogarty, John 116
Foley, Gary 157
Fraser Government 138, 177, 202, 210
Fraser, Malcolm xix, 112, 136
French, Robert 17, 239
Freudenberg, Graham 169
Fryer, CA 117, 118

Gageler, Stephen 239
Garma Festival, Arnhem Land 182, 207, 246, 261
Garrett, Peter 186
Gartrell, Tim 267
Gaudron, Mary 216, 234
general purpose leases 150, 156, 159, 161, 163–4, 171
Gibbs, Harry 223
Giese, Harry 126
Giles, Adam 264
Gillard Government 34, 220, 262
  Expert Panel *see* Expert Panel on Constitutional Recognition
Gillard, Julia xi, 1, 5, 198, 235, 248, 250, 252

Glanville, Jason 252
Gobbo, James 14, 15
Gooda, Mick 267
Gorton Government 61
Gorton, John 59, 60, 63–5, 112, 128, 169, 280
Gove mining case *see* Yirrkala land rights case
Gribble, CF 43, 44, 45, 52, 56–7, 96
Griffith, Samuel 8
Gummow, William 234
Gurindji people 15, 175

Hamer, Rupert 186
Harradine, Brian 214, 226, 230, 232
Harris, Bill 86, 92, 109
Hasluck, Nicholas 76
Hasluck, Paul 9–13, 16, 18, 22–4, 28–30, 37–41, 43, 47–9, 53, 56, 57, 62, 64, 66, 71, 76, 126, 129, 130, 182, 279, 280
Hawke, Bob 186, 192, 286
Hawke Government 191
Hayne, Kenneth 234, 240, 241, 245
Herron, John 205
Hewitt, Len 129, 136
Hiatt, Les 79, 93–4
Highland, Gary 267
Hindmarsh Island Bridge 219, 233
Hindmarsh Island Bridge Act 1997 233–5
Holt Government 18–27, 176, 280
Holt, Harold 18, 19, 21, 22, 23, 26, 59, 60, 128, 130, 147, 148, 219, 280
Hook, Ted 88, 89, 91
Hosch, Tanya 4, 252
House of Representatives
　allocation of seats, excluding races 3–5, 189, 255
　members chosen by the people 255
　motion for constitutional amendment 1988 288
Howard Government 34, 194, 205, 230–3, 235, 264, 272
Howard, John 1, 4, 33, 35, 192, 194, 198, 250–2, 256, 263, 264, 289
Howson, Peter 41, 45, 122–5, 127–30, 133, 135–7, 142–8, 150, 153, 154, 156–9, 167

Huggins, Jackie 253
Hughes, Tom 91
Hunt, Ralph 121, 123, 125, 147, 148, 161, 164
Hutchison, RB 97

ILO *Indigenous and Tribal Populations Convention, 1957* 160, 174
Indigenous Advisory Council 33
Indigenous Land Corporation 217
Indigenous Youth Engagement Council 268
International Convention on the Elimination of All Forms of Racial Discrimination (ICERD) 18, 220–3, 244–5

Jeffrey, Phillip 117
John Paul II, Pope 31
Johnson, Les 162, 172
Joint Select Committee on Constitutional Recognition 197, 250, 260, 262, 266
Joint Standing Committee on Aboriginal Affairs 206
Juddery, Bruce 127, 128

Kartinyeri, Doreen 233
Keane, Patrick 241–3, 245
Keating Government 228–9, 233, 235, 272
Keating, Paul 35, 194, 225, 233, 251, 252, 263
Keeffe, Jim 110
Kelly, Paul (journalist) 151
Kelly, Paul (singer) 15
Keneally, Thomas 186
Kennedy, Ted xiii
Killen, James 194–5
Killoran, Pat 124, 174
Kirby, Michael 215, 234
Koowarta case 222–4
Koowarta, John 222
Kramer, Leonie 195, 197

land councils 202–5, 212–13
land rights xviii, xxii, 24, 29, 34, 35, 68–73, 76, 113, 124, 201–17, 281–2

Aboriginal relationship with land 67–8, 79, 91, 104–7, 114
acknowledgement in Constitution 6
appropriate titleholder 202–5
Arnhem Land 130, 133, 153, 162
assimilation, under 10–11, 50
Blackburn's view 137–40
Canada 102
change of law to recognise 119–21
common law 82, 99, 114, 118
compensation 97, 103
constitutional recognition 6
Ellicott's view 140–2
freehold title, arguments against 136, 142, 159, 162, 202, 212
inalienable freehold 136, 202
leases 132, 138, 146, 150, 156, 159, 177, 202
life choices and 76
McMahon's Australia Day statement 150–4, 157, 163, 165, 167, 171, 280
mining and 42–8, 67–73, 79, 140
native title laws 35
Northern Territory Land Rights Act 120, 136
Papua New Guinea 102
Wave Hill stand-off 15, 74, 100
Whitlam's policy 160–1, 169–76
Woodward Royal Commission xix, 172, 174, 177, 185, 201–12
Yirrkala case 42–59, 67–72, 78–120
Lange, David 266
Langton, Marcia xvi, xx, 37, 217, 248
languages
  Aboriginal, recognition of 5, 6, 250, 262, 275, 278, 297
  clause in constitution 260, 262, 275
leases to Aboriginal groups 132, 138, 146, 177
  general purpose leases 150, 156, 159, 161, 163–4, 171
  long association, on basis of 146
  special purpose leases 164
  sub-leases 102, 132
Leeser, Julian 195, 196
Leibler, Mark 1, 5, 74, 248, 276, 278

Lester, Geoffrey 117
Lingiari, Vincent 15, 100, 175
Lipski, Sam 22–3
Little, John 116–18
local Aboriginal land councils (LALCs) 212–13
Long, Jeremy 77–9, 91, 94

Mabo case xiii, 35, 97, 116, 176, 186, 194, 196, 213–15, 225, 226, 261, 272
Macartney, John Arthur 42
McEwen, John 20, 112
McHugh, Michael 214–15, 233
McLelland, Malcolm 92
McMahon, William 112–13, 119, 121, 124–6, 128, 133–7, 143, 150–4, 157, 163, 165, 167–70, 280
mainstreaming 74–5
Malezer, Les 273
Maloney case 237–9, 245
Maloney, Joan 237
Marika, Roy 105, 121, 159, 160
Marita, Sister 163
Marrantya, Liam 30, 31, 285
Mason, Anthony 91, 97, 224
Menzies, Douglas 115
Menzies Government 9, 16–18
Menzies, Robert 17, 18, 19, 52, 219, 280
Methodist missionaries 43–5, 54–6, 70, 81, 105, 116
Middleton, Karen 253
Milirrpum 51, 80
Milirrpum case *see* Yirrkala land rights case
Minchin, Nick 232
mining Aboriginal land 42–59, 67–72, 78–100, 103, 140
  CAA recommendations 134–5
  compensation 97, 103
  Yirrkala case 42–59, 67–72, 78–120
Morling Review Panel 212
Morling, Trevor 212
Moseley Royal Commission 9
Mulluk Mulluk, Pincher 38
Mungurrawuy 80
Mununggur, Daymbalipu 80, 121

Murphy, Lionel xv, 184, 223, 224
Murray, Les 256

Nabalco 57, 72, 80, 82, 84, 85, 96, 100, 110, 116, 130
  see also Yirrkala land rights case
National Aboriginal Consultative Council (NACC) 172, 176
National Apology 250, 253
  fifth anniversary 250–2
National Congress of Australia's First Peoples 33, 238, 245, 248, 273
National Methodist Church 104
National Press Club 252–3
National Tribal Council 148
native title 35, 214–17, 225, 271–2
  extinguishment 227, 228, 272
  intermediate period acts 231
  Mabo xiii, 35, 97, 116, 176, 186, 194, 196, 213–15, 225, 226, 261, 272
  past acts, validity of 228, 231
  Racial Discrimination Act and 219, 227–33, 236, 261, 272
  registered determinations 216
  Western Australia 226
  Wik xvi, 35, 194, 196, 209, 213, 214, 230, 258, 261, 272
Native Title Act 1993 35, 176, 214, 225–33, 261, 292–5
  acknowledgment of Aboriginal people 292–5
  amendments after *Wik* 230–2
  clause-busting provisions 232
  negotiations 229
  preamble 229
  Racial Discrimination Act and 219, 227–33, 236, 261, 292
Neal, Percy xiv–xv
Nelson, Brendan 250
Nelson, Jock 45
Nicholls, Doug 126
Nixon, Peter 81, 90, 101–3, 158
Northern Land Council 202–4, 209
Northern Territory 42
  administrator 74
  assimilation in 10–14, 39
  equal pay case 13–16, 211
  'federal intervention' laws 1–2, 269
  general purpose leases 150
  Land Board 142, 146, 147
  Land Rights Act 120, 136, 175, 177, 205
  mainstreaming in 74–5
  pastoral leases 13–16, 42
  title or access to lands 133
  traditional land ownership 35
  wards of state, Aborigines as 10, 16, 40, 41
  Welfare Branch 54, 74, 75, 77, 78, 125
  Welfare Ordinance 10

O'Donoghue, Lowitja 194, 253
Office of Aboriginal Affairs 62, 64, 113, 124–7, 160

Palm Island alcohol restrictions 236–45
Papua New Guinea, land rights 102
pastoral leases 42, 141–2, 208
  Aboriginal rights of access 141–2, 158, 209
  Aborigines removed from (NT) 14–16
  equal pay case 13–16, 211
  Macartney lease 42–3
  reversionary interests in 208–9
  sub-leases to Aboriginal groups 102, 132
Pearson, Noel xvi, xx, 28, 34, 36, 182, 216, 246, 248, 258, 274, 276, 283
Peris, Nova 5, 36, 197, 246, 266
Perkins, Charles 22–3, 26, 40–1, 124–7, 148–50, 172–3, 285
Peter, Alwyn xiii, xvii, 37
Pintubi people 77–8
Priestley, Bill 110
Purcell, Frank 70, 82, 83, 86, 93, 121

Queen Elizabeth 192, 194

race power (s 51(26)) 3, 8, 190, 219–27, 235, 257–8
  abuse, possibility of 226–7, 257
  amendment in 1967 3, 16–20, 185, 219, 225, 234

amendment proposed by Expert Panel 257–8, 276, 278, 300
amendment proposed in 1988 190, 191
Hindmarsh Island Bridge Act 233–5
intentions of drafters 8, 225
Kartinyeri case 233–5
Koowarta case 222–4
Native Title Act 226–7
need for amendment 4, 6, 198, 220
original wording 3, 8
Racial Discrimination Act, whether made under 222–3
repeal, proposed 296, 301
special measures 11, 239, 243
Tasmanian Dam case 223–4
use against interests of Aborigines 257
racial discrimination 218–47
   alcohol restrictions 2, 236–45
   constitutional ban on 6–7, 200, 245, 249, 260, 270–3, 275, 297, 298, 299
   determination of electorates 3–5, 189, 255
   Hasluck's view 30
   ICERD 18, 220–3, 244–5
   lack of constitutional protection from 218
   legislation specific to Aborigines 219
   Maloney case 237–43, 245
   Native Title Act 219, 227–33, 236
   race power and 222–5, 235
   s 25 of Constitution 3–5, 189, 255
   special measures 11, 239, 243–4
Racial Discrimination Act 1975 175, 218–22, 227–36, 247
   constitutional validity 222
   discriminatory legislation prohibited 235
   Native Title Act and 219, 227–33, 236, 261, 292
   s 51(26), whether made under 222, 223
   special measures 239, 243–4
Rae, Robert 184
Recognise movement xi, 4, 34, 267, 270
reconciliation 192–4
Reconciliation Australia x, 34, 267
Reeves, John 205–6
Renfree, HE 82

Rice, Walter 153
Roberts, Phillip 126
Robinson, Scott 157
Rowley, Charles 24
Royal Commission into Aboriginal Deaths in Custody xvi
Rubuntja, Wenten 33
Rudd Government 34, 262
Rudd, Kevin 1, 198, 199, 250

Sawer, Geoffrey 17
self-determination xvi, xxi, 28, 29, 32, 34, 72, 158, 165, 178, 192, 268
sentencing principles xv
Shorten, Bill 261
Siewert, Rachel 266, 275
Sinclair, Ian 192
single Australian society 157, 192
Smith, Shirley xiii
Smith, Warwick 146
Snedden, Billy 17
Stanner, WEH xiii, 22, 24, 26, 36–8, 62, 65–73, 80–9, 92–9, 105–10, 120, 122, 128–30, 133, 136, 147–50, 155–6, 163, 165, 167–8, 175–7, 180, 214, 279–81, 284–6
Stephen, Ninian 223, 224, 226
Stoljar, Sam 84
Stone, Julius 71, 72, 84
Strelein, Lisa 267
Sutton, Peter xvi
Swift, Bob 91, 96, 100, 158

Tasmanian Dam case 223–4
terra nullius 32, 34, 39, 58, 131, 175, 176, 196, 281
Textor, Mark 248
Toohey, John 186
Torres Strait Islands 124, 173
Treaty of Waitangi 251, 264–6
Turnbull, Malcolm 194
Turner, Patricia ix–xi, 253

Ungunmerr-Baumann, Miriam Rose 30–1
United States, land rights in 160, 211
   Alaskan Eskimo people xxi, 153

Vestey, Lord 15, 74, 100, 165
Vincent Lingiari Lecture 283
Viner, Ian 138, 177–80, 202

Walker, Denis xiii
wards of the state 10, 16, 40, 41
Watson, Len xiii
Wattie Creek (Daguragu) 100–3, 165, 175
Wave Hill lease 165
Wave Hill strike 15, 74, 100, 281
Wells, Edgar 44, 51, 52, 53, 56–7, 70, 96
Wells, Thomas Alexander 38
Wentworth, WC 45, 59–65, 71, 81, 86, 88, 90, 119, 122, 133, 158
Western Australia, native title in 226
Whitlam, Gough xix, 20, 112, 134, 137, 154, 156, 157, 160, 163, 168–76, 186
Whitlam Government 175, 177, 184
Whitrod, Ray xiii
Wik decision xvi, 35, 194, 196, 209, 213, 214, 230, 258, 261, 272
Willmot, Eric 186
Windeyer, Victor 115
Woodward, Edward 86, 87, 104, 107, 111, 114–16, 122, 138, 171, 185, 201–12

Woodward Royal Commission xix, 172, 174, 177, 185, 201–12
Wootten, Hal 15
World Council of Churches 123, 124
Wunungmurra, Wali Wulanybuma 121
Wyatt, Ken 5, 197, 266, 276

Yirrkala land rights case (*Milirrpum*) 42–59, 67–72, 78–120, 130, 137, 142, 211, 213, 281
  Australian Law Journal letters about 117
  Blackburn's decision 113–18
  change of law after 119–21
  evidence of links with land 99, 104–7, 114
  plaintiffs' claims after 121, 144
  policy developments after 121–54
Yirrkala Methodist church 94–5
Yolngu people 42, 43, 51, 106, 121
Young, Neil 7
Yunupingu, Galarrwuy 98, 104, 207

Zines, Leslie 186

Also by Frank Brennan
ACTING ON CONSCIENCE

Is a Catholic health minister in a fit position to legislate on women's issues such as the right to an abortion pill? When the prime minister invokes church leaders' support in going to war with Iraq – and those church leaders tacitly approve this – is there a moral issue at stake?

In *Acting on Conscience* Jesuit priest, human rights lawyer and academic Frank Brennan tackles these issues head on. He looks at some of the legal, moral and ethical issues capturing the public imagination – and critically examines the figures in public life who pass judgment on them. Issues covered include:

- the war in Iraq
- same-sex marriage and parenting
- late-term abortion
- politics and the judiciary.

Through detailed analysis of examples from both Australia and the US, Brennan asks: Is there a place for personal beliefs in public life? As citizens and voters, how can we responsibly mix law, religion and politics? How can we ensure that in the future, our leaders will speak for us – but not out of turn?

> '*Acting on Conscience* is incredibly timely and game.'
> Geraldine Doogue AO, journalist and broadcaster

> 'In an age of fear and bigotry here is a welcome book of courage and conscience.'
> Bob Brown, former leader of the Australian Greens

ISBN 978 0 7022 3582 2

Also by Frank Brennan
TAMPERING WITH ASYLUM

Revised Edition

In August 2001 a Norwegian vessel picked up 433 asylum seekers from a boat sinking in international waters between Australia and Indonesia. What the Howard government did in response created waves internationally.

By denying the *Tampa* and its cargo of asylum seekers permission to dock at Christmas Island, Australia signalled that it was dramatically closing its national borders. Trading on fear, and rushing in legislation to give their move legal backing, the Howard government effectively excluded asylum seekers from the Australian courts. Brennan argues that the government's response was a massive overreaction, possible only in a remote country such as Australia with few asylum seekers and no land borders. He compares Australia's response with that of the United States and Europe and provides a practical blueprint for countries wanting to humanely protect asylum seekers.

This revised edition includes an epilogue bringing the book up to date with the latest developments. The epilogue covers the Cornelia Rau and Vivian Alvarez Solon cases, Liberal backbencher Petro Georgiou's successful campaign to get children out of detention centres, and the Senate's thwarting of the government's attempt to extend the Pacific Solution in 2006.

'A timely, topical book … penetrating.' *The Canberra Times*

'A powerful book.' *Australian Financial Review*

'Necessary reading' *Australian Book Review*

ISBN 978 0 7022 3581 8